Shadows in the
City of Light

Dan Shiffman, *College Bound:*
The Pursuit of Education in Jewish American Literature, 1896–1944

Eric J. Sundquist, editor, *Writing in Witness:*
A Holocaust Reader

Noam Pines, *The Infrahuman: Animality in Modern Jewish Literature*

Oded Nir, *Signatures of Struggle:*
The Figuration of Collectivity in Israeli Fiction

Zohar Weiman-Kelman, *Queer Expectations:*
A Genealogy of Jewish Women's Poetry

Richard J. Fein, translator, *The Full Pomegranate:*
Poems of Avrom Sutzkever

Victoria Aarons and Holli Levitsky, editors,
New Directions in Jewish American and
Holocaust Literatures: Reading and Teaching

Jennifer Cazenave, *An Archive of the Catastrophe:*
The Unused Footage of Claude Lanzmann's Shoah

Ruthie Abeliovich, *Possessed Voices:*
Aural Remains from Modernist Hebrew Theater

Victoria Nesfield and Philip Smith, editors,
The Struggle for Understanding: Elie Wiesel's Literary Works

Ezra Cappell and Jessica Lang, editors,
Off the Derech: Leaving Orthodox Judaism

Nancy E. Berg and Naomi B. Sokoloff, editors,
Since 1948: Israeli Literature in the Making

Sara R. Horowitz, Amira Bojadzija-Dan, and Julia Creet, editors
Shadows in the City of Light: Images of Paris in
Postwar French Jewish Writing

Patrick Chura, *Michael Gold: The People's Writer*

Nahma Sandrow, *Yiddish Plays for Reading and Performance*

Alisha Kaplan, *Qorbanot*

Shadows in the City of Light

Paris in Postwar French Jewish Writing

Edited by

Sara R. Horowitz
Amira Bojadzija-Dan
Julia Creet

SUNY
PRESS

Cover photo taken by Julia Creet.

Published by State University of New York Press, Albany

For information, contact State University of New York Press, Albany, NY
www.sunypress.edu

Library of Congress Cataloging-in-Publication Data

Names: Horowitz, Sara R., editor | Bojadzija-Dan, Amira, editor | Creet, Julia, editor.
Title: Shadows in the city of light : Paris in postwar French Jewish writing,
    Sara R. Horowitz, Amira Bojadzija-Dan, Julia Creet, editors.
Description: Albany : State University of New York Press, [2021] | Series:
    SUNY series in Contemporary Jewish Literature and Culture | Includes
    bibliographical references and index.
Identifiers: ISBN 9781438481739 (hardcover : alk. paper) | ISBN 9781438481753
    (ebook)
Further information is available at the Library of Congress.

10 9 8 7 6 5 4 3 2 1

Contents

Contents   vii

Illustrations

Acknowledgments

The chapters in this volume were developed from an international symposium, "Paris in Post-War Jewish Literary Memory," convened at the Israel and Golda Koschitzky Centre for Jewish Studies at York University on May 23–25, 2016, by the editors of this collection, Sara R. Horowitz, Amira Bojadzija-Dan, and Julia Creet. The symposium was funded by the Koschitzky Centre for Jewish Studies at York University, York University's Faculty of Liberal Arts and Professional Studies and Departments of English and Humanities, the Social Science and Humanities Council of Canada, and Michael and Amira Dan. We are grateful to them for making this productive scholarly exchange possible. We deeply appreciate the guidance and good judgment of Janet Friskney in developing the Paris project grant. Special thanks to Julie Feinberg for her management, always with grace, of the myriad details entailed in convening the symposium.

We conceptualized this collection of essays as inviting both to specialists and to a broader group of readers interested in Paris, Jewish memory, the aftermath of the Shoah, and other issues treated here. We thank the contributors to this volume for their fine work, and for keeping these audiences in mind. We are grateful to Andrea Knight for her skilled assistance with manuscript preparation and to Phyllis Aronoff for her careful and nuanced translation of Henri Raczymow's essay.

Because Paris as real and imagined space is central to this book, and our ideas came to fruition during several visits to the city, we valued the visual element to help bring readers to the streets and neighborhoods recollected, imagined, and described by the writers treated here, and to remember those who once walked there. We acknowledge with gratitude the United States Holocaust Memorial Museum for granting us permission to use several archival photographs, and to Yad Vashem for providing a

photograph of Sarah Kofman's application on behalf of Mémé. We thank
Judith Cohen, recently retired Chief Photo Archivist for the United States
Holocaust Memorial Museum, for her important guidance; Irena Steinfeldt,
formerly Director of the Department for the Righteous Among the Nations
at Yad Vashem, and Susan Suleiman for the photographs that accompany her
chapter. Thanks, as well, to Michael Dan and Jonathan Richler, who gra-
ciously accepted roving assignments, for their photographic contributions.

1

Introduction

The Long Shadow of the Jewish Question in Paris

SARA R. HOROWITZ
AMIRA BOJADZIJA-DAN
JULIA CREET

The memory has burst, as a balloon bursts, but we spend our time sewing it back up. . . . sewing scraps together is every writer's task, a hypothetically endless task, and impossible task. . . .

—Henri Raczymow

In Search of Shadows Past

On June 1, 2015, the city of Paris designated a broad walkway "Promenade Dora Bruder" after an almost unknown Jewish teenager who was deported in 1943 along with thousands of other Parisian Jews during the Nazi Occupation of Paris. One of many who did not return, Dora was made famous by the Nobel Prize–winning French writer Patrick Modiano years after her murder. A plaque was sunk in the cement of the 18th arrondissement, once the heart of a vibrant Parisian Jewish community. Le Réseau Modiano, a blog dedicated to interpreting Modiano's work, put it this way, "Entre un

livre majeur et une promenade à son nom, Dora Bruder ne pourra pas dis-
paraître de sitôt des mémoires." ("Between a major book and a promenade
in her name, Dora Bruder cannot soon disappear from memory.") Standing
in front of this plaque on a spring afternoon, the editors of this book mar-
veled at the power of literature to invoke history, memory, and melancholy
in Paris, the City of Light, where Jewish life had flourished and perished in
its shadows. Dora Bruder is a shadow, a literary substance, given a concrete
place on the shady promenade between rue Leibniz and rue Belliard in the
quarter between the Clignancourt gate and that of Saint-Ouen, beside a
disused railway line turned into gardens. It's a place of darkness and light.

Shadows in the City of Light is a collection of chapters by fourteen
prominent writers and scholars that explores the significance of Paris in

Figure 1.1. Walking on the Promenade Dora Bruder. (*Photograph by Julia Creet*)

the writing of five influential French writers: Sarah Kofman, philosopher and memoirist; Patrick Modiano, novelist and Nobel laureate; Georges Perec, novelist; and Henri Raczymow, novelist and memoirist—each of whom published in the decades following World War II—and novelist, Irène Némirovsky, who wrote during the war, but whose manuscript about the impact of the war on Parisians was discovered and published decades later. In their writing, these authors walk their readers through streets and arrondissements that bear in powerful ways on the stories they weave, and on the issues they engage. They move their readers through a wartime or postwar cityscape of Paris, where the city functions not merely as a backdrop or setting, but as dynamic space that raises complex questions about absence, survival, ambivalence, secularity, and citizenship.

While Jewish life, culture, and thought both thrived and struggled in other parts of France, the city of Paris holds a special place in the Jewish imagination. During the tumultuous years in turn-of-the-twentieth-century Europe, Paris was a beacon and a magnet for the Jews of central and eastern Europe who flocked there, fleeing social, economic, and political hardship. Those very immigrants and their descendants were the most vulnerable of French Jews under Nazism, deported with the help of French police and bureaucrats, but also sheltered by fellow Frenchmen, in Paris and other areas of France. After the war, Jews from Poland, Russia, and elsewhere gravitated to Paris, some living there temporarily and others settling there, shaped by—and helping to reshape—the Parisian literary, cultural, and philosophical cityscape.

For the writers treated in this volume, neither their Frenchness nor their Jewishness was a fixed point. The chapters in *Shadows in the City of Light* explore the ways in which Paris functions as a fulcrum between cultures, between memory and forgetting, between history and place. The memory of places is a complicated arrangement and one hotly debated in French history.

Pierre Nora argued convincingly that commemoration turns memory into something archival, historical. Commemorative sites, he suggested, substitute for living memory—that is, memory kept alive unselfconsciously in the places where people remembered and the people remembering have always lived. But what of places where memory has been suppressed? Sites that—like "Promenade Dora Bruder"—have to be marked because local memory has tried to forget? The Paris streets remain impassive. And yet we imagine these streets as witnesses who have absorbed what happened there, and have something to impart to us if we know how to look and to listen.

Figure 1.2. A Jewish shopkeeper helps a customer in the doorway of his grocery store in the Jewish quarter in Paris, 1930s. (*Source*: USHMM)

We are drawn into walking and writing in these places, knowing and imagining that we are walking in the footsteps of others, as if the ground, the buildings, the courtyards absorb history and can give back to us a lost past.

But what of this physical relationship between past and present in the streets of Paris? Why do we find the concrete expression of the past so compelling? As Maxime Decout declares in his chapter on *Dora Bruder*, "Topography rather than history brings the dead back to life." You might say that Paris is the main character of this book and our random but orchestrated intersections with her map an elusive dialogue about space, place, and Jewish memory. Jewish memory is inseparable from a history of moving from one place to another, of exile from the promised land and from adopted lands. The Jews of Paris in the books that we study in this volume are mostly from elsewhere, as Annelies Schulte Nordholt and Amira Bojadzija-Dan both show in their contributions to this volume: from Poland, from Germany, from North Africa, contributing to the character of "the wandering Jew" and a "uniquely Jewish anxiety over space and belonging," as Bojadzija-Dan puts it. Jews have occupied temporary spaces in many places, but few have been so compelling as Paris, at once a place of enlightenment ideals and deep disappointment. It is an "extraordinary city," writes Thomas Nolden, "that Jews are permitted to enter and pushed to leave."

Place is one of the great aggregators of collective memory, both figuratively and physically. The collective memories most frequently invoked in the stories that we discuss in this collection are intimate, mostly family memories and memories of family set in the streets and neighborhoods of Paris, representing the larger history of Jewish history in Paris. They are memories lodged in place that offer us a connection between private, family memory and collective tragedy (Henri Raczymow). None of us really remember alone, according to the great French sociologist of memory, Maurice Halbawchs (who died in Buchenwald after protesting the arrest of his Jewish father-in-law), and family memory is one of the most potent forms of collective memory.

All of the writers we read in this volume (save Irène Némirovsky) were children during the war, of the war, or of the immediate postwar, coming of age after the time when the destruction of their families was ordained by the state. We find in these books the "radical loneliness" of remembering alone (Wolf). The implications of these vulnerable families for our understanding of spatial memory are quite profound. French philosopher of literature Gaston Bachelard, in his 1958 book *The Poetics of Space*, looked to psychoanalysis and poetry to map the psychic and physical intimacy of our homes akin to the deepest structures of fairy tales and inscribed in our bodies. The nooks and crannies, attics and cellars, stairs and hallways of houses were the phenomenological embodiment of our dreams, articulated once again through poetry. But what of families that were dispossessed of those private spaces, those safe and nostalgic interior places? It is telling that the Paris we encounter in the stories we write about here is largely topographical, with family memory mourned in the coldness of the city streets more than drawn from the warmth of homes. Most of the narratives we read in this volume are outside stories, expelled from private domains, mapped onto the streets of Paris—only to be forgotten. In *The Practice of Everyday Life* (1980), Michel de Certeau asks us to consider walking as a "pedestrian speech act" (98). When we speak, we occupy or take on all of language and similarly, when we walk in a place, we occupy the topography all around us. When we speak, we perform, as de Certeau puts it, an "acoustic acting-out of language," just as when we walk—our steps performing a movement from one place to another—we perform a "spatial acting out of the place" (98). Finally, when we speak with another, we declare a relationship to our listener and walking, correspondingly, articulates a relationship between places. While walking is both a performative and rhetorical act, it also evokes absence: "To walk is to lack a place. It is the indefinite process of being absent . . ." (103). De Certeau's model of walking seems most salient to us as Scott Lerner observes that our writers search these empty places of Paris pursuing lost parents, a melancholic exercise that treats the topography of Paris as a metaphor for the return of repressed memories (personal and political) themselves.

Strolling along with us for the conversation about presence, absence, and literature, we imagine some of the great walkers of Paris—Charles Baudelaire's flâneur of *Les Fleur du Mal*, Victor Hugo's *Les Misérables*, Marcel Proust's *In Search of Lost Time*—as the prewar Paris intertexts that resituate postwar Jewish writing. We encounter almost immediately in its streets the German Jewish critic Walter Benjamin and his Arcades Project, started in 1927 and unfinished still in 1940, when he fled the Occupation. Strolling through the nineteenth-century Parisian shopping arcades, Benjamin's flâneur, his walker, negotiated the fleeting presence of the past through his material encounters. By the time Benjamin embarked on his Arcades Project, many of the arcades were already memories, their physical presence having been "swallowed up" by the great reconstruction of Paris by Baron Haussmann. Benjamin's mode of walking Paris, a combination of historical materialism with a strong dash of Jewish mysticism, became the model of the Paris rambler who resisted the forces of production by wandering at leisure, finding in the experience of the city, the mystical instant, bringing the past into present. Benjamin's aesthetic walker is now deeply complicated by these Jewish writers in search of memories fixed in time and place only by markers of expulsion. If anything, as Sara Horowitz argues, the Jewish movement in occupied Paris was "anti-*flânerie*," not at all free to roam the city at will.

Dedicated seventy years after the liberation of Auschwitz, the concentration camp and killing center where Dora Bruder and so many others were murdered, the Promenade that bears her name joins other markers of the disappeared and dispossessed of Paris. Some of these are sites of commemoration, memorials that draw local visitors and tourists. The Mémorial des Martyrs de la Déportation (Memorial to the Martyrs of the Deportation),

Figure 1.3. Promenade Dora Bruder. (*Photograph by Sara R. Horowitz*)

for example, is a short walk from the majestic Notre Dame cathedral. Carved into the eastern tip of the Île de la Cité and jutting into the Seine River, it was inaugurated in 1962 to commemorate "the 200,000 French deportees sleeping in the night and the fog, exterminated in the Nazi concentration camps." The inscription gestures toward the German phrase *Nacht und Nebel* that signals the Nazi policy of deliberate obfuscation of their genocidal aim, and toward Alain Resnais's 1956 documentary film, *Nuit et brouillard*, which exposes Nazi atrocity and the killing centers in the east that enacted the genocide. Neither Resnais's film nor the Deportation Memorial note the deportation and murder of Jews as a distinct category. That omission is characteristic of the conversation in France about Nazis and the Occupation that was current in the decades following World War II.

Physically absent after the war, the deported Jews were also missing in French national memory. As philosopher François Azouvi insists in his 2012 *Le Mythe du Grand Silence*, postwar acknowledgment of the geno- cide of the Jews of Europe found its way into journalistic reportage and intellectual exchange. Still, as the works of the writers treated in this book attest, French public discourse about the war, its victims, and the ethical implications were couched most often in universal, rather than particular, terms—effectively effacing the specific circumstances and experiences of the disappeared French Jews. These unnoted Jewish deportees cast a shadow in the City of Light. It is their unremarked absence that drew Patrick Modiano in search of a trace of Dora Bruder, and Georges Perec in search of traces of his parents and the other disappeared Jews of the Belleville neighborhood. The recurring mapping and remapping of Paris in their writing, and in the writing of Sarah Kofman and Henri Raczymow, bring the absent past into the present, layering past and present cityscapes over one another. Thanks to their engagement with the sights, textures, and sounds of a part of Paris that is no more, the city itself remembers its past.

A Brief, Modern History of the Jews of Paris

Lebn vi got in Frankraykh—Un juif est heureux comme Dieu en France

The eighteenth century helped usher in a new era for the Jews of Europe and, particularly, of France. The French Revolution of 1789, so central to the Enlightenment project, initiated the political philosophy that led to the emancipation of the Jews—that is, extending to Jews benefits of citizenship—first in France, then in other European countries. Although it was a deeply contentious issue, the French revolutionaries who set the ideals of their movement—*liberté, égalité, fraternité*—argued in favor of according the full rights of citizenship to France's native Jews.

The integration of Jews into the French nation emerged out of Enlightenment ideas about human and social perfectability. In a speech now famous for setting the terms by which liberal democracies would regard minorities, Count Stanislas de Clermont Tonnerre insisted that the French Republic must grant equal rights to French Jews if it was to honor its own principles of equality, secularity, and human rights. "The Jews should be denied everything as a nation, but granted everything as individuals. . . . they must constitute neither a state, nor a political corps, nor an order; they must individually become citizens. . . . The existence of a nation within a nation is unacceptable to our country." This formulation responded to fears that the Jew harbored dual loyalties and, as such, posed a danger to France. Count Clermont-Tonnerre's language articulated a neat divide between private and public life, and between personal (that is, religious) and national identity. Religion was seen as a personal and domestic option shared with one's coreligionists. Citizenship was a public and collective commitment, shared with all French people.

But the laws that emancipated the Jews also threw the Jewish community into one of its many identity crises, which, according to the French historian Léon Polyakov, strikes individuals whose belonging to a particular group is questioned, or who are subject to exclusion, discrimination, or violence. For Jews, Polyakov observes, such identity crises are endemic. The emancipation put many Jews in the impossible position of having to choose between Jewishness and Frenchness. Moreover, the proponents of the emancipation, such as Abbé Grégoire, hoped that it would bring Jews, by "gentle means" to become Christians—in other words, that it would result in their disappearance as Jews. Thus pressured to abandon who they were to become something else, the Jews of France were subjected to the opposing forces of tradition and the affective pull of Jewish community life, on one side, and economic opportunity and social emancipation, on the other.

It was not until the nineteenth century that a significant Jewish population took root in Paris. From a meager population of 3,000 in 1808, by the middle of the nineteenth century Paris housed the twelfth largest Jewish population of any city in the world. And when France lost the territories of Alsace-Lorraine to Prussia in 1871, the Jews from that region gravitated in large numbers to Paris. They formed a distinct cultural group and, like the Jews who already called Paris home, they aspired to assimilate—that is, to maintain both a French and a Jewish identity.

By the nineteenth century, a Yiddish expression common in Poland and Ukraine encapsulated the eastern European image of Jewish France: *Lebn vi got in Frankraykh* (Live like God in France). Or, as rendered more expansively into French: *Un juif est heureux comme Dieu en France* (A Jew is as happy as God in France). Although the long-standing fears of the Jewish presence endured in France, in the eyes of Jews elsewhere, the rights enjoyed by French Jews as citizens of a liberal democracy made their position enviable. And for them, as for other Europeans, Paris was the symbol of France. Indeed, responding to both economic crisis and renewed waves of pogroms, some 35,000 Jews left eastern Europe for Paris between 1880 and 1914, with the number of immigrants mounting after 1905.

The pogroms in Russia left the French public puzzled. In Paris, the frenzied antisemitism of the populace in eastern Europe was, according to Polyakov, considered a "bewildering foreign mania." As a whole, as he points out, "the French people took some time before they danced to the foreign tune, whether that of Berlin, Saint Petersburg, or Rome." The French

Revolution swept aside the history of exploitation, plunder, persecutions, and murder of the French Jews but it didn't take long for the indigenous antisemitism to manifest itself. In spring 1886, Édouard Drumont's tract *La France juive* fostered a new climate and paved the way for the rapid spread of large-scale antisemitic propaganda. In 1890 the Catholic newspaper *La Croix* proudly proclaimed itself "the most anti-Jewish newspaper in France."

It was in this climate that the infamous Dreyfus affair hit the press. In December 1894, Captain Alfred Dreyfus, a young Jewish military officer, was falsely accused of passing along French military secrets to Germany, convicted of treason, and imprisoned on Devil's Island. Exonerating evidence soon emerged—evidence that identified the real culprit to be Major Ferdinand Walsin Esterhazy. But military authorities suppressed the evidence and introduced falsified documents that further incriminated Dreyfus. As a result, in 1897, Esterhazy was acquitted and Dreyfus's conviction stood. Two years later, Dreyfus was retried. He was again convicted, although this time he was pardoned and released. Not until 1906 was Dreyfus exonerated.

For Theodore Herzl, the Dreyfus affair was proof that Jews had no real future in Europe. Notwithstanding the legal rights Jews claimed as citizens, Herzl concluded that antisemitism precluded real equality. He attended the Dreyfus trial as a journalist and saw Dreyfus being stripped of his rank, writing, "They didn't shriek 'Down with Dreyfus!' but 'Down with the Jews!'" French sociologist Emile Durkheim, who, like Dreyfus was from an Alsatian Jewish family, bitterly remarked on the "burst of joy on the boulevards instead of what should have been public mourning." French Prime Minister Léon Blum, then a young man who was also from an assimilated Alsatian Jewish family, was appalled by the "mood of the scalp dance, a ferocious joy of reprisal." The Dreyfus affair unleashed a cold civil war in France. In spite of the letters published by *Le Figaro* demonstrating Esterhazy's hatred of France and proving his guilt, and in spite of novelist Émile Zola's *J'accuse* (1898)—which accused the French government of antisemitism—the majority of the French public and its political establishment remained staunchly anti-Dreyfus. Even when new information made a review of the Dreyfus verdict inevitable, the *anti-Dreyfusard* camp did not relent. Violent incidents multiplied and as the victory of the *Dreyfusard* camp became imminent, the risk of a coup d'état and civil war grew. Polyakov points out that the social fabric in France suffered consequences that persist to this day: on one side were the conservative forces, the torch bearers of the traditional Catholic values; on the other side were the progressives, the partisans of a secular republic founded on the ideals of human rights.

Figure 1.4. Grave of Alfred Dreyfus. (*Photograph by Jonathan Richler*)

Nonetheless, French immigration policies were far more liberal and welcoming of Jews than those of other Western countries. The 1905 Aliens Act of Great Britain, for example, kept the wave of Jewish immigration from the east to a trickle. France's relatively liberal policies toward Jews between the two world wars were beckoning. Jews saw France as land of equality and opportunity. Paris developed a thriving Jewish cultural life. Many foreign-born Jews enlisted in the French army and—like Alfred Dreyfus after he was exonerated—fought in World War I. At the same time, many French continued to harbor deep ambivalence towards Jews, with mounting xenophobia and antisemitism.

French Jews, too, were ambivalent about the new arrivals. In Paris, the newcomers were not warmly welcomed by the native French Jews of the city, who numbered approximately 40,000. Still, many Jewish organizations in Paris helped the eastern European immigrants to acclimate to French life. The Jewish immigrants pouring in from eastern Europe at turn of century were largely poor, Yiddish speaking, often religious, and working class, among them skilled workers and artisans. Some, however, were well-educated, secular, acculturated Jews seeking to escape the violent antisemitism of eastern Europe, and political refugees and intellectual exiles. Existing Jewish organizations offered education on Jewish culture in the French context. They provided economic assistance to the newcomers, and encouraged them to assimilate culturally and adopt French ways of being.

Figure 1.5. A view of rue des Rosiers in the Jewish quarter in Paris, 1930s. (*Source*: USHMM)

However, the two populations—the long-standing Jewish community and the more recent immigrants—maintained a high degree of cultural separateness. For the most part, the immigrants established and clung to their own institutions. For example, the established French synagogues felt alien to the Jews of eastern Europe, modeled as they were on French Catholic churches, so they founded their own synagogues and retained customs from home. They formed cohesive religious, cultural, social, and economic networks. They created their own newspapers, schools, philanthropic organizations, trade unions, and cultural institutions. They frequented their own theater and restaurants, and patronized their own kosher butchers. Jewish neighborhoods developed beyond the Marais—in the area of Belleville, in the 11th, 19th, and 20th arrondissements; in Montmartre, in Clignancourt. These neighborhoods figure in important ways in the works of the authors examined in this book.

The 1930s in France were marked by economic crisis and political instability. The charismatic, Jewish Léon Blum was the head of the Parti populaire français and president of the council (prime minister) of the leftist coalition government. Another Jewish political figure, Georges Mandel, was a minister in the same government. This decade would witness the emergence of fascist movements and xenophobic writers such as Louis-Ferdinand Céline, who used his talent to promote hatred of Jews. A slew of newspapers such as *L'anti-juif*, *La Gerbe*, or *Je suis partout* were at the forefront of a campaign of hatred against Léon Blum. Patrick Modiano's first novel, *La Place de l'étoile* (1968), echoes the savage antisemitism in France during the years leading up to World War II.

Vichy France and the Paris Cultural Scene

On May 10, 1940, German forces attacked France. On June 14, Paris fell, undefended. On June 22, the capitulation of France to Germany was signed, ushering in the period known as Vichy France, or *Régime de Vichy*. On Hitler's orders, the railcar where the 1918 armistice ending World War I was signed—the ultimate humiliation of Germany in Hitler's eyes—served this time as the stage for the final act of France's defeat. As part of the armistice agreement, the country was divided into two parts. The north and the Atlantic coast of France—including Paris—were directly controlled by the Nazis and the city thus came under German military rule in collaboration with their chosen French officials. The southeastern part of the country was governed by the French and the capital was moved from Paris to the city of Vichy, some 250 miles to the south.

The stunned Parisians witnessed Hitler's triumphant tour of the city on June 23, 1940. Soon after, on July 10, in an extraordinary session of the two chambers of representatives meeting at the theater of the Grand Casino in Vichy, President Albert Lebrun accorded General Philippe Pétain full powers to form a government and introduce a new constitution. The vote took place in the absence of 20 percent of the members of both chambers, some exiled, some dead. The majority of those present voted yes, effectively ending the Third Republic.

By the time the German army invaded France in May 1940, roughly 175,000 Jews lived in Paris—some of them long-time residents, others recent refugees from other places under Nazi control. Realizing the danger to their own status in France and intensely loyal to the French Republic, many Jews joined the French resistance. When northern and western France came under Nazi occupation, many of the Jewish inhabitants fled Paris, hoping to find haven in southern France, helped by secret Jewish organizations such as the Communist Solidarité, the Bundist Amelot, the Oeuvre de Secours aux Enfants, or the Children's Aid Society (OSE), and several clandestine Zionist groups. A September 1940 German census records 150,000 Jews living in Paris, 64,000 of them designated as foreign Jews. This latter group was the first to be targeted for arrest and deportation.

In the parts of France under their direct control, Nazis instituted race laws identical to those applied in Germany. The so-called free zone, controlled by the Vichy government, had its own rules, but, according to the terms of the 1940 armistice, the Vichy government was to collaborate with Germany in the implementation of the Final Solution. With Maréchal Pétain as head of government, joined by Pierre Laval as vice president of the Council of Ministers, the government initiated a slew of measures that established antisemitism as the official state policy and Jews were excluded from social and political life. The government established a special ministry and police force for the "Jewish question" (CGQJ). Foreign Jews—50,000 persons by the end of 1940—were imprisoned in the territory under the control of the Vichy government. Later on, Vichy civil servants continued to collaborate with the occupier by giving lists of the Jewish citizens to the Gestapo and the municipal police of Paris. The Police Préfecture of Paris for example, handed in the so-called Tullard file, containing the names of all the Jews living in the Paris region.

Figure 1.6. "For one hundred years, the verminous Jew has come from his ghetto and invaded France." One of a series of cartoons from a French language, anti-Jewish pamphlet titled, "The Canker Which Corroded France," published by the Institute for the Study of Jewish Questions in Paris, 1940–1941. (*Source*: USHMM)

Between 1940 and 1941, with the help of the French police, the Germans arrested 10,000 Jews. On July 22, 1940, less than a month after it was formed, the Vichy government stripped all Jews naturalized after 1927 of their French citizenship. As a result, more than 15,000 people became stateless, and therefore further marginalized and more exposed to persecution. Then, in the fall of 1940 and in June 1941, Vichy enacted additional laws regarding the status of the foreign Jews. These new laws differentiated between Jews born in the countries under the Nazi occupation, Jews born in France, and Jews from the rest of Europe. The laws applied also to Jews living in French colonies such as Algeria. All foreign Jews were to be interned. Two additional categories of citizens subject to these laws were communists and Freemasons. So proactive were the antisemitic measures of the Vichy government that by early 1943, the head of Pétain's civil cabinet boasted that France outdid the rest of Europe, rivaling Germany in its persecution of Jews.

Between July 1940 and November 1942, when the Germans invaded the free zone in response to the landing of the Allied troops in Tunis and Algeria, the pressure of the race laws made life untenable. Starting in 1940, Jews could no longer be civil servants, soldiers, teachers, or journalists; in 1941 the list of proscribed professions expanded even further. Jews were excluded from the census, and they were limited in the practice of medicine and dentistry. From June 1942, Jews could no longer be artists.

The arrival of the German army also gave rise to an eruption of reactionary forces in France: the puritanism that characterized Vichy merged with the antisemitism and anti-Modernism that had marked French public discourse in the late 1930s. Prominent writers such as Louis-Férdinand Céline, Drieu La Rochelle, and Robert Brasillach openly welcomed the Nazis. Cries against the moral corruption, perversion, and decadence spread by modern art, and the need for it to reform itself, came from even the most respected daily newspapers such as *Le Temps* and *Le Figaro*. Céline, Drieu La Rochelle, Brasillach, and figures such as Alain Laubreaux, the theater critic of the fascist weekly *Je suis partout*, served as models for the characters of Patrick Modiano's *The Occupation Trilogy*, only recently translated into English.

When the Germans marched into Paris in the spring of 1940, it was not only France that lost; according to Frederic Spotts, what followed was a unique historical phenomenon in which a genuine "cultural International" composed of writers, painters, sculptors, composers and musicians, filmmakers and art collectors, both French and foreign, was irreparably shattered. He describes it as follows:

> Twentieth-century Paris was to culture what nineteenth-century England had been to industry. Paris had fostered Impressionism and post-Impressionism, Cubism, Fauvism, and Symbolism as well as Dadaism, Futurism, Purism, Realism and Vorticism, not to mention Existentialism, Neo-Plasticism, Orphism, Pointillism, Simultanism, Surrealism and Transhylism. It enjoyed what seemed to be a predestined superiority, taking for granted that the best art was made in Paris and would go on being made there for evermore. (Spotts, 167)

By the time of the armistice, this unique community of intellectuals and artists was scattered across France and beyond.

Most foreigners, Spotts points out, had already fled Paris ahead of the advancing German forces: Nabokov was on his way to the United States, Walter Benjamin was in a transit camp near Nevers, and Max Ernst was in an internment camp near Nimes. Many others also left Paris: Picasso, Matisse, Duchamp, Dalí, Chagall, Kandinsky, Sonia Delauney, Magritte, Léger, philosopher Henri Bergson, and Simone de Beauvoir were spread across the south of France in search of shelter and a source of income. Writers such as Malraux, Sartre, Jeanson, Desnos, and Anouilh, were all made prisoners of war. Irène Némirovsky's *Suite Française* captures the full extent of the chaos among Parisians, and her own life is a poignant example of the horrors that befell the Jews of France.

Some cultural figures remained in Paris, especially those of an older generation. Some were opportunists who hoped to take advantage of the Occupation for their personal gain. For French intellectuals, the decision to stay or leave Paris presented itself as a moral dilemma. For the foreigners, many of whom also happened to be Jewish, leaving, if possible, represented the only possibility for survival. Chagall nearly did not make it: in April 1941 he was picked up in a surprise roundup of Jews and was saved by the urgent intervention of the American Emergency Rescue Committee.

A few days after the armistice Albert Camus wrote, "Life in France is hell for the mind now." This, however, did not prevent him from getting married and moving to Paris from Algiers, then publishing *L'Étranger* and *Le Mythe de Sisyphe* in 1942. Sartre, who also worked and published during the Occupation, is still the subject of much debate. According to Ingrid Galster, Sartre was "neither saint nor criminal. He was neither a pure resistant, nor a collaborator. . . . During the occupation he did not want to renounce his vocation of a writer . . . even though, to support himself, he took the job of a Jewish professor who was fired by the Vichy government." The response of French artists and intellectuals to the Occupation, remains, to this day, subject of discussion and a matter of controversy: Was staying on and continuing to work equal to collaboration with the enemy? Was it courageous or cowardly? What about the *attentistes*, the ones who thought the best thing to do was wait and see? In the words of Alan Riding, France is still trying to answer the question, "where did accommodation leave off and collaboration begin?"

In 1942, these efforts were stepped up as Germans began systematically rounding up and deporting foreign Jews from Paris to transit camps in Drancy, Pithiviers, and Beaune-la-Rolande. In mid-July 1942, 13,000 Parisian Jews were rounded up and confined to the Vélodrome d'Hiver, or Vél d'Hiv, a sports arena in the southern part of the city. This was the largest roundup of Jews in France. There they were confined under abysmal conditions, without food or water, with poor sanitation and no ventilation. After several days, the Jews were deported to the internment and transit camp in Drancy, a northeastern suburb of Paris. The camp was initially staffed by French police and while they were there, the Jews were held in buildings that had once served as police barracks. From Drancy, they were sent on to Auschwitz-Birkenau. Between August 1941 and August 1944, approximately 70,000 people passed through Drancy en route to the concentration camps and killing centers in the East. Most of the deportees were Jews, along with about 5,000 or 6,000 non-Jews who were active in the French resistance. One-third of Jews deported from Drancy were French citizens. Of those interned in Drancy, fewer than 2,000 survived the war.

By the middle of 1943, about 60,000 Jews remained in Paris. The Germans began to deport Jews from orphanages, hospitals, and nursing homes. Then, early in 1944, they concentrated on arresting and deporting all Jewish French citizens. On August 25, 1944, Allied forces liberated Paris. In all, more than 50,000 Parisian Jews, mostly foreign-born, had been deported and murdered. Nonetheless, antisemitism had always been

Figure 1.7. Foreign-born Jews arrive at the Gare d'Austerlitz station during a deportation action from Paris, 1941. (*Source*: USHMM)

rejected by a part of the French people that included progressive women and men of all walks of life: Émile Zola and Georges Clemenceau, the leading *Dreyfusards*; members of the resistance; and the approximately 4,000 people who helped rescue Jews and were later honored by the Israeli government with the designation "Righteous among the Nations." Also included in this group were courageous members of the Catholic clergy who were involved in hiding the Jews of France and helping them to escape. This, together with the fact that many people managed to hide or escape on their own, explains how more than three-quarters of French Jews survived World War II.

The Authors and Their Contexts: The Paris of the Postwar Literature

Because he was a Jew, my father died in Auschwitz. How can it not be said?

—Sara Kofman

. . . the Paris of the occupation was always a kind of primordial darkness. . . .

—Patrick Modiano

In the aftermath of the war, Paris, along with the rest of France, reluctantly confronted questions of occupation, resistance, and collaboration. But the Jewish question—the deported Jews of Paris who never returned, the deep antisemitism in Nazi ideology, and, more specifically, French responsibility for Jewish deaths, deportations, and suffering—was excluded from the national conversation about the war for more than two decades. After World War II, many European intellectuals found themselves in exile in Paris, making the city the postwar center for European intellectual life. As historian Tony Judt declared in *Postwar*, "Paris was the capital of Europe." In universities and cafés, the Paris intellectuals talked about evil, suffering, and atrocity without accounting for the yellow star or the moral compromises of the Vichy government. Jewish deportations were swept into the broader discussions of deportations under Nazism. The Nazi genocidal actions against Jews, and French participation in those actions, were not part of a public conversation. Judt acerbically observes that "the narcissistic self-importance of Paris within France was projected un-self-critically onto the world at large."

Beginning in the late 1960s, Jewish writers and intellectuals in Paris began to push for a reconsideration of French wartime behavior and a more explicit record of the fate of Jews in France under Nazi occupation and under the Vichy government. Many of these writers were born during or after the war, often into immigrant families. Some identified strongly as Jews, others acknowledged Jewish ancestry but regarded their own identity as ambiguous. They looked back at the war and its aftereffects partly to account for past events, and partly to understand themselves and the deep currents that stirred inside them. As novelist Patrick Modiano noted in his Nobel Prize acceptance speech, "Like everyone else born in 1945, I was a child of the war and more precisely, because I was born in Paris, a child who owed his birth to the Paris of the occupation. . . ." He noted the silence of those around him who had been adults during the Occupation of Paris. In a sense, one might say he speaks for all the writers treated in this volume when he says, "[W]hen their children asked them questions about that period and that Paris, their answers were evasive. Or else they remained silent as if they wanted to rub out those dark years from their memory and keep something hidden from us. But faced with the silence of our parents we worked it all out as if we had lived it ourselves."

This volume considers five Paris writers who, like Modiano, grappled with the effects or the aftermath of the Nazi occupation, and its imprint on their own lives and on their Paris. The chapters that follow explore the significance of Paris in the postwar writing of Sarah Kofman, Patrick Modiano, Georges Perec, and Henri Raczymow—each of whom published in the decades following World War II. Although Irène Némirovsky did not survive the war, her novel, discovered and published much later, describes the impact of the war on Parisians with the immediacy that only her tragic proximity to those events could afford. Paris was the topography of memory, recording the impact of the Holocaust on Jewish and French identity, on literature and literary forms, on adaptation, identity, displacement, belonging, and haunting.

Sarah Kofman (1934–1994) was a prominent philosopher interested in psychoanalytic approaches to art, film, and literature. Her parents were Orthodox Jews who had come to Paris from Poland in 1929. Her father, Berek Kofman, the rabbi of a Paris synagogue, was among the 13,000 Jews arrested in the Vel d'Hiv' Roundup; he had refused to go into hiding in the hope that his capture would buy his family time to hide. He was deported to Auschwitz and murdered there. With the help of Jewish organizations and the kindness of non-Jewish French people, Sarah's mother was able to secure safe havens for each of her six children and for herself. While Kofman's brothers and sisters lived out the war in the French countryside under false, Catholic identities, Sarah and her mother survived the Nazi occupation in the Paris apartment of a French Catholic woman. Although she was a prolific writer, for most of her life Kofman wrote little of her experiences as a hidden child, or about the Jewish experience of the Nazi genocide. In 1987 she published *Paroles suffoquées*, translated as *Smothered Words*, her first attempt to contend with the Holocaust in writing. Rather than narrate her own experiences, she wrote more theoretically about the impossibility and necessity of writing about Auschwitz. Although the book memorializes her father and discusses his Jewishness, it also incorporates her response to the writing of two non-Jewish French writers who wrote about Auschwitz: Robert Antelme, a member of the French resistance deported to labor camps, and Maurice Blanchot, a French fiction writer and literary theorist who grappled with the effect of Nazi atrocity on language. It was not until 1993 that Kofman wrote a belated memoir of her childhood in occupied Paris, *Rue Ordener Rue Labat*. In it, she describes the war years, spent with the French Catholic woman who concealed Kofman and her mother in a Paris apartment. The memoir traces the ambivalences of that rescue, as the rescuer disengages the girl from her mother and from Judaism, and introduces her to French writers and French culture. Kofman wrote the novel in the sixtieth year of her life and, soon after, committed suicide by gassing herself in her apartment.

Patrick Modiano (b. 1945) is a French novelist and Nobel laureate whose writing engages the challenging ethical legacy of World War II. Although he wrote more than forty novels and screenplays, his work has been little studied outside of France. Until he was awarded the Nobel Prize for Literature in 2014, few of his works were available in English translation. Born in the outskirts of Paris in July 1945 to parents who met during the Nazi occupation, he saw himself as a creation of occupied Paris. His mother was a Belgian actress and his father was a Jewish man of Greek and Italian descent who was born in Paris in 1912. Both of his parents lived on the fringes of Paris society. There is some evidence in his son's writing that Albert Modiano may have been a Nazi collaborator. In his 2005 memoir, *Un Pedigree*, Modiano writes, "I was born . . . to a Jewish man and a Flemish woman who had met in Paris under the Occupation. I write 'Jewish' without really knowing what the word meant to my father, and because at the time it was what appeared on the identity papers." In *Dora Bruder*, Modiano examines loss, complicity, absence, and memory under the shadow of the war as he traces the attempt of the narrator to determine the destiny of an eponymous Jewish teenage girl reported missing by her parents in 1941. As the narrator walks the streets of Paris imagining Bruder's routes, he mediates his own relationship with the city, on the absent Jewish deportees, and on French complicity.

Irène Némirovsky (1903–1942) immigrated to France with her parents from Ukraine in 1918 and settled in Paris. After studying at the Sorbonne, Némirovsky embarked on a career as a writer, becoming a popular fiction writer by the time she was in her mid-twenties. She was unable to obtain French citizenship and her continued status as a foreign Jew placed her among the most vulnerable under the Vichy government. In 1939, she was baptized as a Catholic. Nonetheless, in 1942, she was arrested and then deported to Auschwitz, where she was murdered. Her novel *Suite française* has been included under the rubric of postwar Jewish literary memory because, although it was written during World War II, it remained tucked away in a trunk and unread for decades. Its publication in 2004 brought posthumous attention to Némirovsky and some measure of controversy. Some critics see her writing as peppered with antisemitic tropes and refer to her as a "self-hating Jew." Other critics see her negotiating within limited and lethal parameters under the threat of genocide, and see her life as exemplifying some of the ambivalences of modernity for the secular Jew in Europe.

Georges Perec (1936–1982) was a celebrated novelist, playwright, and filmmaker who experimented with aesthetic form. He particularly engaged in constrained writing—a form of experimental writing in which the author applies artificial constraints. Examples of this are his 1972 novel, *Les Revenentes*, in which the only vowel permitted is the letter *e*, and 1969 novel, *La Disparition* (*A Void*), written without the letter *e*. Born in Paris to Polish Jewish parents who immigrated to France in the 1920s, Perec is a descendent of the Polish Yiddish writer Isaac Leib Peretz (1852–1915). The family lived in the neighborhood of Belleville, among other Jewish immigrants from eastern Europe. Perec's father enlisted in the French army and died in 1940 from battle wounds inflicted during the German invasion of France. To shelter her son from the dangers of occupied Paris, Perec's mother sent him to the southern part of France, the *zone libre*, or free zone, in 1941, when he was five years old. She herself did not survive the war. In 1943, she was rounded up and interned in Drancy. From there, she was deported to the East and murdered, most likely in Auschwitz, that same year. The young Georges spent the war hidden in a Catholic school in Villard-le-Lans. After the war, his paternal aunt and uncle, secular, affluent Parisian Jews, adopted him. No one, he recollects, uttered the word *Auschwitz*; no one told him directly about what had happened to his mother. Like Kofman, his early works did not overtly deal with the Holocaust or the fate of Parisian Jews. But increasingly, his writing began to contend with issues of Jewishness, the effects of the war, and bereavement. Many of his works focused on the neighborhood of Belleville, and with the absent Jews. He grew critical of French cultural amnesia about the Nazi occupation and French collaboration. His 1975 semi-autobiographical novel, *W, ou le souvenir d'enfance* [*W, or the Memory of Childhood*], contains two narratives that, taken together, examine the implications of the Shoah. One narrative portrays a utopian society on a mythic island called W that is eventually revealed to be a totalitarian society and prison camp. The second narrative, autobiographically based, engages with the absences that shaped Perec's own wartime childhood in Paris.

Henri Raczymow (b. 1948) is a novelist and essayist, and one of the cofounders of the journal *Traces*, which explores aspects of contemporary French Jewish culture. He was born in Paris, the city where his paternal grandparents settled after leaving Poland in the 1920s, and his maternal grandparents did the same after leaving Germany during the same period. Both of his parents were born in Paris soon after the families arrived there. During World War II, Perec's father fought with the Jewish Communist partisans against the Nazi occupiers. Many of Raczymow's extended family, on both the maternal and paternal sides, were murdered in Nazi death camps and labor camps. His paternal grandmother was caught up in the Vel d'Hiv' Roundup and deported to the East, most likely to Auschwitz. His paternal uncle was arrested by the French police and deported to Majdanek. Neither returned. Raczymow's parents were assimilated, secular Jews, distanced from Jewish and Yiddish cultures, and Raczymow himself grew up as a secular Jew. In the late 1960s, he began to explore and reclaim the Judaism and Yiddish culture of his grandparents. Both a fiction writer and a literary critic, Raczymow writes about Jewish and French cultures, and has translated Yiddish literature into French. Like Modiano, Raczymow is part of the second, or postwar, generation—a generation whose memory Raczymow has famously described as "shot through with holes." *Un Cri sans voix* [*Writing the Book of Esther*], one of the few works in the Raczymow oeuvre to be translated into English, imagines the relationship of a postwar Jewish writer to the wartime past and to his vanished relatives. In addition to discussing Raczymow's literary writing, this volume includes an original essay by him.

The writing of these five authors pulls us with them through a city of memory. Not far from Notre Dame, in the Marais—the Paris neighborhood across the river from Île de la Cité known for its large Jewish population—a much more recent memorial site restores the murdered Jews to contemporary memory. The Wall of Names, inaugurated in 2005 on the grounds of the Fondation pour la Mémoire de la Shoah (Foundation for the Memory of the Holocaust), lists all the known names of deported French Jews. Among them are relatives of the authors treated in this volume. Our fingers brush the letters that remember Berek Kofman. Nearby, on the Wall of the Righteous, inaugurated in 2006, are the names of French people who saved the lives of Jews targeted by the Nazi genocide. Listed among them is the Catholic woman who sheltered Sarah Kofman and her mother on rue Labat.

Walking through the neighborhoods of Paris today, we walk past schools bearing plaques that commemorate the Jewish schoolchildren of

Figure 1.8. Wall of Names, Fondation pour la Mémoire de la Shoah, Paris. (*Photograph by Sara R. Horowitz*)

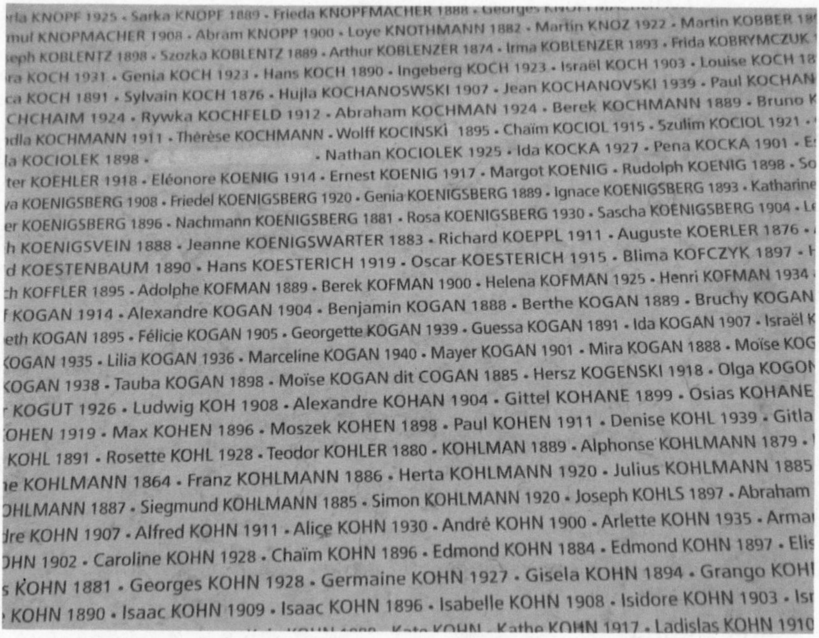

ría KNOPF 1925 · Sarka KNOPF 1889 · Frieda KNOPFMACHER 1888 · Georges KNO...
muí KNOPMACHER 1908 · Abram KNOPP 1900 · Loye KNOTHMANN 1882 · Martin KNOZ 1922 · Martin KOBBER 18
eph KOBLENTZ 1898 · Szozka KOBLENTZ 1889 · Arthur KOBLENZER 1874 · Irma KOBLENZER 1893 · Frida KOBRYMCZUK 1
ra KOCH 1931 · Genia KOCH 1923 · Hans KOCH 1890 · Ingeberg KOCH 1923 · Israël KOCH 1903 · Louise KOCH 18
ca KOCH 1891 · Sylvain KOCH 1876 · Hujla KOCHANOSWSKI 1907 · Jean KOCHANOVSKI 1939 · Paul KOCHAN
CHCHAIM 1924 · Rywka KOCHFELD 1912 · Abraham KOCHMAN 1924 · Berek KOCHMANN 1889 · Bruno K
ıdla KOCHMANN 1911 · Thérèse KOCHMANN · Wolff KOCINSKI 1895 · Chaïm KOCIOL 1915 · Szulim KOCIOL 1921 · ·
la KOCIOLEK 1898 · . Nathan KOCIOLEK 1925 · Ida KOCKA 1927 · Pena KOCKA 1901 · Es
ter KOEHLER 1918 · Eléonore KOENIG 1914 · Ernest KOENIG 1917 · Margot KOENIG · Rudolph KOENIG 1898 · So
ya KOENIGSBERG 1908 · Friedel KOENIGSBERG 1920 · Genia KOENIGSBERG 1889 · Ignace KOENIGSBERG 1893 · Katharine
er KOENIGSBERG 1896 · Nachmann KOENIGSBERG 1881 · Rosa KOENIGSBERG 1930 · Sascha KOENIGSBERG 1904 · Le
h KOENIGSVEIN 1888 · Jeanne KOENIGSWARTER 1883 · Richard KOEPPL 1911 · Auguste KOERLER 1876 · ·
d KOESTENBAUM 1890 · Hans KOESTERICH 1919 · Oscar KOESTERICH 1915 · Blima KOFCZYK 1897 · H
ch KOFFLER 1895 · Adolphe KOFMAN 1889 · Berek KOFMAN 1900 · Helena KOFMAN 1925 · Henri KOFMAN 1934 ·
f KOGAN 1914 · Alexandre KOGAN 1904 · Benjamin KOGAN 1888 · Berthe KOGAN 1889 · Bruchy KOGAN
eth KOGAN 1895 · Félicie KOGAN 1905 · Georgette KOGAN 1939 · Guessa KOGAN 1891 · Ida KOGAN 1907 · Israël K
KOGAN 1935 · Lilia KOGAN 1898 · Marceline KOGAN 1940 · Mayer KOGAN 1901 · Mira KOGAN 1888 · Moïse KOG
KOGAN 1938 · Tauba KOGAN 1898 · Moïse KOGAN dit COGAN 1885 · Hersz KOGENSKI 1918 · Olga KOGON
r KOGUT 1926 · Ludwig KOH 1908 · Alexandre KOHAN 1904 · Gittel KOHANE 1899 · Osias KOHANE
OHEN 1919 · Max KOHEN 1896 · Moszek KOHEN 1898 · Paul KOHEN 1911 · Denise KOHL 1939 · Gitla
KOHL 1891 · Rosette KOHL 1928 · Teodor KOHLER 1880 · KOHLMAN 1889 · Alphonse KOHLMANN 1879 · ·
ıe KOHLMANN 1864 · Franz KOHLMANN 1886 · Herta KOHLMANN 1920 · Julius KOHLMANN 1885
OHLMANN 1887 · Siegmund KOHLMANN 1885 · Simon KOHLMANN 1920 · Joseph KOHLS 1897 · Abraham
dre KOHN 1907 · Alfred KOHN 1911 · Alice KOHN 1930 · André KOHN 1900 · Arlette KOHN 1935 · Armaı
OHN 1902 · Caroline KOHN 1928 · Chaïm KOHN 1896 · Edmond KOHN 1884 · Edmond KOHN 1897 · Elis
s KOHN 1881 · Georges KOHN 1928 · Germaine KOHN 1927 · Gisela KOHN 1894 · Grango KOHI
KOHN 1890 · Isaac KOHN 1909 · Isaac KOHN 1896 · Isabelle KOHN 1908 · Isidore KOHN 1903 · Isr
...KOHN 1888 · Kate KOHN · Kathe KOHN 1917 · Ladislas KOHN 1910

Figure 1.9. Berek Kofman's name on the Wall of Names, Fondation pour la Mémoire de la Shoah, Paris. (*Photograph by Sara R. Horowitz*)

Paris, arrested and deported to their deaths during the Nazi occupation. Less obtrusive than the *Stolpersteine*, or stumbling stones, that protrude from the pavement in front of the homes of deported Jews in Berlin and other German cities, these plaques bring the memory of genocide down to the local level. And in three locations—if one knows to look—are the sites of internment camps that once functioned in the heart of Paris itself.

Together, these sites form a network of shadows that point to what once was—or more properly, to those who once were. Their absent presences—like Dora Bruder, or Sarah Kofman's father, or Georges Perec's parents, or Irène Némirovksy and her husband, or Henri Raczymow's uncle and grandmother, or thousands of others—hint at those who disappeared abruptly, violently, and irreversibly. Captured by the Nazi authorities, arrested by the Paris police, betrayed by neighbors and colleagues, their memory-traces draw the authors into the neighborhoods, streets, parks schools, synagogues, and markets where they once led their lives. Through their language and silence, their memory and imagination, the shadows of the revenants shimmer and beckon. We follow.

Figure 1.10. Memorial plaque. (*Photograph by Sara R. Horowitz*)

We have organized the chapters collected in *Shadows in the City of Light* into five broad themes—Topography, Familiar Strangers, Ambivalences, Mourning, and Past Imperfect. These themes allow us to think about our physical, political, psychic, historical, and emotional encounters with the postwar Paris literature of Jewish memory. We hope you will find these categories useful.

Bibliography

Azéma, Jean Pierre. "La vérité sur le fichier juif" (interview). *L'Histoire*, no. 163 (February 1993): 58–60.

Azouvi, François. *Le Mythe du Grand Silence: Auschwitz, les Francais, la mémoire.* Paris: Fayard, 2012.

Benbassa, Esther. *The Jews of France: A History from Antiquity to the Present*, translated by M. B. DeBevoise. Princeton, NJ: Princeton University Press, 1999.

Berkovitz, Jay R. *The Shaping of Jewish Identity in Nineteenth-Century France.* Detroit, MI: Wayne State University Press, 1989.

Burton, Richard D. E. *Blood in the City: Violence and Revelation in Paris, 1789–1945.* Ithaca, NY: Cornell University Press, 2001.

Cosnard, Denis. "Une promenade Dora Bruder bientôt à Paris" Blog. January 20, 2015. https://lereseaumodiano.blogspot.com/2015/01/une-promenade-dora-bruder-bientot-paris.html.

Curtis, Michael. *Verdict on Vichy: Power and Prejudice in the Vichy France Regime.* New York: Arcade Publishing, 2002.

Deak, Istvan, Jan T. Gross, and Tony Judt, eds. *The Politics of Retribution in Europe: World War II and Its Aftermath.* Princeton, NJ: Princeton University Press, 2000.

Dreyfus, Jean-Marc, and Sarah Gensburger. *Des camps dans Paris: Austerlitz, Lévitan, Bassano.* Paris: Fayard, 1995.

Fine, Ellen. "The Absent Memory: The Act of Writing in Post-Holocaust French Literature." In *Writing and the Holocaust,* edited by Berel Lang. New York: Homes & Meier, 1988, 41–57.

Galster, Ingrid. "Sartre: Années noires" (interview). *L'Express* (September 1994). https://www.lexpress.fr/culture/livre/sartre-annees-noires_1578702.html. Accessed January 15, 2019.

Hand, Seán, and Steven T. Katz, eds. *Post-Holocaust France and the Jews, 1945–1955.* New York: New York University Press, 2015.

Hofmeester, Karin. *Jewish Workers and the Labour Movement: A Comparative Study of Amsterdam, London and Paris 1870–1914,* translated by Lee Mitzman. Aldershot, Hants, UK; Burlington, VT: Ashgate, 2004.

Horowitz, Sara R. "Sarah Kofman et l'ambiguïté des mères." In *Témoignages de l'après-Auschwitz dans la littérature juive-française d'aujourd'hui: Enfants de survivants et survivants-enfants,* edited by Annelies Schulte Nordholt. Amsterdam and New York: Rodopi, 2008, 101–20.

———. "Lovin' Me, Lovin' Jew: Gender, Intermarriage, and Metaphor." In *Antisemitism and Philosemitism in the Twentieth and Twenty-first Centuries: Representing Jews, Jewishness, and Modern Culture,* edited by Phyllis Lassner and Lara Trubowitz. Newark: University of Delaware Press, 2008, 196–216.

Hyman, Paula E. *From Dreyfus to Vichy: The Remaking of French Jewry, 1906–1939.* New York: Columbia University Press, 1979.

Judt, Tony. *Postwar: A History of Europe since 1945.* New York: Penguin, 2005.

Kaplan, Alice Yaeger. *Reproductions of Banality: Fascism, Literature, and French Intellectual Life.* Minneapolis: University of Minnesota Press, 1986.

Klarsfeld, Serge. *Vichy-Auschwitz: Le rôle de Vichy dans la solution finale de la question juive en France, 1942.* Paris: Fayard, 1983.

Kramer, Lilian, ed. *Holocaust Literature.* New York: Routledge, 2003.

Lévy, Claude, and Paul Tillard. *Betrayal at the Vél d'Hiv.* New York: Hill and Wang, 1969.

Marrus, Michael R., and Robert O. Paxton. *Vichy France and the Jews.* New York: Basic Books, 1981.

Paxton, Robert O. *Vichy France: Old Guard and New Order, 1940–1944.* New York: Columbia University Press, 1972.

Poliakov, Léon. *The History of Anti-Semitism.* Vol. IV, *Suicidal Europe, 1879–1933.* Translated by the Littman Foundation and Vanguard Press. Oxford: Oxford University Press, 1985.

Poliakov, Léon. *L'impossible choix: Histoire des crises d'identité juive.* Paris: Editions Austral, 1994.

Raczymow, Henri. "Memory Shot Through with Holes." Translated by Alan Astro. "Discourses of Jewish Identity in Twentieth-Century France." *Yale French Studies* 85 (1994): 225–27.

Raczymow, Henri. "Pourquoi écrire." *Traces* 3 (1981): 98–99.

Rajsfus, Maurice. *La Police de Vichy—les forces de l'ordre françaises au service de la Gestapo: 1940–1944.* Paris: Le Cherhe midi, 1995.

Rayski, Adam. *The Choice of the Jews under Vichy: Between Submission and Resistance.* South Bend, IN: Notre Dame University Press, 2015.

Riding, Alan. *And the Show Went On: Cultural Life in Nazi-Occupied Paris.* New York: Knopf, 2010.

Sicher, Ephraim, ed. *Holocaust Novelists,* vol. 299, *The Dictionary of Literary Biography.* Farmington Hills, MI: Gale, 2004.

Spotts, Frederic. *The Shameful Peace: How French Artists and Intellectuals Survived the Occupation.* New Haven: Yale University Press, 2008.

Suleiman, Susan Rubin. *The Némirovsky Question: The Life, Death, and Legacy of a Jewish Writer in Twentieth-Century France.* New Haven, CT: Yale University Press, 2016.

Zalc, Claire. *Dénaturalisés. Les retraits de nationalité sous Vichy.* Paris: Seuil, 2016.

Zuccotti, Susan. *The Holocaust, the French, and the Jews.* Lincoln: University of Nebraska Press, 1999.

PART 1   TOPOGRAPHY

The three chapters in this part of the collection focus on the cityscape of Paris in the aftermath of the Shoah. They contrast the immutable character of the city, its monumental stability, with the fleeting character of Jewish lives lived in its midst.

Through an examination of maps used in the 1999 English translation of *Dora Bruder*, Julia Creet follows Modiano on his quest for Dora Bruder. Creet argues that Modiano's is "a tour of melancholic absence." Visiting the places in which he imagines Dora walked and bestowing significance on unremarkable places, Modiano produces a "psychogeography" of her existence. Creet argues that the intersection of four axes of place, time, memory, and emotion involved in the making of the map of Dora's life create a kind of palimpsest within the layers of time.

Gary Mole ventures into Sarah Kofman's neighborhood and its surroundings, mapping out the events from his life onto Kofman's. The neighborhood of rue Ordener and rue Labat hasn't changed much; but its Jewish residents are long gone along the path of suffering and destruction, itself immutable: Vel' d'Hiv', Drancy, Auschwitz. Gary Mole uncovers the ways in which Kofman's belated autobiography bares the inner workings of trauma.

Finally, Anneliese Schulte Nordholt points out that the fundamental theme of much of Patrick Modiano, Georges Perec, and Henri Raczymow's work is absence and loss of an irretrievable past. However, one place that maintains an intense presence and definite fullness is the cityscape of Paris. She raises the key question of this section of the book: Might our revisiting of sites or premises connect us in a deeper and more meaningful way with the past?

2

A Psychogeography of *Dora Bruder*

JULIA CREET

Two sections of an old Paris map serve to introduce readers to the 1999 English translation of Patrick Modiano's *Dora Bruder*. The maps are details at different scales of the 12th and 18th arrondissements, almost certainly extracted from the iconic A. Leconte, *Plan de Paris par arrondissement* tourist guide books of the 1940s.[1]

Consider what Dennis Wood says about maps in his seminal work of cartography, *The Power of Maps*: "They make present—they *re*present—the accumulated thought and labor of the past . . . about the milieu we simultaneously live in and collaborate on bringing [into] being. In so doing they enable the past to become part of our living . . . *now . . . here*" (Wood and Fels 1, ellipses and italics in the original). Unlike a time machine that would eliminate the present, the map works, Wood says, because we see the past in the present. So past and present exist in a palimpsestic relationship, where one layer obscures yet reveals another.

Wood stresses that maps re-present, that they make present again, so that "whatever invisible, unattainable, erasable past or future can become part of our living" (Wood and Fels, 7). Wood's emphasis on the relationship between the map's "there and then" and the "here and now" assumes a walker, a body occupying the space and place that the map describes. Paul Ricœur, the great philosopher of history, observes that the body "constitutes

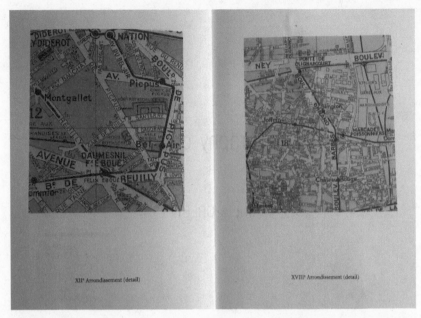

XII⁰ Arrondissement (detail)   XVIII⁰ Arrondissement (detail)

Figure 2.1. Frontispiece of *Dora Bruder*. (*Source: Dora Bruder*, English edition [University of California Press, 1999])

the primordial place" of memory (Ricœur, 43). When we walk in these places, following a map (either physically or at a remove) we experience memorial sites as the here and now of the one who remembers.

Michel de Certeau, emphasizing a very similar point to Wood and to Ricœur, writes in his landmark work, *The Practice of Everyday Life*, that the "rhetoric of the walker" enunciates "both a near and a far, a *here* and a *there*." De Certeau adds that this location, the here-there "necessarily implied by walking" means that we appropriate these places as if they were our own (Certeau, 99). He reinforces the "parallelism between linguistic and pedestrian enunciation." This parallel between the pointer words that locate us in linguistic time and space—"here," "there," "now," "then," which are always relative to our own positions—and the experience of walking (even in our imagination) is vitally important to how we inhabit mnemonic space and particularly the maps that mark both presence and absence in works of postwar literary Paris.

In his densely descriptive and intensely topographic *Dora Bruder*, Patrick Modiano searches the streets of Paris for the traces of a young Jewish girl, Dora Bruder, deported from Paris to Auschwitz, along with her parents, during the Nazi occupation of France in the early 1940s. Many of the essays in the book engage with the melancholic loneliness of Modiano's literary pursuit of the fragmentary evidence of Dora and her parents. He conjures the apparition of Dora out of an exquisite narrative tension between fact, memory, and imagination, grounded in the details of otherwise insignificant streets, addresses, and buildings. As Maxime Decout writes in his contribution to this volume, "Topography more than history brings the dead back to life." Topography as word derives from the Greek "topos" (place) and "graphia" (writing), and we retain that original meaning when we map in detail a small area or local place paying attention to the contours of the land and its structures. Modiano's topographical precision of places Dora lived, walked, and might have walked acts as a defense against how little he knows of Dora and her parents, drawing readers imaginatively into the physicality of his mapping of Paris. "Often, what I know about them amounts to no more than a simple address. And such topographical precision contrasts with what we shall never know about their life—this blank, this mute block of the unknown" (Modiano, 20).

The original French edition of *Dora Bruder*, without the maps, invoked this topographical precision through description rather than the visual *eikon* or image of the map—the present representation of an absent thing. Here is the description that invokes the locale *re*-presented in first detail of the 12th arrondissement: "The buildings of the Saint-Cœur-de-Marie no longer exist. Modern apartment blocks have taken their place, giving an idea of the vastness of the grounds. I don't possess a single photograph of the vanished school. On an old map of Paris, its site is marked 'House of religious education.' Four little squares and a cross symbolize the school buildings and chapel. And a long, narrow rectangle, extending from the Rue de Picpus to the Rue de la Gare-de-Reuilly, outlines the perimeter" (Modiano, 33). Dora had run away from this house of religious education, a Catholic school and a place of relative safety for a young Jewish girl. It was her escape that prompted her parents' ad for her safe return that caught Modiano's eye forty years later in *Paris-Soir* of December 31, 1941.

We might expect then that the opening map would be the one on which Modiano found the school—given the importance of the school and its environs to the narrative, to which Modiano returns several times in the story. But, if we examine the detail of the map closely, the school is not there, though many of the other institutions and buildings in those adjacent blocks that Modiano also describes as loci or "places" of memory are. The *re*-presentation of this map is presence—Dora walked here and Modiano

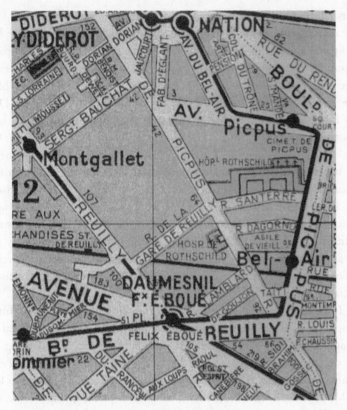

Figure 2.2. Detail of frontispiece of *Dora Bruder*. (*Source*: *Dora Bruder*, English edition [University of California Press, 1999])

followed—but more so absence: the absence of the school and the absence of Dora, both missing from the locale that is pictured in detail.

These maps provide a paratextual frame of reference—something "outside" the text that shapes our reading, particularly for readers outside of Paris who might not readily bring to mind the precise locations of the narrative, or provide our own phenomenological experience of wandering through the twelfth district. And yet, the map is also beyond the narrative, convening the place of the school, but not its *eikon* or image, as schematic as it would have been, a series of rectangular boxes and a few crosses.

Normally, we would consider Modiano's verbal pictures to be a kind of ekphrasis, an expository, descriptive exercise that vividly brings a visual scene (sometimes a work of art) before our eyes—one of the things that readers agree Modiano does brilliantly for the Paris streets of *Dora Bruder* (Howell). But, in this case, it seems that our imaginative reception of that visual exposition is an insufficient response. The impulse to find a map (as Modiano does) or to study iteration after iteration (as I did for decades of *Plan de Paris par arrondissement* editions) or to, finally, create one's own, indicates another kind of mnemonic topography at work. Strangely, the descriptions fuel another urge, one that surfaces strongly for me in reading *Dora Bruder* and a response that I have seen in other readers, something we might call "reverse ekphrasis"—a very common impulse to plot the places Modiano describes linguistically back onto a topographic iconography. In other words: to draw maps.

Following Modiano tracking Dora Bruder, we track Modiano, solidifying his presence in the streets of Paris, even though Modiano is as much an apparition as Dora: "I merged into that twilight, into those streets, I was non-existent," he writes of a memory of dusk in January 1965. To be swept into the power of Modiano's memory is to encounter the urge to reorient the ephemeral in the concrete, even if abstractly.

From Modiano's footsteps tracing Dora emerges an assortment of readers' maps that betray a similarly obsessive but impossible desire to pin Modiano in place, much as he tried to pin Dora. I discovered that I was not alone in my impulse to make maps. Phillip Azoury and Joseph Ghosn, the authors of a Google Maps rendition of *Dora Bruder*'s places, were also self-conscious about their impulse toward cartography, asking, "Que la tentation est grande, aujourd'hui, désormais, de relire Modiano une application Google Map à la main—au risque d'en briser le charme?" ("How strong the temptation today, now, to reread Modiano with a Google Map in hand—at the risk of destroying the spell?") (Azoury and Ghosn). As they put it, "Dora Bruder a remplacé le vertige de l'évocation par l'abîme de la précision. Paris s'est refermé sur la petite Dora." ("Dora Bruder has replaced the vertigo of evocation with the abyss of precision. Paris closed on little Dora.")

More than 64,000 people have looked at Azoury and Ghosn's map. Clicking on any location on the map will take us, in the manner of all Google Maps, directly there, providing both a contemporary detail and a street view. Yes, indeed, the charm is fully broken.

Further, flat maps don't seem sufficient. Hélène Visentin, a digital humanities French studies scholar at Smith, mapped *Dora Bruder* into a 3D pedagogical model, as part of a larger project to explore and study the historical layers of Paris. Her project, "Mapping Paris, a Cultural Capital," uses "interlinked digital maps of Paris from the 16th through 19th centuries," again using a contemporary Google Map of the city as the final coordinator of the past. Three-dimensional Geographic Information System (GIS) technology gave Visentin's students "a way to synthesize much more information about the story and the city Modiano portrays for this dark hour of Paris history." "Now," Visentin explains, "we can map those locations, make them visible, add images and descriptions, write notes on each address, follow the path of the main character" (Ebbets).

These are curious responses to a book that admits most of the things that might have taken place at these locations are illusory, though so suggestive that we want them to be true. It is relatively easy to argue, as Marja Warehime does in "Paris and the Autobiography of a *Flâneur*," that "Dora Bruder evokes the [postmodern] Baudelairian and Surrealist/flâneur because the narrative emphasizes the physical presence of the walker in the city, his solitude in the crowd and . . . the melancholy and nostalgia that sharpen his perceptions" (Warehime). Absolutely true, and the book invites us to concretize the narrative by place, compelling scholars like Stephen Ungar to take pictures as he walks in Modiano's footsteps (Ungar).

But in the face of all of these mappings of *Dora Bruder* that seem even more precise than Modiano's, the text suggests to me another kind of walker, one more in keeping with Modiano's postwar context: that of Guy Debord and his psychogeographers, who walked in absurdist fashion. They used the map of one city to negotiate another, or followed an algorithm, "first left, second right . . . repeat." They walked in ways that bestowed significance on unremarkable places like "an empty alley, a fresh tree stump, a set of hidden stairs, a bank sign, an abandoned church" (Hart). Nicholas Mirzeoff claims that the postwar psychogeographers were obsessed with the "old Jewish districts of European cities that had recently been the scene of Nazi violence." According to Mirzeoff, Debord himself initiated a *derive*—a random drift—through the Marais in 1950, only to escape hostility from a group of Hasidic Jews by running up a staircase painted by the Jewish artist Camille Pissaro at the turn of the century (Mirzoeff, 64). These random intersections revealed the historical and emotional layers of a city "where building, route, or decoration expanded with meaning or disappeared for the lack of it" (Marcus, 127).

Debord asserts in the introduction to *A Critique of Urban Geography* (1955) that "People are quite aware that some neighbourhoods are sad and others pleasant. But they generally simply assume elegant streets cause a feeling of satisfaction and that poor streets are depressing, and let it go at that. In fact, the variety of possible combinations of ambiances, analogous to the blending of pure chemicals in an infinite number of mixtures, gives

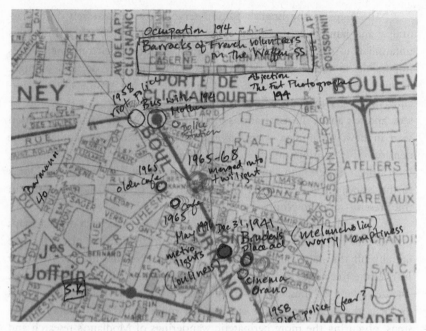

Figure 2.3. Mapping Affect. (*Photograph by Julia Creet*)

rise to feelings as differentiated and complex as any other form of spectacle can evoke." Here, before the spectacle turned to capitalist circus, Debord accords the visual impact of a scene or an event to the experience of place, calling for the production of psychogeographic maps not subordinated to randomness, but insubordinating habituation. Modiano offers us a tour, a tour of melancholic absence, which disturbs his habitual experience of familiar places. Through his physical encounters with the places in which he imagines Dora walked, he produces axial coordinates of time, location, history, memory, and absence, expressed emotionally.

I think the concept of psychogeography, of mapping geographies with emotions, gets closer to Modiano's Paris. We need not a logical, topographical map, but a psychic one. Others hear Debord's soft footsteps lurking in Modiano's geographies: "C'est un Paris, au contraire, de la dérive amnésique, de la dérive psychogéographique (Debord où es-tu? as-tu jamais croisé Modiano? que ne vous a-t-on jamais fait vraiment converser?)" (It is the Paris, on the contrary, of the amnesic drift, of the psychogeographic drift [Debord, where are you? Have you ever crossed paths with Modiano? What have you ever really done to converse?]) (Azoury and Ghosn).

The maps in the English edition serve not as maps often do to nat-
uralize and familiarize us with a place, but to make those selected quarters
unfamiliar, to tag them with a very specific history, albeit one that proves
impossible to locate, because the maps aren't, in fact, detailed enough.
Though he walks with more purpose than the aimless wanders of the psychogeographers through which a street, a neighborhood, a city would be
seen and felt anew, the associations of those places—a familiar neighborhood
seen in new, unfamiliar, ways—is essentially the mode of Modiano. The
density of his locations and their associations all have their deictic functions,
indicating the here and now of the writing, the there and then of Dora's
furtive appearances, and other theres and thens of Modiano's memory in
the present—and now ours.

While the details, in the sense of selection, of these two district maps
pull us into them, they also serve to exclude somehow all the places that are
literally off the map: Sevran, Drancy, the winter velodrome, the Palace of
Justice, the free zone, the hospital in which Modiano fails to find his father.
The selections of these maps—maps that are themselves selections—pull
or focus the attention of the story much more squarely to Dora's furtive
steps, obscuring the more peripatetic wanderings of Modiano's research and
associations. They close down the text in some significant way.

My draw to these maps then was to further concretize the ephemeral, to follow in Modiano's footsteps, visualizing the landscape of memory
through which he travels in his search for Dora. Modiano became my lost
object, and Dora at second remove, and I thought to illustrate the opera-
tions of Modiano's personal and manufactured memories through a model
that could capture the dynamics of memory itself as it surfaces itself in
and out of place. If Dora Bruder speaks to us about that impossible nexus
of absence and presence that we call Jewish memory, surely remapping in
intricate detail, mapping the psychogeography of the book, would produce
a physical model of that impossible-to-capture, that only-ever apparitional
capacity that we call in hopeless and hopeful shorthand, memory itself.

My inclination toward this concretization of Modiano's truth effect
took several almost forms, themselves imagistic efforts to illustrate the
four-dimensional qualities of Dora Bruder, and memory in general, visualizing time and memory beyond geographic three-dimensionality. It was
those four axes of place, time, memory, and emotion that I found myself
wanting to plot some three-dimensional palimpsest in layers of time. My
vision was that each layer would plot the place and its associated emotion
in three eras: the facts of and Modiano's reimagining of Dora's existence

between 1941 and 1942; Modiano's memories of the mid-late 1960s when he walked similar streets knowing nothing of Dora, and then again in 1996 as he wrote the story.

I first reproduced the map of the 18th arrondissement, for it is here that the temporal layering of the narrative is the most dense and its emotional hues most pronounced.

My associations produced emotional readings that were mine more than Modiano's. The fat photographer seemed abject to me; the Bruders' address became a place of melancholia, of emptiness and historical anxiety; the barracks located political amnesia. Soon, my emotional topographies became exhausting and I gave up.

The detail of the map of the 12th arrondissement is quite flat in comparison and of a larger scale, suggesting a smaller scope of action. Modiano places himself there at age eighteen when he is treated for something at a nearby infirmary; in 1971 when he wanders the neighborhood feeling in an uncanny moment that he was following the footsteps of someone else, back shadowing Dora Bruder; and in 1996 when he goes to visit the office

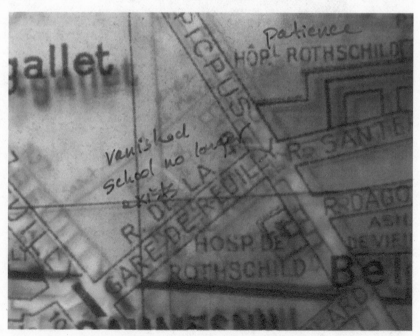

Figure 2.4. Dimensions of Time and Memory. (*Photograph by Julia Creet*)

of the Civil Registrar looking for Dora Bruder's birth certificate. Other than that he has few associations and can form only a limited imaginary since the buildings on which he bases the precise contours of emotional emptiness elsewhere have been torn down. In the end, ground itself is more permanent than the maps, but maps are more enduring than the structures, and structures outlive most people.

I made transparencies, plates, and digital images. No matter how I tried to layer them—projecting them in one, two, three layers on an overhead projector, enlarging them again many-fold, layering them in Photoshop—the layers refused to be read through each other, blurring into unreadable solidity rather than allowing the eye to discern the feelings written in one time in one place on top of another written in the same place in another time and another in an adjacent place by another in yet another time. And quickly, my precision turned against Modiano's, becoming swiftly not a

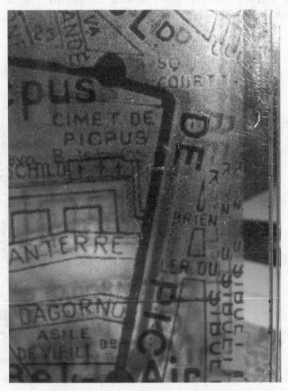

Figure 2.5. (*Photograph by Julia Creet*)

rendition of his feelings and his imagined feelings for Dora, but a map of my own feelings about these places in which I had never set foot. Such is the force of prosthetic memory.

They all failed in the end. But, these failures revealed something interesting about a need to solidify the spectral, much in the mode of Modiano himself—and the ultimate impossibility of such a gesture. Nonetheless, I find the objects that I created from these maps quite beautiful. They are not precious, only ink on plastic, the spacing between them arbitrary, the locations now devolving into notations completely imprecise and no longer only Modiano's—and the erased Serge Klarsfeld (Morris)—but belonging to all those who would pinpoint the life of Dora Bruder as a metonym of every obscure Jewish victim long forgotten.

Of course, my instinct to make the ephemeral solid is similar to Modiano's relationship to the streets and the less permanent structures of

Figure 2.6. Promenade Dora Bruder. (*Photograph by Julia Creet*)

Figure 2.7. Plaque dedicated to Modiano's Dora Bruder. (*Photograph by Julia Creet*)

history, a manifestation of anxiety in relation to the mobility of memory (Creet & Andreas Kitzmann). That anxiety was enacted most manifestly when, in the best tradition of Pierre Nora's sites of memory, Promenade Dora Bruder was inaugurated in 2015 in the 18th arrondissement—just off the edge of our map.

Modiano was present for the inauguration, declaring: "Dora Bruder has become a symbol. This is the first time that an anonymous adolescent has been inscribed forever in the Parisian geography. Today we are gathered in this alley that bears her name, I cannot help but think that Dora was quite simply a child of the 18th arrondissement, a child of Montmartre." A child, we might add, whose fleeting steps have now been made concrete, inscribed in a place for the benefit of our need to make an absence permanent.

Bibliography

1991: Literary Pyschogeography. http://imaginarymuseum.org/LPG/Litpsy91.htm. Accessed March 31, 2016.

Classic Cafes/Psychogeography. http://www.classiccafes.co.uk/Psy.html. Accessed March 31, 2016.

Azoury, Phillip, and Joseph Ghosn. "Le Paris de Modiano, Version Google Map." *Bibliobs,* http://bibliobs.nouvelobs.com/romans/20141010.OBS1793/le-paris-de-modiano-version-google-map.html. Accessed November 9, 2017.

Benjamin, Walter. *The Arcades Project.* Cambridge, MA: Harvard University Press, 1999.

Certeau, Michel de. *The Practice of Everyday Life.* Berkeley: University of California Press, 2011.

Crampton, Jeremy W., and John Krygier. "An Introduction to Critical Cartography." *ACME: An International E-Journal for Critical Geographies* 4, no. 1 (2005): 11–33.

Creet, Julia, and Andreas Kitzmann, eds. *Memory and Migration: Multidisciplinary Approaches to Memory Studies.* Toronto: University of Toronto Press, 2011.

Debord, Guy. "Introduction to a Critique of Urban Geography." *Situationalist International Online,* http://www.cddc.vt.edu/sionline/presitu/geography.html. Accessed April 6, 2016.

Debordpsychogeo.jpg (JPEG image, 755 × 600 pixels); scaled (96%). http://imaginary museum.org/LPG/debordpsychogeo.jpg. Accessed March 31, 2016.

Ebbets, Jan. "With Digital Mapmaking, Scholars 'See' a New Virtual Landscape of Paris." *Smith College: Insight* (Oct. 2011), http://www.smith.edu/insight/stories/paris.php.

Grenaudier-Klijn, France. "Street Names in Patrick Modiano's Work: La Place de l'étoile and the Case of Rue Lauriston." *Neohelicon* 44, no. 1 (June 2017): 217–27.

Hart, Joseph. "A New Way of Walking." *Utne,* http://www.utne.com/community/a-new-way-of-walking.aspx. Accessed April 6, 2016.

Howell, Jennifer. "In Defiance of Genre: The Language of Patrick Modiano's Dora Bruder Project." *Journal of European Studies* 40, no. 1 (March 2010): 59–72.

"Le Paris de Modiano, Version Google Map." *Bibliobs.* http://bibliobs.nouvelobs.com/romans/20141010.OBS1793/le-paris-de-modiano-version-google-map.html. Accessed May 18, 2016.

Marcus, Greil. *Lipstick Traces.* Cambridge, MA: Harvard University Press, 2009.

Mirzoeff, Nicholas. *Watching Babylon: The War in Iraq and Global Visual Culture.* New York: Routledge, 2012.

Modiano, Patrick. *Dora Bruder.* Translated by Joanna Kilmartin. Berkeley: University of California Press, 1999. Originally published as *Dora Bruder.* Paris: Gallimard, 1997.

"Modiano's Dora Bruder—With & without Images." *Vertigo* (February 22, 2015).

Morris, Alan. "'Avec Klarsfeld, Contre l'Oubli': Patrick Modiano's Dora Bruder." *Journal of European Studies* 36, no. 3 (September 2006): 269–93.

"Psychogeography of Memory." *Place Called Space*. http://placecalledspace.org/content/
    psychogeography-of-memory/. Accessed March 31, 2016.
Ricœur, Paul. *Memory, History, Forgetting*. Chicago: University of Chicago Press, 2004.
Wood, Denis, and John Fels. *The Power of Maps*. New York: Guilford Press, 1992.
Warehime, Marja. "Paris and the Autobiography of a Flâneur: Patrick Modiano and
    Annie Ernaux." *French Forum* 25, no. 1 (2000): 97–113.

3

"Ô popoï, popoï, popoï"

Breathless Sobs, Displacement, and Parisian Cartography in Sarah Kofman's *Rue Ordener Rue Labat**

GARY D. MOLE

Memories, Places, Encounters

I would like to begin with a brief personal anecdote related to the way memory, especially emotional memory, conjures spatial locations as much as it disturbs the temporal order.

Prior to 1995, my knowledge of Paris's 18th arrondissement was limited to Zola's working-class neighborhood of the Goutte d'Or in his 1877 novel *L'Assommoir,* to Montmartre's Sacré-Cœur, and to the artists and caricaturists of the Place du Tertre. But before moving to Israel in late September 1995, I spent the academic year on sabbatical leave in Paris and for three months of the summer I changed accommodation and rented a small fourth-floor apartment in the rue Léon, a relatively small street where, unbeknownst to me at the time, a young Jewish girl named Sarah Kofman had had her tonsils removed in a clinic back in 1943. Rue Léon is just around the corner, in fact, from the rue de la Goutte d'Or and runs parallel to the rue des Poissonniers where the Yiddish-speaking Polish immigrant

*This research was supported by the Israel Science Foundation (grant no. 746/13).

Rabbi Bereck Kofman had lived with his wife and six children in the late 1930s before moving to the rue Ordener, itself just up the street from the rue Léon. It was in my apartment on the rue Léon on July 16, 1995, that I listened on the radio to Jacques Chirac's watershed presidential speech during the commemoration of the Vel d'Hiv' Roundup of July 16, 1942, the date that Rabbi Kofman was arrested, interned in Drancy, and subsequently deported to Auschwitz. At last, I remember thinking, as did no doubt many others, a French president was acknowledging the complicity of the French in the persecution and deportation of some 75,000 Jews. . . . It was from the rue Léon too that I would make my way to a small synagogue on the rue Doudeauville, the street where Sarah Kofman attended primary school. The Métro stations of Marcadet Poissonniers, Jules Joffrin, the streets of the rue Ordener, rue Labat, rue Marcadet, rue Custine, rue Lamarck, all these constituted the compass points of my daily life. It was here, too, on the rue Marcadet—the same street, I would reflect later, from which Mémé, Kofman's antisemitic surrogate mother, had telephoned her friend Paul fifty-one years earlier to announce that she had been given legal custody of the young Kofman—that I was attacked with an open canister of tear gas while making a call in a telephone booth. I was wearing a kippah. I have always liked to think that the attacker I glimpsed was a staunch Republican manifesting his displeasure at my flouting of the principle of *laïcité*. . . . It was in my apartment on the rue Léon in any case that in August 1995 I first read Sarah Kofman's *Rue Ordener Rue Labat*, published just the year before. I had read in the press about Kofman's suicide in the previous October and, although I was familiar with Kofman's *Comment s'en sortir?* (How to get out of this?), *Lectures de Derrida* (Readings of Derrida), and *Paroles suffoquées* (*Smothered Words*) from my doctoral studies, *Rue Ordener Rue Labat* had a profound emotional impact on me. This was mostly, of course, because of the distressing and tortured account of a child torn between two mothers, but partly, too, because of my intimate familiarity with the local Parisian landscape of Kofman's wartime memories. I would subsequently read other texts by Kofman in the course of my teaching and research, but it would be another twenty-one years before I would return to *Rue Ordener Rue Labat*.

Mapping Readings of *Rue Ordener Rue Labat*

In the intervening years, Susan Rubin Suleiman has coined the term "1.5 generation," referring to child survivors of the Shoah who were "too young to have had an adult understanding of what was happening to them, and sometimes too young to have any memory of it at all, but old enough to have been there during the Nazi persecution of the Jews" ("The Edge of Memory," 179), subsequently placing Kofman squarely in the company of such writers, psychoanalysts, and historians as Georges Perec, Raymond Federman, Berthe Burko-Falcman, Boris Cyrulnik, Pierre Vidal-Naquet, and Saul Friedlander ("Orphans of the Shoah"). Steven Jaron has preferred the term the "liminal generation," whose members have in common a condition at once historical, existential, and psychical, occupying a Freudian *Zwischen-reich*, an "in-between"—between childhood or adolescence and adulthood, Judaism and Christianity, memory and history, fiction and historiography, French citizenship within the Republic and Jewishness (209). At the same time, a plethora of critical writing on Kofman's philosophical corpus has emerged, including significant psychoanalytical studies of her last autobiographical text *Rue Ordener Rue Labat*.

For many readers, Kofman's suicide in October 1994 was a direct consequence of what Lars Iyer intimates as her "public act of mourning." For Françoise Duroux, the redaction of Kofman's memoir, far from being a therapeutic activity, represented a "suicidal plunge into her own melancholy" (138); Rachel Rosenblum talks of the "dangers of testimony"; and Griselda Pollock explores the inability, in the end, of using art for what the artist and psychoanalyst Bracha Ettinger calls a "transport-station of trauma." Critics would seem to concur, therefore, that despite what Ann Smock, Kofman's English translator, refers to as Kofman's "sense of unexpected renewal" (xi) as she began to write *Rue Ordener Rue Labat* at the beginning of 1993, Kofman's text ultimately offers "no sense of understanding or ultimate resolution, no relief, no consolation whatsoever" (xii), as Smock herself finally concedes. Accordingly, for Kathryn Robson, Kofman's text is without closure, open and undecided (621), while Solange Leibovici writes that Kofman's memoir offered its author no reparation toward the mother nor toward herself, no sublimation or discharge, no love, no pleasure, no visible guilt, only never-ending hatred and pain. The wound, concludes Leibovici, never healed; worse still, in writing *Rue Ordener Rue Labat*, her identity disintegrated. Sara R. Horowitz has given perhaps the most cogent expression to this aspect of Kofman's text, linking the radical deterioration of the mother-daughter relationship to what she sees as the deconstruction of Kofman's very self-foundations.

Whether or not one agrees with interpreting Kofman's suicide as the inevitable result of psychical wounds and the failure of writing about them to heal them, most psychoanalytical readings of Kofman's text quite rightly give prominence to patriarchal/matriarchal distinctions (Dobie, Hoft-March, Oliver). Some emphasize the physical cruelty of the Jewish biological mother and the emotional (and perhaps unavowed sexual) abusiveness of the Christian surrogate mother Mémé (Cairns, Chanter), while others negotiate Kofman's trauma through its encoding not in the mind but in the body, exploring images of bodily ingestion and expulsion, eating and vomiting, the intake and rejection of food as the young Kofman is shifted between maternal and paternal laws to the complete rejection of Jewish identity and dietary habits under the influence of Mémé (Robson). All these readings are also ineluctably drawn to chapters 18 and 19, namely, Kofman's brilliant yet laconic apparent digressions—curious deviations for Pollock, doubling procedures for Horowitz, a layered mise-en-abîme for Cairns—in which Kofman, through Da Vinci's 1499 cartoon of the *Madonna and Child with Saint Anne* and Hitchcock's 1938 film *The Lady Vanishes*, effectively plays out her inner dramas of maternal abandonment and attraction.

Yet as a number of critics have argued, taking their cue from Kofman's own comment at the very beginning of her text that maybe all her books were the "detours required" to bring her to write about "that" (3), in other words, the experience of one father too few, one mother too many, Kofman never actually stopped writing about her childhood during the war, though Ashlee Mae Cummings has contested this, arguing that *not* writing about "that" in her works was the only way Kofman could arrive at the moment of writing about it later (13). Still, there remains sufficient evidence to demonstrate that Kofman *did* write about "that" well before *Rue Ordener Rue Labat*, as shown by the short texts " 'Ma vie' et la psychanalyse ("My life" and Psychoanalysis), "Tombeau pour un nom propre" (Tomb for a Proper Name), "Sacrée nourriture" (Sacred Food), "Cauchemar" (Nightmare), and "Les 'Mains' d'Antelme" (Antelme's "Hands"), as well as *Paroles suffoquées* (*Smothered Words*), her extremely personal 1987 reading of Robert Antelme's *L'Espèce humaine* (*The Human Race*), and Maurice Blanchot's short story "L'Idylle" (The Idyll), in which she explicitly evokes the deportation of her father. Moreover, Jacques Derrida suggested in a 1996 homage to Kofman that retrospectively her first work *L'Enfance de l'art* (*The Childhood of Art*) was already her *autobiogriffure*, an autobiographical anamnesis (152). Sara Horowitz has similarly argued that Kofman's later philosophical works are also disguised autobiographies, and Rachel Rosenblum has given an excellent study of how Kofman's three "pharmaceutical styles"—the philosophical, the aesthetic, and the intellectually autobiographical—all ceded in the end to a fourth style that had nothing pharmaceutical about it at all but was concerned with the direct and brutal exhibition of the death of the father, the conflict between the mothers, and the horror linked to the display of hatred, a process of thirty years of transposition and transfiguration of the distress of a little girl.

A Gift as Yet Unfully Unwrapped

Yet despite the numerous commentaries and attempts to unpack the text's double binds, aporias, and narrative impasses, *Rue Ordener Rue Labat* remains a bewildering and deeply troubling *enigma*. Not that *Rue Ordener Rue Labat* is a fable, or speaks allusively, as the Greek etymology of the word *enigma* would suggest—*ainos, ainissesthai*. But neither, I would argue, is it "bathed in a lucidity unclouded by insight" (xii) or "plainly legible" (xi), as Ann Smock would have it. True, as Lucille Cairns has suggested, Kofman's text employs "fairly conventional narrative means" (219), but despite its apparent simplicity, clarity, and narrative conventions, *Rue Ordener Rue Labat*, torn from Kofman's entrails and offered to the reader as a gift—to use Kofman's own terminology in " 'Ma vie' et la psychanalyse"—retains its enigmatic air, a gift we are not quite sure what to do with and certainly one, I believe, that has not yet been fully unwrapped.

For example, if the fountain pen belonging to her father—all she has left of him, she writes (3)—has been analyzed and psychoanalyzed, what are we to make of the other *memory-objects* in her possession—at the very least nuancing her initial claim—such as the "old worn-out brown photo" of her father that still "overwhelms" her and "pierces" her heart (53), or her father's letters written in Yiddish retrieved, along with other photos of her father, in Israel by her sister Rachel, provoking the recollection that during the entire war she never ceased drawing her own hands (53)? Why has there been no commentary, to my knowledge, on the fact that Kofman insists on proper names throughout the text, even Mémé's, which is Claire (39), except for Mémé's family in L'Haÿ-les-Roses where individual members are referred to merely by their initials H., L., M., C., R., and S. (51)?

Perhaps more telling is the refusal to name the Jewish butcher-turned-kapo who supposedly murdered her father in Auschwitz and who reopened his shop after the war on the rue des Rosiers (10), or the "Jewish friend" who had taken in Kofman and her mother but upon hearing of Kofman's mother's physical abuse of her daughter "promptly switched sides" during

the Free French Tribunal (60). How should we interpret the faulty trans-
literations of Hebrew terms (in the original French edition and taking into
account possible pronunciation difficulties of certain Hebrew consonants for
native French speakers) such as *tvilim* (14) for *tfillin* (phylacteries), *Simra-
thorah* (15) for *Simhat Torah*, *Shoukkot* (16) for *Sukkot*, all corrected in the
English translation, not to mention just plain errors such as *Kiddush* (11)
for *Havdalah* or the "seven [instead of ten] plagues of Egypt" (15) recited
by her father during the Passover seder? Are these signs of a Jewish heritage
never fully reclaimed, or a simple lack of copyediting by the French publisher Galilée? Why does Kofman give roman numerals to her twenty-three
chapters but add a brief title to each one in the table of contents? Would
this reflect the tension of absence and presence played out thematically, men-
tally, memorially, throughout the text? How can one not have noticed that
Gustav Mahler, whose music was banned from public performance during
much of the Nazi era, is intimately associated with Kofman's father (11),
while Beethoven, second only for Hitler to Wagner as a master composer,
is the surrogate mother Mémé's "passion" (48, 85)? Finally, what of the host
of literary and nonliterary texts—what I would call the text's "auto*bibli-
o*graphical" feature—that Kofman constantly mobilizes in her memoir, such
as La Fontaine's fables "The Cockerel, the Cat, and the Mouseling" (24),
"The Grasshopper and the Ant" (45), and "The Cat, the Weasel, and the
Bunny Rabbit" (47); novels such as Louis Desnoyer's 1832 serialized novel
The Misadventures of Jean-Paul Chopard (20), Swift's *Gulliver's Travels* (31),
Zenaïde-Marie-Anne Fleuriot's 1881 story of impossible love, honor, family,
and money, *Raoul Daubry* (51), or Sartre's *Roads to Freedom* (83), which the
adolescent Kofman had to read by torchlight under the bedclothes because
her mother, after the war, would cut off electricity to her room; short stories
by Dickens (68), children's tales such as "The Pied Piper of Hamelin" (19)
or "The Children's Friend" by Arnaud Berquin (36); Louis Forton's comic
strips Bibi Fricotin and Les Pieds Nickelés (29); or the Vermot Almanach
(76) and Maurice Maeterlinck's 1930 essay "Life of the Ants" (76). What
do all these tell us of Kofman's return to the past and her subsequent back
to the future, Kofman's writing present? Should they tell us anything? Or
are they simply part of memory's unpredictable *mapping*?

Temporality and Displacement

This notion of mapping, together with my own predominantly spatially oriented memories of my first encounter with *Rue Ordener Rue Labat* recounted

in my opening anecdote, as well as what has or perhaps has not been said of Kofman's text, brings me at last to the significance of the title of the present study. Detours are often the better (and necessary) part of arriving at one's destination, as Kofman's text would perhaps teach us.

I would note, first of all, that no attentive reader of *Rue Ordener Rue Labat* can possibly fail to notice its temporal disjunctions, the constant time-jumps from the narrative present (both the narrating present and the historical present) to a series of narrative pasts (the recounting of events from before, during, and after the war), with the dominant past historic and imperfect tenses frequently ceding to a direct or implied narrative future. The father's arrest during the Vel d'Hiv' Roundup of July 16, 1942, for instance, is retrospectively read through the lens of the future philosopher's reading of ancient Greek tragedy: the breathless sobs and "Oh papa papa papa" of six children at the terrifying and confusing moment of separation from their father, "knowing they would never see him again" (7), become the Ancient Greek lament of fate "Ô popoï, popoï, popoï." But there is more than just *temporal* displacement here (in other words, the superimposition of two pasts, one during and one after the war). There is also *cultural* and *linguistic* displacement (from Jewish/Yiddish to Greek, via the homophony *papa/popoï* where the two expressions nevertheless have different orthographical forms and different meanings). These displacements clearly and quite consciously play out the principal drama of the physical and emotional displacements of Kofman's childhood during the Occupation.

Displacement—from one place and/or person to another—is also ultimately and intimately related to the Parisian *street-mapping* at the heart of the text and far outweighs its narrative temporalities. Lucille Cairns correctly writes that the title of Kofman's memoir signals a schism, metonymically designating Kofman's two mothers (217), while Rachel Rosenblum speaks, in relation to Kofman, of a "cartography of writing" but all too rapidly reduces the trope to a simple question of style (97). Even Griselda Pollock, whose otherwise brilliant psychoanalytical reading takes issue with the whole idea of the conflict of Kofman's life being a "tug of war between two maternal subjects for one child" (209), mentions only as if in passing the "topographical distance between the two apartments signaled by the two addresses" (210). Rare, then, are the readers who, like Verena Andermatt Conley, seriously raise the question of the role that geography and toponyms (place names) play in Kofman's "working through" of her trauma—or rather, for many readers, in the light of her suicide, her *failure* to *durcharbeiten*, to work through. The title, writes Conley, "invites us to look at the geography of the story as if it were of the allegorical density that characterizes the two roads or directions in *À la recherche du temps perdu—Swann's Way* or *Guermantes' Way*" (156). Proust's almost protean influence on writing and memory in the twentieth century can, of course, hardly be underestimated, but the analogy is nevertheless wrong, as Conley later points out: one of Proust's revelations in *Le Temps retrouvé* (*Time Regained*), the final volume of *À la recherche du temps perdu* (*In Search of Lost Time*), is that the two paths meet. This is patently not the case in Kofman's text. Divided by the rue Marcadet, running almost parallel to them and directly connected by only three streets (rue de Clignancourt, Boulevard Barbès, and rue des Poissonniers), the two metonymic toponyms never cross. In fact, I would add, in the title they are not even grammatically or syntactically coordinated by a conjunction, not even related by a comma. The paratactic title (the juxtaposition of the street names without the use of coordinating or subordinating conjunctions) already testifies to the lack of the either/or option, pointing rather to a deeply ambivalent irresolvable simultaneity. Conley characterizes this as Kofman's "commanding art of refusal," whereby the text invites and rejects our desire to see in "rue Ordener"—linked to the space of the "real" mother, the father, and the inherited Judaic faith—anything "ordonné" (orderly) or "ordinaire" (ordinary), just as "rue Labat"—linked to the Christian mother/other—refuses that "là-bas," "over there," be a simple haven of warmth and pleasure (156). By contiguity, however, concludes Conley, the two streets "make up a marvelously layered story of real space, real in the sense that the reality of the past only merges through the practice of language and affect, seeping into the most common toponyms made available here to sparkle in a subject's most common memories" (156).

Reading the Mappings of *Rue Ordener Rue Labat*

These insights are crucial to any understanding of Kofman's memoir, but they also underestimate the full extent to which cartography governs the structure and narrative of Kofman's tortured text that obsessively attaches a memory to a particular place, situates people and events in a toponym, brings absence into presence. There are clear similarities here with certain texts by Georges Perec, Patrick Modiano, and Henri Raczymow as contributions to the present volume of chapters patently make clear, and as Annelies Schulte Nordholt has intimated in her excellent study of these three writers and the interconnectedness in their work (despite significant differences) of the representation of places, urban space, and memory, be it Perec's "workings of memory," Modiano's "superimpositions," or Raczymow's "absent memory" or "memory shot through with holes." There is also, no doubt, some justification in relating what I am calling here Kofman's cartography to what Michel de Certeau argues in his influential *The Practice of Everyday Life*, namely, that by the nineteenth century, cartography, particularly urban cartography, far from being, as was thought, a faithful description of reality, was both representation and discourse, a Barthesian "reality effect." As Michel de Certeau suggests too, in the distinction he makes between static "place" and dynamic "space," the city is "inhabited," "transhumant," it never sleeps, and is traversed by movement, a succession of meetings and trajectories of its inhabitants. Yet I would hardly characterize Kofman in *Rue Ordener Rue Labat* as a Certelian "practitioner of urban space." On the contrary, if de Certeau makes a valid distinction between a "tour," which tells us of space, and a "map," which involves action and tells us of place, I would say that in terms of the representation of Kofman's memories, her text offers not so much a tour of Paris but activates a map meant to tell us (and herself) very precisely of *place* or *places*, of the people long since gone who occupied them, and of the events that took place there. In other words, in reading *Rue Ordener Rue Labat*, we are not a comfortably ensconced "reading-tourist" of Paris's 18th arrondissement and elsewhere, but the uncomfortable voyeur of Kofman's *sites of memory*, the sites of her painful memories as they regress, like etymological research, to the origins of her traumatized self.

There are in fact four main geographical locations or places mapped out in Kofman's text, all traversing the three temporal zones of events that took place prior to, during, and after the war. The first, spotlighted in the title, concerns the 18th arrondissement, though if all the streets and Métro stations mentioned by Kofman were to be highlighted on a map, the sinewy network that would emerge, like a nervous system, would cover but a fraction of the arrondissement's myriad of boulevards and streets. Nevertheless, street names are cited with such insistence, the mapping of memory onto topography so pointed, that we cannot but read the phenomenon as a textual *duty of memory*, Kofman's imperative so to speak, her need in returning to the past to specify that her father, Bereck, was rabbi in a synagogue on the rue Duc (5); that her primary school was on the rue Doudeauville (23); that her parents had previously lived on the rue des Poissonniers where they had first met their neighbor the "lady on the Rue Labat" (31); that the close family friends, the Adler family, lived on the rue Simart (14); that Hélène Goldenberg, the best pupil in class, lived on the rue Émile-Duployé before being deported (18); that Mme Fagnard, one of the primary school teachers, lived at 75 or 77 rue de la Chapelle (20); that Kofman would fetch cigarette papers, the famous Zig-Zag brand, for her father from a tobacconist on the rue Jean-Robert (11); that the Jewish children's home where she spent just a few hours—saved from deportation by her stubborn refusal to be separated from her mother—was situated in the rue Lamarck (30); that she vomited along the rue Marcadet on the way to Mémé's for the first time (31); that she had her tonsils removed in a clinic on the rue Léon (35); that it was in a shop on the rue Custine, on the *fête des Mères*, that Kofman bought a hairnet, a comb, and two postcards for her two mothers and realized that her preference for Mémé was patent (45); that after the Liberation Kofman shared a bed with her mother in a miserable hotel room on the rue des Saules (58); that when Mémé won the court case to keep Kofman, it was from a café on the rue Marcadet that she called her friend Paul to announce the news (60); that, finally, though I have hardly been exhaustive, after the war Kofman and her family were housed in an unsanitary slum building on the Impasse Langlois near the Porte de la Chapelle, provisional housing that would last until 1957 (33). How utterly significant that Kofman should end the war in an *impasse*!

The second series of mappings takes us further afield, to other parts of Paris and its suburbs, beginning with Drancy from which her father would be deported (9); on to Mont-Valérien and the Zoo in Vincennes to which Mme Fagnard would take Kofman and her sisters (20); then taking in the rue des Charbonniers in the 12th arrondissement where Kofman accompanied her mother to consult a reader of Tarot cards for news of her father (28); the Institute of Notre-Dame-de-Sion on the rue Notre-Dame-des-Champs from which the nine-year-old Kofman fled without ado (36); the bookshop of Mémé's friend Paul on the rue de Flandre (40); the hotel near the Gobelins Métro station where Kofman spent a night with Mémé (55); and the Champs-Élysées where Mémé took Kofman to see De Gaulle the day Paris was liberated (49). After the war, we learn that Kofman and her family would eventually move to an HLM (*Habitation à Loyer Modéré*, a form of cheap rent-controlled public housing) at the Buttes-Chaumont in the 19th arrondissement (34); that Kofman would finish her school education at the Lycée Jules-Ferry in the 9th arrondissement (17) before completing *hypokhâgne* and *khâgne* (preparatory classes) while living in student accommodation on the rue du Docteur-Blanche in the 16th arrondissement (84); and, finally, as a student at the Sorbonne, residing at the Cité Universitaire in the Deutsch de la Meurthe house in the 14th arrondissement (84). And as I noted earlier, we also learn, as if the (non-)memory of Auschwitz were to invest the memory of Paris, that the butcher who killed her father returned from the death camp and reopened his shop on the rue des Rosiers (10).

The third set of Kofman's cartographical memories evokes events outside Paris and involves places either to which Kofman's mother sent her and her siblings for hiding or are intimately associated with Mémé and her family. Between July 1942 and February 1943, for instance, we learn that brothers Isaac and Joseph were placed in an infant-care home in the north of France; sister Annette with a Jewish Communist woman in Nonancourt in the Eure; and the other siblings, Rachel, Aaron, and Kofman herself, in Merville, near Nonancourt (23). Before the war, Kofman reveals, while a three-year-old on a summer camp at Berck-Plage in the Pas-de-Calais, she was already physically rendered ill by the fear of abandonment (27). During the war, Mémé's family would be encountered in its entirety at L'Haÿ-les-Roses, a southern suburb of Paris in the Val-de-Marne (51). Later, after the war, Kofman would find herself with all her siblings and her mother back in Nonancourt at a hospice, from which she promptly fled in an effort to reunite with Mémé, only to be detained at the gendarmerie in Saint-Rémy-sur-Eure (72) and sent back to her family in Nonancourt. In one of her many attempts to distance her daughter from her attachment to Mémé, Kofman's mother sends her with her sister Annette to a preventorium in Hendaye in the Pyrénées-Atlantiques for nine months (79), and then to the well-known Jewish children's home in Moissac in the Tarn-et-Garonne (79). Finally, while Kofman was a university student, Mémé left Paris and moved to Les Sables-d'Olonne, a seaside town in the Vendée (84), where she would live until her death shortly prior to Kofman's redaction of her text.

The fourth and final mental mapping of Kofman's past takes us outside France altogether and concerns events all related to the Shoah: Auschwitz, where her father was murdered (10); the Warsaw Ghetto, where almost all of her grandmothers, aunts, uncles, and cousins died (52); Yugoslavia, to which the one survivor of Kofman's father's ten brothers and sisters escaped only to be shot by the Nazis (52); and Israel, where his non-Jewish widow who would later convert to Judaism took her two children to found a moshav (53). These details and their geographical complements, I should add, fall more specifically under the purview of Marianne Hirsch's "postmemory," in the sense that Kofman had no personal experience of these events and learned about them after the war, highlighting Kofman in these instances as what Froma Zeitlin has called a "vicarious witness." They also raise the question of the role of letters and photographs in Kofman's text, those *memory-objects* other than her father's fountain pen with which the text opens.

Place-mapping the Past

What does this "*ancrage/encrage*" (to borrow Perec's terminology), this *anchoring* of memory in place and the *inking* of memory in text, tell us of Kofman's final memoir? It tells us first and foremost that Kofman's dangerous plunge into her past, into the guilt, betrayal, shame, and self-punishment related to the two mothers; into the Jewish/Christian overdetermination of her conflict; into the inconsolable loss of the father, beaten with a pickax and buried alive for not working on Shabbat in the *place* of Auschwitz "where no eternal rest would or could ever be granted" (10), was less temporal than spatial, more precisely toponymical, cartographical. Is it by chance, one may wonder, that the writing and publication of Kofman's text coincided with what the cultural theorist Frederic Jameson in the early 1990s called the "spatial turn" of postmodernism, the realization that "we now inhabit the synchronic rather than the diachronic, [. . .] that our daily life, our psychic experience, our cultural languages, are today dominated by categories of space rather than by categories of time" (16)? Whatever the case, when Conley calls Kofman's twenty-three chapters "memory-flashes" and "paratactic units" (157), she is right, but the spatial mapping—I would call it *place-mapping*—she recognizes in relation to the title of the book is of far greater consequence than she acknowledges. Kofman, I believe, in finally broaching "that," the trauma of her childhood experience, in a sustained narrative form, could not do so—consciously or unconsciously—without mapping that experience in geographical terms. The initial Yiddish sobbing "Oh papa papa papa" and the Ancient Greek lament "Ô popoï, popoï, popoï," related to patriarchal loss and subsequent physical and psychical maternal displacements, could not be negotiated in temporal terms alone.

Cartography, I would claim, understood here in its psychological rather than in its political and social dimension, is as central to an understanding of Kofman's autobiographical project as psychoanalytical readings of unresolved issues of doubled mothers, two sets of breasts, physical abuse, and the historically and ethnically determined conditions of desubjectivization. No doubt, in the end, the places Kofman revisits, in and around Paris, in France and outside it, are the *nonplaces* of her memory she should not but could not *not* have returned to.

Bibliography

Cairns, Lucille. *Post-War Jewish Women's Writing in French*. Oxford: Legenda, 2011, 181–237.

Certeau, Michel de. *The Practice of Everyday Life*, translated by Steven F. Rendall. Berkeley: California University Press, 1984.

Chanter, Tina. "Eating Words: Antigone as Kofman's Proper Name." In *Enigmas: Essays on Sarah Kofman*, edited by Penelope Deutscher and Kelly Oliver. Ithaca, NY: Cornell University Press, 1999, 189–202.

Conley, Verena Andermatt. "For Sarah Kofman, *Rue Ordener rue Labat*." *SubStance* 25, no. 3 (1996): 153–59.

Cummings, Ashlee Mae. "The Shelter of Philosophy: Repression and Confrontation of the Traumatic Experience in the Work of Sarah Kofman." MA Thesis. Miami University, 2009.

Derrida, Jacques. "D'abord, je ne savais pas . . ." In *Les Cahiers du Grif*, edited by Françoise Collin and Françoise Proust. Paris: Descartes & Cie, 1997, 131–65.

Dobie, Madeline. "Sarah Kofman's *Paroles suffoquées*: Autobiography, History, and Writing 'After Auschwitz.'" *French Forum* 22, no. 3 (1997): 319–41.

Duroux, Françoise. "How a Woman Philosophizes." In *Enigmas: Essays on Sarah Kofman*, edited by Penelope Deutscher and Kelly Oliver. Ithaca, NY: Cornell University Press, 1999, 134–40.

Hirsch, Marianne. *The Generation of Postmemory: Writing and Visual Culture after the Holocaust*. New York: Columbia University Press, 2012.

Hoft-March, Eilene. "Still Breathing: Sarah Kofman's Memoires of Holocaust Survival." *Journal of the Midwest Modern Language Association* 33, no. 3; 34, no. 1 (2000–2001): 108–21.

Horowitz, Sara R. "Sarah Kofman et l'ambiguïté des mères." In *Témoignages de l'après-Auschwitz dans la littérature juive française d'aujourd'hui. Enfants de survivants et survivants-enfants*, edited by Annelies Schulte Nordholt. Amsterdam: Rodopi, 2008, 101–20.

Iyer, Lars. "Lament." 2003. http://spurious.typepad.com/spurious/kofman/index.html. Accessed March 23, 2017.

Jameson, Frederic. *Postmodernism or the Cultural Logic of Late Capitalism*. Durham, NC: Duke University Press, 1991.

Jaron, Steven. "Autobiography and the Holocaust: An Examination of the Liminal Generation in France." *French Studies* 56, no. 2 (2002): 207–19.

Kofman, Sarah. "Cauchemar." *Comment s'en sortir?* Paris: Galilée, 1983.

———. *Lectures de Derrida*. Paris: Galilée, 1984.

———. "Les 'Mains' d'Antelme, post-scriptum à *Paroles suffoquées*." *Lignes* 21 (1994): 159–63.

———. "'Ma vie' et la psychanalyse (janvier 76, fragment d'analyse)." *Première livraison* 4 (1976).

———. *Paroles suffoquées*. Paris: Galilée, 1987.

———. *Rue Ordener Rue Labat*. Translated by Ann Smock. Lincoln: University of Nebraska Press, 1996. Translation of *Rue Ordener Rue Labat*. Paris: Galilée, 1994.

———. "Sacrée nourriture." In *Manger*, edited by Christian Besson and Catherine Weinzaepflen. Liège: Yellow Now; Chalon-sur-Saône: Maison de la culture, 1976, 71–74.

———. "Tombeau pour un nom propre." *Première livraison* 5 (1976).

Leibovici, Solange. "Conceptualizing Trauma: Remembering, Acting-out, Working-through: The Case of Sarah Kofman." *PSYART: A Hyperlink Journal for the Psychological Study of the Arts*. February 16, 2004. http://www.psyartjournal. com/article/show/leibovici-conceptualizing_trauma_remembering_actin. Accessed March 23, 2017.

Oliver, Kelly. "Sarah Kofman's Queasy Stomach and the Riddle of the Paternal Law." In *Enigmas: Essays on Sarah Kofman*, edited by Penelope Deutscher and Kelly Oliver. Ithaca, NY: Cornell University Press, 1999, 174–88.

Perec, Georges. "Vilin Souvenir no. 2." "Vilin-Souvenir: Georges Perec, par Philippe Lejeune." *Genesis: Revue internationale de critique génétique de l'ITEM* 1 (1992): 127–49.

Pollock, Griselda. "Art as Transport-Station of Trauma? Haunting Objects in the Works of Bracha Ettinger, Sarah Kofman, and Chantal Akerman." In *Representing Auschwitz: At the Margins of Testimony*, edited by Nicholas Chare and Dominic Williams. London: Palgrave Macmillan, 2013, 194–221.

Robson, Kathryn. "Bodily Detours: Sarah Kofman's Narratives of Childhood Trauma." *Modern Language Review* 99, no. 3 (2004): 608–21.

Rosenblum, Rachel. "And Till the Ghastly Tale Is Told: Sarah Kofman—Primo Levi: Survivors of the Shoah and the Dangers of Testimony." *European Judaism: A Journal for the New Europe* 33, no. 2 (2000): 81–103.

Schulte Nordholt, Annelies. *Perec, Modiano, Raczymow: la génération d'après et la mémoire de la Shoah*. Amsterdam: Rodopi, 2008.

Smock, Ann. "Translator's Introduction." *Rue Ordener Rue Labat*. By Sarah Kofman. Translated by Ann Smock. Lincoln: University of Nebraska Press, 1996, vii–xiii.

Suleiman, Susan Rubin. *Crises of Memory and the Second World War*. Cambridge, MA: Harvard University Press, 2006, 178–214.

———. "Orphans of the Shoah and Jewish Identity in Post-Holocaust France: From the Individual to the Collective." In *Post-Holocaust France and the Jews, 1945–1955*, edited by Seán Hand and Steven T. Katz. New York: New York University Press, 2015, 118–38.

Zeitlin, Froma. "The Vicarious Witness: Belated Memory and Authorial Presence in Recent Holocaust Literature." *History and Memory* 10, no. 2 (1998): 5–40.

4

Perec, Raczymow,
and Their Sites of Memory

ANNELIES SCHULTE NORDHOLT

On May 14, 1940, the German bombs that destroyed Rotterdam also erased a long, lively shopping street, the Hoogstraat, killing many of its inhabitants and passersby. The photographs taken after the bombing show a flat expanse of rubble, no single wall left standing. Nowadays, if you go there, you will find a new Hoogstraat, rebuilt a short distance from there. But you can also walk the virtual street—the old one—recently reconstructed on an internet site. After years of research, we know again who lived or had a shop at what number, and for each house number we find a short biography on its inhabitants. This wonderful memory project reminded me of Georges Perec's work on the rue Vilin, in Paris, where he was born. For six years, in the early 1970s, he paid a yearly visit to the rue Vilin to make an inventory of the street, house by house. Of course, there are huge differences with the Rotterdam project: the rue Vilin was not destroyed by bombs, but by urban renewal (although the effect was almost the same). Moreover, his yearly descriptions did not resurrect the street as it was, but witnessed and documented the process of its demolition: these texts are at the heart of his work of memory.

"La rue Vilin" is a series of five texts, originally a part of his experimental project called *Lieux*. He published "La rue Vilin" as a newspaper article in 1977 and it was republished in his posthumous volume *L'Infra-ordinaire*. The *Lieux* project, of which this text was initially a part, explains many things about "La rue Vilin." Perec started working on *Lieux* in 1969, when he chose twelve Paris sites for which he had a strong personal attachment and decided to describe these over a range of twelve years, writing two texts a year about each of them. One is a factual description made on the spot (a "Réel"), the other is a series of memories about it, which could be written anywhere (a "Souvenir"). Apart from the rue Vilin, the sites included the Square Franklin Roosevelt, where Perec spent a long day when he fled home as a twelve-year-old boy, and the rue Saint-Honoré, where he lived in an attic as a student, and the Place d'Italie, where he typed his first novel. The aim of it all was both to construct an archive of personal and collective memories and to track change, to see how places and his memories would shift in the course of time. After six years, Perec dropped the project and most of these texts were never published. The seven-hundred-leaves-long manuscript, which also includes series of photos taken on the premises, is kept at the Bibliothèque de l'Arsenal in Paris.

These two examples—the destroyed Rotterdam and the Paris street, and the work of memory that was done on them—reveal an interesting paradox that occurs to me whenever I turn to the work of French-Jewish postwar authors like Georges Perec, Henri Raczymow, and, of course, Patrick Modiano: the fundamental theme of much of their work is absence, void, the loss of an irretrievable past, but there is one thing that is intensely present, that has a definite fullness—Paris urban space. Their texts are full of precise sites and streets, street names, itineraries, and topography. Theirs is, in Raczymow's famous metaphor, "memory shot through with holes," an absent memory, yet writing on urban sites seems an exceptional way to remember. The first question is: why this paradox? Modiano gives a limpid answer in his 1997 novel *Dora Bruder*. His obsessive haunting of the streets where Dora has lived is due to his belief that "premises retain some stamp, however faint, of their previous inhabitants. Stamp: an imprint, hollow or in relief" (21). The second question is: how does this memory work? May sites or premises enable a sort of contact with the past? Is there some kind of metonymy between sites and the memories they retain? Or are they only visible signs referring to an absence, speaking indirectly about it? And how does imagination come in when writers work on their sites of memory? In order to deal with these questions, I will confront two contemporary but very different texts on the same Paris site: the quarter of Belleville, in northern Paris. One is Perec's work on the rue Vilin, the other is Raczymow's novel *Rivières d'exil* (Rivers of Exile).

The Belleville Neighborhood in the Works of Perec and Raczymow

The Belleville neighborhood is a key site in the work of Perec and Raczymow; they were both born there, the former in 1936, the latter twelve years later, in 1948. But these twelve years of difference make Perec into a child survivor, whereas Raczymow is a "Juif de l'après," a Jew born after World War II, belonging to the second generation. Apart from "The rue Vilin," Perec wrote a few other descriptions of the rue Vilin. In chapter 10 of his novel *W, or the Memory of Childhood*, he recounts a period of almost total amnesia about the rue Vilin, roughly between 1946 and 1962; he had forgotten all about this street, to the point of not being sure where exactly it was located. When he returned there for the first time, in 1962, he did not recognize anything, nor was he able to point out the house where he had lived. A few years later, he returned there by chance, saw that it was on the point of being demolished and took up the *Lieux* project, returning there from 1969 to 1975, just in time to document this demolition.

Whereas the war abruptly put an end to Perec's childhood on the rue Vilin, Raczymow spent his whole childhood in Belleville, in the 1950s. In much of his autobiographical work and some of his novels, Belleville is very present, but most of all in *Rivières d'exil*, a novel published in 1982.[1] Mathieu, its protagonist, is a sensitive young boy growing up in this working-class area where many recently emigrated Jews from eastern Europe were living at the time. Two stories are told here, in alternating chapters: on the one hand are Mathieu's childhood memories of daily life in Belleville, and, on the other, are his grandfather's bedtime "stories from Poland." In a gentle, humorous way, the grandfather, who emigrated from Poland in the 1920s, transmits to his grandson a treasure of tales about Jewish exile. The stories come from the Bible, from Jewish history, but above all from legend. What happened to the ten lost tribes of Israel after the Babylonian exile? What about their 2,000-year wanderings, from Babylon to the Caucasus and from Poland to Western Europe? He also tells him all about false Messiahs and about the incredible story of the Khazars, a Central Asian nomad people who converted to Judaism in the seventh century CE and managed for some time to maintain an independent Jewish kingdom. He suggests that in the end, all Ashkenazic Jews may descend from these Khazar converts.

Since Arthur Koestler's 1973 book *The Thirteenth Tribe*, the rather controversial Khazar story regularly turns up in public discussion.[2] However, in the first chapter of *Rivières d'exil*, Raczymow warns that these stories are nothing more—and nothing less—to him than wonderful legends, "an unknown, obscure, nearly crazy genealogy" of the Jewish people, belonging not to memory but to fabulation (9). For Polish Jews, he says, no family genealogy is possible beyond one's grandparents because all roots have been cut off first by emigration and after that by the Shoah, which "erased from all archives the very trace of their passage in the Polish landscape" (10).

At this point, in spite of their difference in age, Raczymow and Perec have their most fundamental experience in common: that of living on the edge of a huge void, of being, in a sense, a survivor (be it first or second generation). In *Writing the Book of Esther*, Raczymow's great novel about second-generation Jews and the Holocaust, the protagonist's postwar family is described as a circle with a hole in the middle; the more the family grows, the more the hole widens itself, becoming the size of "a sea of ashes" (185). This is why, both for Perec and for Raczymow, Belleville has an ambiguous character. In *Rivières d'exil*, postwar Belleville—although it is home and the site of a happy childhood—is also the symbol of a double exile: the exile of his family from Poland—due to emigration and to the Shoah—and historical exile from the Promised Land. Mathieu's grandfather feels "exiled from his own exile" (115). But given this absence of origins, Belleville becomes the only site of memory available, however ambiguous. It is the place where the child feels the presence of several lost worlds: not only the prewar Poland, but also the immemorial past of the exile and peregrinations of the Jewish people. Similarly, for Perec, the rue Vilin is the place where he briefly lived with his mother and family but also where he lost all of them; a place of security but also of destruction. Let us see now how this overdetermination of streets and places works out, on the two levels of proper names and of topography.

The City as a Book

In order to become sites of memory, streets have to be invested with meaning, with language, and, we could say, with desire. The most obvious way in which this happens here is through proper names and text in general.

Streets are full of words. They are text, if one pays attention to street names, house numbers, signboards, words and slogans on walls or fences.

To the child Mathieu in *Rivières d'exil*, Belleville is his world. Many streets in this neighborhood have the name of waters: rue de la Mare (Pond Street), rue des Rigoles (Canal Street), rue du Jourdain (Jordan Street), rue des Cascades (Waterfall Street) . . . To the child, it is absolutely clear why: the neighborhood is one of the most hilly in Paris and these streets are like rivers streaming downhill; they spring from high Belleville, from the rue des Pyrénées—which is paramount to a mountain chain. Like the young hero of Proust's *In Search of Lost Time*, Mathieu is at the age of nouns: he believes that proper nouns correspond to their object; that is why these streets have "wet names" (16). But there is more to it. Proper names *are* what they refer to and in this sense, "the rue du Jourdain *is* the river Jordan itself. And the Jordan is Palestine" (71). This new layer of meaning stems from the stories of the grandfather. In his tales about the wanderings of the Jewish people, rivers play a prominent role: the river Jordan makes Belleville into a kind of Promised Land. Moreover, his stories are full of rivers of exile. According to the grandfather, the migrations of the Jewish people always begin or end in view of a river: first of all, the "Rivers of Babylon," where, according to the psalmist, the Jewish people lamented their exile.

"By the rivers of Babylon we sat and wept When we remembered Zion." (Psalm 137:1)

The grandfather particularly cherishes the story of the mythical river Sabbation, which is said to stop flowing on Sabbath. Later "rivers of exile" are the Vistula, the Volga, the Rhine, and, finally, in the case of Mathieu's family, the Seine. All these stories give a magic aura to the streets of Belleville. This beautiful image of the "rivers of exile" is what tightly knits together both threads of the novel: a childhood in Belleville, on the one hand, and the wanderings of the Jewish, people on the other. It also makes clear that Jewish life in Belleville, in the 1950s, is still a life in exile. In its habits, its language—largely Yiddish—and its way of life, this community is still similar to prewar Polish Jewish communities. Ashkenazic Belleville after the war was "a semblance of a shtetl, a simulacrum of Yiddishkeit, [but] a shtetl, a Yiddishkeit shot through with holes, with missing links: the names of the dead" ("Memory Shot Through with Holes," 102).

In "The Rue Vilin" (Perec, *Species of Spaces and Other Pieces*), there is no such Proustian fabulating about street names, except of course in his awareness of the pun: vilin = *vilain*, ugly. "The rue Vilin" is not fiction but a "sociological" inventory of the street. His first aim is to be complete: he wants to "exhaust a Parisian space" (*épuiser un lieu parisien*), to record every slight detail of it, every house, in a factual, neutral style. Only in this way may he document the progressive demolition of this street. In these rather dry listings of facts, one can nevertheless detect a strong investment of emotion and desire, but its style is much more indirect than Raczymow's. In the first place, this indirectness appears in the house numbers. Perec's method is the same at every yearly visit: he walks up and down the street and jots down, for every building, what it is. Is it a private house, a shop (what does it sell?), a hotel? Is it still in use or abandoned? Is it shut? This method necessarily makes him come across the two house numbers that are the reason for his presence there: number 1, where his grandparents lived, and number 24, where he lived with his parents and where his mother had a small hairdressing salon. But this principal fact is mentioned only very briefly, between parentheses—and the trauma of his mother's deportation not at all. His trauma is expressed indirectly, in a subdued, muted way; the letters "Coiffure dames" on the wooden door of number 24, become fainter every year. In Perec's descriptions, not only number 24 but all house numbers are overdetermined. They come to coincide metonymically with the building concerned, speaking indirectly about the past and becoming expressions of absence. Perec had a fascination for numbers, which he often used as autobiographical signals, as he does here. In his later work, autobiographical elements are often encrypted in numbers, for instance the numbers 11 and 43, which compose the date of his mother's deportation (on of February 11, 1943). Numbers thus form a numerology and a fantasmatic arithmetic, recurring in many of his works (see Magné, 1999).

Signboards are another type of texts that make a street speak, even when it is dying like the rue Vilin. Some refer—in a comical way—to the hilly character of Belleville: in the upper part of the rue Vilin, there is the wine and charcoal shop "Au repos de la montagne," and even the "Hotel du Mont-Blanc"! But most of these signboards refer to the past, when Belleville was a flourishing working-class area with many shops and workshops. Some of these signposts now seem ironic, like the electrician's sign advertising "Power and Light," but plunged into darkness (Perec, 2008, 215). On number 27, he notes "a shop, closed, 'La Maison du Taleth,' with, signs in Hebrew still to be seen and the words MOHEL, CHOHET, BOOKS, STATIONERY, RELIGIOUS OBJECTS, TOYS" (214). One would expect here a translation or short explanation of those Hebrew words—*taleth*, or prayer shawl; *mohel*, or ritual circumcisor; *chohet*, or ritual slaughterer—but

Perec gives none, as if to say that they have lost their meaning in this neighborhood and at this time, where traditional Jewish life has almost disappeared. It may also be taken as an indication of Perec's conception of his own Jewish identity as he expressed it in *Ellis Island Revisited: Tales of Vagrancy and Hope*: "[B]eing Jewish is not a belonging, it is not related to a belief, to a religion, a way of life, a folklore or a language; it is rather a silence, an absence, a question, a putting into question, a hesitation, a disquiet" (Perec, 1994, 58, my translation).

In Raczymow's novel, Belleville is still teeming with (Jewish) life. Rue de Belleville is "full of life, of shops, of pedlars, of glaziers who shout: Here comes the glazier! of knife-grinders, of chair-menders, of ice-cream sellers, of red and golden books, a street full of things to see" (Raczymow, 1982, 95). Perec's rue Vilin, only ten years later, seems an empty, dying place.

(Re)mapping Belleville and the rue Vilin

Topography is another way in which Belleville becomes a site of memory in these two texts. Both Perec and Raczymow give great importance to the shape, to the spatiality of the neighborhood or street. But they do this, again, in entirely different ways. In *Rivières d'exil*, Raczymow does not return to the premises but takes an imaginary walk through Belleville, resurrecting its colorful inhabitants. Imagination invests urban space with meaning, giving it an aura of exile. Perec, in contrast, is a lonely, obsessive walker. His recurring visits to the rue Vilin have a single aim, which remains unsaid: by describing them every year, he hopes to force his memory to produce some recollection of his mother and of their short common life there. That is why the *Lieux* project not only includes descriptions of the present state of a site, written on the premises but also recollections of people or events belonging to it. The "Souvenirs" of the rue Vilin have never been published; they are only available in manuscript (see Lejeune, 1991). Studying them at the Bibliothèque de l'Arsenal in Paris, I was struck by how meager and confused they are (Schulte Nordholt, 2008 and 2016). In these texts, relying only on a faulty memory and refusing to verify facts (this was part of the rules of the *Lieux* project), Perec is in total confusion about crucial details. Was he born in the rue Vilin or in another, nearby street? And to what arrondissement did the rue Vilin belong? How old was he when he left for his hiding place in the Alps? And so on. Perec's childhood memories, as they are told in *W, or the Memory of Childhood*, may seem slight/insignificant and uncertain, but turn out to be quite substantial!

His inability to remember anything about his parents and childhood may explain why Perec wanted to be so precise and exhaustive in his writing. The first sentence of chapter 10 in *W, or the Memory of Childhood* also reveals his will to establish topographical facts, however meager and banal they may seem: "We lived in Paris, in the 20th arrondissement, in the rue Vilin; it is a small street starting at the rue des Couronnes and going uphill, while vaguely tracing the shape of an S, to the steep stairs leading to the rue du Transvaal and the Olivier Metra Street [. . .]" (Perec, 1995, 67, my translation). This cartographic precision about the premises is even clearer in the five descriptions composing "The rue Vilin." Here he acts as a true geometrician, estimating the angle of inclination at different points of the street, measuring its length between side streets and accurately describing the two turns and their incline: "On the odd number side, on the left, level with number 49, the street bends for a second time, also through about 30 degrees. This gives the street the general appearance of a very elongated S (like in the high tension symbol SS)" (Perec, 2008, 215).

The manuscripts show that, on location, Perec made several sketches of the shape of the street. It was only later that day, in a café, when he copied out his notes, that he added the comparison to the SS symbol. Years later, Robert Bober, a friend of Perec's, made a striking film on the rue Vilin, *En remontant la rue Vilin* (1992). In this ode to Perec, where he reconstitutes the street using hundreds of old photographs, he also examines the shape of the street from the air and discovers that it does not at all have the shape of an S! In spite of Perec's near-scientific approach of the rue Vilin, his description of it is saturated with the imaginary and the past, making it into a fantasmatic street, a symbol of trauma and loss.

Whereas Perec sees the SS symbol in the shape of his street, Raczymow's topography of Belleville is altogether different but is also marked by a geometrical figure heavily loaded with symbolism, the Jewish star: "The windows of the dining room of 71, rue de la Mare, look out on a small square where one may take a rest, when one is tired of ascending the long way from low to high Belleville. It is like a small square of the David's star, if you like." My translation alas cannot account for the pun in this sentence: "C'est comme une minuscule petite *place de l'étoile* de David, si on veut" (Raczymow, 1982, 47, my emphasis). Here, Raczymow implicitly refers to the title of Patrick Modiano's first novel, *La place de l'étoile* (1968). Modiano's title refers both to the famous Paris square and to the yellow star and finally, to the Magen David as a symbol of Jewish identity. Taking up all these different layers of meaning, Raczymow underscores the last one, seeing the shape of the Jewish star in the form of Belleville streets. Here—at least in the 1950s—he seems to say, there still was a Jewish land, a kind of homeland, with its river Jordan and other geographic memory markers, even if it was a land of exile. Belleville is indeed a homeland because these streets are called "les rues de par chez soi," the familiar, everyday streets.

Raczymow then gives us a playful guided tour of this star of streets. After the rue des Envierges, we come to the rue Botha, "where the movie *Casque d'or* was made with the beautiful Signoret and the skinny Reggiani" and then to the stairs of the rue Vilin "where *Le ballon rouge* was shot with kids of the Levert school, and from where one sees the whole of Paris" (Raczymow, 1982, 48). This approach—making memories surge from sites—is comparable to that of Perec in his "Souvenirs," the main difference being that memories seem to freely flow in Raczymow's case, whereas in Perec's they seem to have dried up entirely.

Both authors apprehend urban space by projecting symbolical forms on it, be it the SS sign or the Star of David. Both of them also give a great importance to roaming through the city, according to precise, predetermined trajectories. Walking the streets of Belleville, whether literally, like Perec, or in the imagination, like Raczymow, is a privileged way of experiencing the neighborhood. In his 1974 essay "Species of Spaces," Perec called himself "a user of space" ("un usager de l'espace"). This active conception of urban space is closely related to the findings of the French anthropologist Michel de Certeau. In his famous inquiry on daily life, *The Practice of Everyday Life*, he showed how everyday experiences like walking the streets, consuming, living, or cooking are "practices" through which we "invent city space": in many, often playful, ways, we create spaces of our own, and personal and collective forms of appropriation of them. This is certainly also visible in the texts we are considering here. Another one of the rules of the *Lieux* project, underlying Perec's descriptions of the rue Vilin, is the obligation to return every year—in principle for approximately twelve years—to the same street, and to walk it through, always in the same direction, from the bottom to the top, making an inventory of all the buildings, number by number, as we have seen. Perec has thus established beforehand a trajectory meant to be repeated once a year, like a pilgrimage; the intended result of this being the creation of some kind of archive of memory.

In Raczymow's case, we see something similar: the memories of the child's daily trajectories through the neighborhood map the space of daily life. In *Rivières d'exil*, an invisible frontier seems to divide upper and lower Belleville. This is, first, perceived as a social divide: the narrator lives with

his parents in the more elegant upper quarter, whereas his maternal grandparents still live in the lower quarters, in a tiny apartment and workshop
where they collect and repair rags. The child is therefore forever walking
from one address to the other, using different, but always preestablished
itineraries. How then does the child "invent" his own city spaces? For him,
these humble streets become a ground where he goes treasure hunting: with
his grandfather, who is a rag picker, he explores the trash cans in search of
things to sell; at other times, he roams the gutters, which magically become
"rivers of precious or archaeological objects: screws, needles, old coins with
a hole in the middle, pieces of industrial metal" (Raczymow, 1982, 94–95),
all to become part of his private collection of "useless waste objects, but
loaded with journeys, wanderings, exiles, fugues and transits" (95).

Let us now return to Modiano's dictum about how sites retain a stamp
of the people who lived there. We may say that in Raczymow's case, this
stamp is in relief, present and visible. The Belleville he describes is "shot
through with holes," but it still is—or rather was—a neighborhood teeming
with life and stories, and these stories are told in a direct, uncomplicated
way, often in daily conversation. On the contrary, in Perec's meticulous
descriptions of the rue Vilin, the stamp of its former inhabitants—especially
of the unnamed mother—is hollow, their absence is felt everywhere, but
it may only be expressed indirectly, by means of street numbers, fading
signboards, and the uncanny shape of the street. This account of the demolition of a street is a perfect metaphor of absence, Perec's central theme.
In short, *Rivières d'exil* is a "happy" text, whereas Perec's texts on the rue
Vilin are profoundly melancholy. Apart from their very different personal
history, the reason for this may be that Raczymow allows his childhood
memories to be invested with imagination and the power of literature: by
means of the tales on Jewish exile, they become inhabited, enchanted. In
Perec's attempts to describe the rue Vilin, nothing of the like is allowed to
happen. However precise his descriptions are, the street remains empty and
desolate; it is unable to make memory speak.

Notes

1. All quotations from *Rivières d'exil* are my translations.

2. Recently, for instance, the books of the Israeli historian Shlomo Sand (2009
and 2012) gave rise to a great deal of controversy.

Bibliography

Certeau, Michel de. *The Practice of Everyday Life*. Translated by Steven Randall. Berkeley: University of California Press, 1984.

Lejeune, Philippe. *La mémoire et l'oblique. Georges Perec autobiographe*. Paris: P.O.L., 1991.

Magné, Bernard. *Georges Perec*. Paris: Nathan, 1999.

Modiano, Patrick. *Dora Bruder*. Translated by J. Kilmartin. Berkeley: University of California Press, 1999.

Perec, Georges. *L'Infra-ordinaire*. Paris: Seuil: 1989.

Perec, Georges. *Récits d'Ellis Island. Histoires d'errance et d'espoir*. Paris, P.O.L., 1994.

———. "The Rue Vilin." In *Species of Spaces and Other Pieces*. Translated by J. Sturrock. London/New York: Penguin Classics, 2008, 212–21.

———. *W, or the Memory of Childhood*. Translated by David Bellos. Boston: David R. Godine, 2002.

———. *W, ou le souvenir d'enfance*. Paris: Gallimard/L'imaginaire, 1995.

Raczymow, Henri. *Contes d'exil et d'oubli*. Paris: Gallimard/Le Chemin, 1979.

———. "Memory Shot Through with Holes." "Discourses of Jewish Identity in Twentieth-Century France," edited by Alan Astro. *Yale French Studies* 85 (1994): 98–105.

———. *Rivières d'exil*. Paris: Gallimard/Le Chemin, 1982.

———. *Writing the Book of Esther*. Translated by D. Katz. New York: Holmes & Meier, 1995.

Sand, Shlomo. *The Invention of the Jewish People*. London and New York: Verso Books, 2009.

———. *The Invention of the Land of Israel*. London/New York: Verso Books, 2012.

Schulte Nordholt, Annelies. "Georges Perec, 'La rue Vilin': écrire la double disparition." In *Lire, écrire, pratiquer la ville*, edited by Nathalie Roelens and Thomas Vercruysse. Paris: Kimé, 2016, 251–64.

———. *Perec, Modiano, Raczymow. La génération d'après et la mémoire de la Shoah*. Amsterdam: Rodopi, 2008.

Sheringham, Michael. *Everyday Life: Theories and Practices from Surrealism to the Present*. Oxford: Oxford University Press, 2006.

PART 2 FAMILIAR STRANGERS

"Comme Dieu en France?" could have been an alternative title for this group of chapters. France in general, and Paris in particular, held a special place in the eastern European Jewish imaginary in the decades between the two world wars. Nadia Malinovich focuses on continuity and ruptures in portrayals of the French capital among the Yiddish writers of the 1920s and in the writing of the Sephardic Jews who moved to France after the Algerian war. From enchantment to disillusionment; from the desire to embrace everything Parisian and the feeling of not fitting in, Malinovich follows the stories of identity crises that seem to accompany every big historical change in Jewish life.

In his chapter, Henry Raczymow explores the territories of the real, the ideal, and the symbolic: the destruction of the Jewish community in Paris, the ideal of the Republic, and the demands that the Shoah places on the Jewish intellectuals. In this respect, Sarah Kofman's situation is emblematic: she simultaneously feels the pull and repulsion of the warmth of belonging, and relishes being an intellectual in a country that places very high value on its thinkers. Simultaneously, the psychic wound of the Holocaust that must be addressed makes her different from her peers, a "familiar stranger," a writer with an unhappy destiny, unlike anyone else's. "I have only one country, and it is Paris," writes Raczymow, thus encapsulating the terrible task of a Jewish writer as the keeper of memory of a murdered people in a city that he identifies as his home.

5

Comme Dieu en France?

Disillusionment and Dreams in Twentieth-Century
French Jewish Immigrant Literature

NADIA MALINOVICH

Over the course of the twentieth century, French Jewish writers have imagined and experienced Paris as both a city of dreams and a city of disillusionment. There is simultaneously a continuity and rupture in their portrayals
of the French capital; this is particularly evident in the ways that Jewish
immigrant and first-generation writers have experienced and represented
Paris in two significant periods: the early twentieth century (1905–1932)
and the post–World War II years (the 1950s to 1980). Both of these eras
saw an important influx of Jewish immigrants to France, the majority of
whom settled in and around Paris. Most Jewish immigrants to Paris in the
early twentieth century were Ashkenazim from eastern Europe who were
driven from their countries of origins for primarily economic reasons. Jewish
arrivals in the 1950s and 1960s, by contrast, were mainly Sephardim from
North Africa, whose departure was linked to decolonization.

Despite these important differences in geographical origins and historical context, we see a number of parallels between the experiences of new
Jewish arrivals to Paris in the pre– and post–World War II eras. Both eastern European and North African Jews usually brought with them idealized

73

images of France and Paris and, as a result, their immigration stories often center on the collision between the Paris of their dreams and the Paris of reality. The very positive reputation that both France and Paris traditionally held in the eastern European Jewish imagination strongly colors the image of Paris that emerges in eastern-European immigrant and first-generation literature of the 1920s. Upon arrival, the protagonists make the city their own and immerse themselves in its pleasures and freedoms. Ultimately, however, they see their dreams of melting seamlessly into Parisian life, and into France more generally, thwarted by outside forces beyond their control. In the novels and memoirs of post–World War II immigrant writers from North Africa, we once again find an idealized image of both France and Paris stemming from the privileged relationship with French language and culture that North African Jews had developed in the colonial period. These immigrants—like their eastern European counterparts who had arrived a half century before—were often disappointed as their idealized Paris confronted the real Paris. More often than not, however, for these people, the city was ultimately able to fulfill its promise as a site of sophistication, pleasure, and personal liberation. I will explore these themes through a study of two Jewish-themed novels published in the 1920s—*L'Epopée de Ménaché Foigel* (The Epic of Ménaché Foigel) by André Billy and Moïse Twersky and *Jacob* by Bernard Lecache—as well as two postwar memoirs, *Mémoire illettrée d'une fillette d'Afrique du nord à l'époque colonial* (The Illiterate Memoir of a Girl from North Africa in the Colonial Era) by Katia Rubinstein (née Taïeb) and *Les Jours innocents* (Days of Innocence) by Jean-Luc Allouche.

France in the Eastern European Jewish Imagination

Beginning in the late nineteenth century, worsening political and economic conditions sparked a massive emigration of eastern European Jews out of the tsarist empire. While most of those individuals made their way to the United States, France was also a major destination, with approximately 200,000 Jewish immigrants settling in the country between 1881 and 1939 (Hyman, 64, 68). France was anything but a random destination for those who chose it. Just as eastern European Jews developed a mythology around the United States as the "goldene medina," Nancy Green explains, so too did France hold a special place in the eastern European Jewish imagination. The mystique of France's appeal—linked to its strong association with the ideals of liberty, equality, and fraternity embodied in the French Revolution—had

particular significance for Jews because France was the first European country to have politically emancipated its Jewish population. With its relatively
high salaries and advanced worker protection laws, France was also attractive
for practical purposes (Green, 27, 28).

Gilbert Michlin, who was born in Paris in 1926, nine months after
his parents' immigration from the Russo-Polish territory of Niezwiej, sums
up this eastern European Jewish attraction to France in his memoir, *Of No
Interest to the Nation*. Recalling his mother's "French dream," he notes that
whereas his father had longed to go to America, "My mother, Riwka, a
French teacher, dreamed of living in France where her brother and cousin
were living. . . . France was, of course, the country of Human Rights. The
first country to emancipate the Jewish people, it was a place they could live
well. *Lebn vi Got in Frankrayk*, As Happy as God in France, they would
say" (7).

While the Dreyfus Affair (1894–1906) was covered in the eastern
European Jewish press and naturally garnered dismay in certain circles, there
is no evidence that it slowed immigration or seriously tarnished the image
of France in the eastern European Jewish imagination. Ironically, the very
fact that the entire scandal of the affair centered on an openly Jewish army
officer in the high command of the French army cast France in a positive
light: neither in the tsarist empire nor in Imperial Germany could a Jew
ever have hoped to obtain such a position (Green, 28). The post–World
War I years were a high-water mark for Jewish immigration to France. The
passage of new, restrictive legislation in 1923 had all but shut the door to
eastern Europe immigration to the United States. France, by contrast, eased
its immigration laws after its devastating population loss during World War
I, paving the way in the 1920s for the country to become the primary
destination for eastern European Jews from the former tsarist empire.

City of Dreams, City of Temptations:
Paris in French Jewish Literature of the 1920s

This influx, combined with the coming of age of second-generation French
Jews whose parents had arrived before World War I, gave rise to a new
flourishing of literature written in French by Jewish writers of east European
origin. This literature provides a rich source of immigrants' impressions of
France and, more specifically, Paris, where the overwhelming majority of the
new arrivals settled. *L'Epopée de Ménaché Foigel*, the collaborative effort of

Moïse Twersky, an immigrant from Ukraine, and prominent French novelist and literary critic André Billy, exemplifies this genre. As Billy (1882–1971) explains in his preface to a postwar edition of the trilogy, he based the novels on details of Jewish history and culture that Twersky, an eccentric and endearing character whom he met at an artist's studio in Montparnasse, had shared with him.

L'Epopée de Ménaché Foigel recounts the adventures of Ménaché and his wife, Haïkélé, first in fin-de siècle tsarist Russia, then in Paris, and finally in England during World War I. The first volume, *Le Fléau du savoir* (The Plague of Knowledge) focuses on the encounter between the traditional religious culture of eastern European Jews and Enlightenment secularism through the story of a traditional, pious Jew as he ventures outside the sheltered world of the shtetl. Billy and Twersky use the analogy of a "plague" to describe, with irony, the destabilizing effect that the Haskalah (Jewish enlightenment) has on their protagonist, Ménaché Foigel, and on the Jewish communities of eastern Europe more broadly. Steeped in religiosity and tradition, the authors suggest, the Jews of the shtetl lived happily among themselves with little concern about the goings-on of the "goyim." It is only when the "sickness" of the Haskalah descends on a town that its residents become discontent and newly resentful of the restrictions placed on them by both the tsarist government and their own religious tradition. Ménaché soon succumbs to this "plague of knowledge," losing his faith and ceasing to be a practicing Jew (109). This part of the story is loosely autobiographical. As we learn from Billy's preface, Twersky was the son of an unnamed "miraculous rabbi," who had abandoned all religious practice by the time that Billy met him in the early 1920s.[1]

For Twersky himself, this loss of religious faith had gone hand in hand with the dissolution of an arranged marriage (v), whereas, for his fictional hero, the move from the shtetl to the city marks a rupture with tradition that liberates him to find a spouse outside of that constraint. Ménaché meets, falls in love with, and marries Haïkélé, a fellow modern, secular Russian Jew. The impetus for the couple's departure from Russia is Ménaché's desire to avoid military service, which the narrator portrays as only natural given both the Jews' lack of political rights in tsarist Russia and their traditional condition of statelessness: "this necessity [military service] was as inconceivable to [Ménaché] as the possibility for a Christian of not having a country, not having enemies, not doing military service" (156).

It is at this point that Paris is first mentioned in the novel, as Ménaché's uncle Schmuel advises him to set his sights on the French capital, where

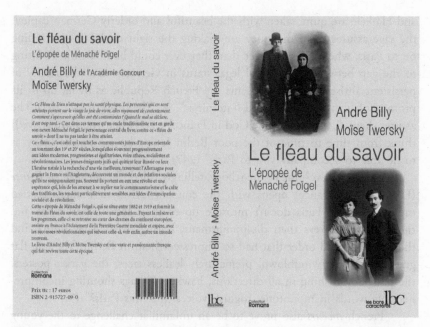

Figure 5.1. Cover of *Le fléau du savoir: L'épopée de Ménaché Föigel*, published by Éditions Les Bons Caractères (2006). (*Source*: Photos collection Bérezné)

his brother-in-law has already immigrated and made a fortune in business (161). By contrast, Sarah, an elderly, pious, traditional shtetl Jew who is a friend of Haïkélé's mother, warns the couple against the move. In a scene that underlines the generational clash between traditional religious Jewish culture and secular modernity, Sarah speaks with horror of her experience visiting her son in the French capital. Through Sarah's account, the authors portray eastern European immigrants to Paris as assimilating at a rapid clip, happily abandoning their religious practice, and readily embracing inter-marriage. The image of Paris as a site of debauchery and sin, which the already secularized Haïkélé and Ménaché clearly take with a grain of salt, is presented in a comic light. This scene was surely modeled on Twersky's story of own mother's trip to visit him in Paris, in which she refuses to leave her son's apartment and its immediate surroundings for fear of being tainted by "the most corrupt city in the world" (vi).

This volume ends, by contrast, with a very positive image of the French capital given to the protagonists by an old Jewish sage in Berlin, where the couple lives for a brief period on their journey westward. While Ménaché and Haïkélé are quite taken with the beautiful and orderly German capital, the sage assures them that they are making the right choice in continuing on to Paris, where Jews are freer than they ever could be in Berlin. Pointing to the gap between Jews' equal legal status in Germany and the reality of persistent antisemitism, he presents the French Republic as living up to its promise of liberty, equality, and fraternity: ". . . The proverb is correct," he assures them, ". . . 'to live like God in France' . . . [when you have arrived] think from time to time of the poor Berlin Jews who are not so lucky as to be able to accompany you to Paris" (247).

The second volume of the trilogy, tellingly titled *Comme dieu en France* (Like God in France) opens with the couple's arrival in France's storied capital. Initially, Paris doesn't measure up to their lofty expectations and the narrator conveys their disappointment, noting that: "They didn't find the discipline and order that had so impressed them in Berlin. The tall, flat gray houses, the windblown, prematurely leafless trees, the garish posters, the passersby rushing in all directions, hawkers in rags shouting incomprehensible words in monotone, roguish voices: this was Paris?" (5).

French *moeurs* also prove to be an unfamiliar challenge to the young couple. Haïkélé is shocked when her brother, who had settled in Paris several years prior, takes them to a restaurant where she is sure that the provocatively dressed female patrons are prostitutes. Though she remains skeptical, Haïkélé ultimately accepts her brother's assurances that they are in fact perfectly respectable women whose code of fashion is simply different from that to which she and Ménaché are accustomed. After the initial culture shock of their arrival, Ménaché and Haïkélé quickly find themselves adapting to Paris life. They find work easily, begin to learn French, and to look and act like Parisians: "For two thousand years, the life of the chosen people had required continual adaptation. Following in the footsteps of an incalculable number of their fellow Jews, Ménaché and Haïkélé easily adapted to Parisian mores. By the end of one month, the tailor already was able to understand French, and Haïkélé's progress was even more remarkable. She now dressed as fashionably as Marcelle [her non-Jewish, Parisian sister-in-law], and with even more happiness" (87). While the degree to which eastern European Jews maintained religious practice and intercommunal relations after immigration no doubt varied, the trajectory of rapid secularization and acculturation attributed to Ménaché and Haïkélé reflects the majority tendency among the eastern European Jewish immigrant population in Paris in the pre–World War II years (Malinovich, 108–15).

The next turn in the plot, however, suggests that that Twersky was among the minority of Russian Jews who resisted the patriotic fever that spread through France in 1914.[2] As we have seen, the desire to avoid military service was the decisive factor in the couple's decision to leave Russia. This concern becomes determinate in sparking their decision to immigrate once again after the outbreak of World War I, this time to England. Haïkélé and Ménaché do not share their neighbors' patriotic enthusiasm, which they rather see as foolish jingoism. This comes across in a scene in which the concierge in their apartment building reports with great excitement and pride that their upstairs neighbor has been called up for military service. When Ménaché and Haïkélé react with puzzled surprise at the concierge's excitement about the war, she remarks by way of parting, "It is true that you people cannot understand." Reflecting on the encounter, Ménaché does not disagree with her assessment, ruminating that that "there were many things, over these last few days, that he felt incapable of understanding" (175). The narrator goes on to describe an antinationalist, cosmopolitan view of the world that he understands as a natural outgrowth of the Jewish condition of exile. Patriotism, he explains, can be equated with religious belief, and Haïkélé and Ménaché, "who have lived without a country for two thousand years" are, understandably, not believers (136).

The final volume of the trilogy, *Le Lion, l'ours et le serpent* (The Lion, the Bear, and the Snake) finds Ménaché and Haïkélé rather unhappy in London, where they are disappointed to discover English Jews living a much more ghettoized existence than their French counterparts. "Everything in Whitechapel is for the Jews," Ménaché remarks disparagingly. "A 'real Jew' could live here without ever leaving the neighborhood" (31). On occasion, Twersky and Billy show Ménaché and Haïkélé taking pleasure in the warm and welcoming feeling of being surrounded by fellow eastern European Jews. When they attend a Yiddish theater performance, for instance, they marvel over the fact that "the Jews of Whitechapel, from the richest to the poorest, form one big family" (38). Overall, however, the couple finds the ethnic insularity of Whitechapel stifling; they are nostalgic for Paris, where they were able to assimilate much more effortlessly into the mainstream culture.[3]

In Bernard Lecache's 1925 novel *Jacob*, we find another example of a semi-autobiographical novel that explores the possibilities and limits of the integration of eastern European Jews in France. A journalist and left-wing political activist, Lecache is best known as the president of the Ligue internationale contre l'antisémitisme (International League against Antisemitism) that he founded in 1929 and remained at the head of until his death in 1968. Lecache tells the story of a first-generation French Jew who, like himself, is the Parisian-born son of Ukrainian immigrants. The first section of the book, like *Comme dieu en France*, is set before World War I, and we find a similar portrait of Paris as a kind of antighetto. On the occasion of his younger brother Avrum's visit, Jacob—who has moved away from home and integrated into mainstream bourgeois Parisian society—proposes a "trip down memory lane" to a restaurant on the rue des Rosiers, the Jewish immigrant district where the brothers used to enjoy Sunday lunches with their parents. The neighborhood is described as loud, unrefined, and impoverished, but also homey and warm, a place where Jews—even newly arrived immigrants—and non-Jews mix freely. The sidewalks are lined with pregnant women, crying babies in their arms, chatting with one another while their husbands smoke and socialize among themselves. In the meanwhile, the narrator explains, "Their sons and daughters jumped rope, happily pushing and shoving one another, sympathized with the little *goïm*. A distorted Yiddish sounded from all around, cut with a thick French pouring out from the sad cafes where *maçons* from the Limousin region, sat and drank . . . at the angle of Charlemagne and de Jouy streets, an adolescent Jewish girl flirted with a maladroit worker with a provincial accent. She flayed, with her pretty broken voice, the words of France" (176).

As is the case for Twersky and Billy's protagonists, however, the seemingly successful assimilation of Jews into French society that we find in the first half of the book turns out to be but a bitter illusion. Jacob Randansky, shortening his name to Randan, makes the fateful decision to move away from his Jewish identity in order to further climb the social ladder. He then falls from grace when an antisemitic newspaper denounces him as a Jew after he is involved in a financial scandal.

In the Paris of Lecache's novel, working-class Jews and gentiles can mix amiably, but once Jews climb the social ladder this open and uncomplicated "French and Jewish" identity is no longer possible. Jacob feels pressured to reject his Jewish identity in order to become French, which Lecache associates with a loss of faith and the adoption of a secularized lifestyle. In the end, Lecache offers a pessimistic view of the possibilities of Jewish acceptance in France. No matter how much the Jew attempts to assimilate, the plotline of *Jacob* tells us, his Jewish background will inevitably be called out, revealing him, in the eyes of the surrounding population, to be not authentically French.

A City of Dreams (and Disappointments) Once More: Paris in the Postwar Sephardic Literary Imagination

While France's Jewish population prior to World War II was overwhelmingly Ashkenazi, beginning in the 1950s and 1960s that demography changed dramatically. Decolonization led to the mass migration of Jews from the former French colonies to the French mainland. This population transfer was most dramatic in the case of Algeria, which saw its Jewish population—along with the *pied noir* French settlers—relocate to France almost overnight after the French withdrawal from Algeria in 1962. While more Moroccan and Tunisian Jews—who had not, like their Algerian counterparts, been granted French citizenship during the colonial era—relocated to Israel, substantial numbers of Jews from these countries also immigrated to France. As a result of these migratory trends, France's current Jewish population is more than 70 percent Sephardic.

We find many of the same tropes in the literature of French Jews from North Africa—France as an idealized promised land that both lives up to its promises and disappoints—that we find in the literature of the pre–World War II eastern European immigrants. Over the course of the late nineteenth and early twentieth centuries, the Jews of French colonial North Africa increasingly came to identify with French culture, and—especially among the more educated—to see France as their spiritual home. This phenomenon was the result of colonial policies that tended to favor Jews and other minority groups as intermediaries between the colonial powers and the indigenous Muslim population and furthered by the work of the Alliance Israelite Universelle, a French-based international human rights organization that set up a very successful network of French-language schools for Jewish children all across the Muslim world. These developments meant that for most Sephardic immigrants in the postwar years—even more than for their Ashkenazi counterparts earlier in the century—both France and Paris were places with strongly positive associations. Furthermore, the majority of these immigrants were already French-speaking and familiar with French culture before their arrival.

Katia Rubinstein's semi-autobiographical novel, *Mémoire illettrée d'une fillette d'Afrique du nord à l'époque coloniale* (The Illiterate Memoir of a Girl from North Africa in the Colonial Era) illustrates the affinity of North African Jews to France, especially among the younger generation. The book tells the loosely autobiographical story of a young girl growing up in Tunis in the 1950s and follows her to Paris after the family's immigration in 1959. For Rubinstein's protagonist, Kadem, Paris is a city of dreams, a city of freedom—she cannot wait to arrive. A conversation between her grandmother and another older relative relating to the family's immanent plan of immigration reveals the young girl's exuberant excitement at the prospect of relocating to the French capital: "That girl, marriage? . . . she spits on the idea, I tell you. Strolling and dreaming, on l'Avenue de Paris [the main boulevard in Tunis]; all she wants to do is to flee to the real Paris as soon as she can! She dreams of taking the city by storm, one day or another; What hasn't she heard about Parisian women? The most educated, the most elegant, the freest in the whole world!" (226).

In his memoir *Les Jours Innocents*, the Algerian-born Jean-Luc Allouche similarly recalls his excitement at the prospect of living in Paris. "I was excited by the promise of an adventure, by the idea of enlarging my horizons . . . I savored the unknown and discovery. I was twelve years old, I could think of nothing but Paris" (18).

For both Allouche and Rubinstein's loosely fictionalized Kadem, growing up in French colonies and being educated in French, made both France and Paris seem familiar to them in a way that they were not to Haïkélé and Ménashé in *L'Epopée de Ménaché Foigel*. That sense of familiarity, however, often made the encounter with the real Paris even more stark and tinged with disappointment than it was for the Yiddish-speaking eastern Europeans who had arrived earlier in the century. Novelists and memoirists writing about the relocation of North African Jews to France, notes Ewa Tartakowsky, "are very often imbued with a sense of regret for the life left behind, if not a real sense of nostalgia and profound deception, which could lead them to question their place in metropolitan France, this France that they had once so idealized" (177).

This is painfully true for Katia Rubinstein's main character, and in her case the disappointment is exacerbated by the fact that it is not only France, but Paris itself, that disappoints. The Paris that she was promised, Kadem explains wistfully in a letter to a friend back home, was not the Paris she found: "the sky is obstinately gray, neither the perfumes of cooking, not flowers, not soap fills the air, but rather the odor of burning coal; there is no colorful laundry hanging from the windows, the colors are all washed-out" (289). Even more important than Kadem's disappointment at the physical character of the French capital is her disappointment with Parisians themselves. Students don't share their snacks in the school yard as they did in Tunis, and Kadem's mother is shocked at the unfriendliness of her new neighbors who seem to take no note of her existence: "Had it not been repeated to us incessantly that Parisians were the most generous, the most open-minded and the most cultivated of creatures? How is it possible that the reality is so different? I only see dry and empty arrogance, intolerance, stinginess, and devious sophistication (289).

Allouche and his family experienced a similar sense of disillusionment when they arrive in the French capital. "Paris was no party," he explains to the reader, describing their disappointment at the gray, drab buildings and weather, and, even more importantly, the family's loss of social status. He feels self-conscious of both his appearance and accent when he begins high school in France just two days after the family arrives. "I still had 'the dark complexion of a barely civilized alien, a heavy sing-song accent' " (20). Feeling awkward and out of place, he naturally gravitates toward others from marginalized backgrounds rather than the "real" French students, whom he finds alien and intimidating. Furthermore, Allouche is simultaneously embarrassed by his family's religiosity and disappointed by the lack of festivity surrounding the celebration of holidays in their new home: "Despite my feeling of detachment, I consented to accompany my father to religious services for the High Holy Days. They took place in a garage: the community, too poor, consisting of survivors from North Africa, did not have the means to build an oratory worthy of its name" (43). "This world that had so seduced me was not, in fact, mine," Allouche goes on to reflect. "Paris, so desired, escaped me" (45).

The dramatic tensions in prewar Ashkenazi immigrant literature, as illustrated in both *L'Epopée de Ménaché Foigel* and *Jacob*, center on the contradictory pulls of Frenchness and Jewishness. In these novels, Jewishness is associated with the Jews' status in Christian Europe as the perpetual outsider, who even in the "promised land" of France, cannot ever fully attain insider status. For North African Jews, by contrast, Jewishness in their native lands had given them a privileged status vis-à-vis the indigenous Muslim population and offered them a ticket into European and French culture. Once they had arrived in France, however, it was their North African otherness—rather than their Jewishness—that came most prominently into play.

Paris, City of Dreams Fulfilled?

Despite his initial sense of disappointment and the difficulty of his family's experience when they arrived in Paris, Allouche excelled at school, went on to study at the Sorbonne, and became a successful journalist and writer. He also came to develop a genuine affection for the "real Paris" that was now his home: "I loved Paris—far from the tumult and drama of the Mediterranean. The city cured me of the pungency of Africa; its lightness and its air, the carefree urbanity of its people, the calculated indifference of its people, the precarious, fleeting exhilaration of friendships, all distancing me from incandescence of Algeria, from the burn of the betrayed land" (36). As he began to appreciate the advantages of life in France and Paris, the early alienating and shocking aspects of the city eventually became normal, desirable, and liberating.

The theme of Paris as city of liberation is particularly strong in the fiction and memoir literature of North African Jewish women writers. For these immigrant women, burdened with the weight of traditional female roles and expectations, Paris most often represents social freedom and hope for the future (Tartakowsky, 214). This trope of Paris as a site of liberation comes across very strongly in Rubenstein's novel. At the same time that she conveys Kadem's disappointment at the disjuncture between the idealized Paris of her dreams and the Paris that she finds when she arrives, Rubenstein also describes the sense of personal liberation that Kadem finds in the French capital. While she and the rest of her family are a bit put off by their French cousins' lack of religiosity, Kadem is surprised and pleased by the progressive attitude the husband of one of her cousins shows toward women and family life: "Affirming the value of being single, of the pleasures of a free life, of having a child eventually, but not necessarily . . . finally! Someone who didn't lie and, moreover, spoke the words that I had always wanted to hear!" (278). Despite all its shortcomings, for Kadem, Paris is associated with liberation, with possibilities and pleasures that—especially for a woman—would not have been possible in the land of her birth. While she was aware that she enjoyed more Western-style freedoms than did her Muslim compatriots in Tunisia, the extent to which she was part of an Arab culture that put more restrictions on women's possibilities for self-fulfillment than the European culture becomes clear to her in France.

Bernard Lecache's novel ends with Jacob's brother Avrum making a bittersweet comment when he sees a young, pregnant Jewish woman and her husband speaking Yiddish on the streets of Paris: "They were poor, they must still believe in *Adonai*. But the little one, who she is carrying in her belly, he will be like us" (247). The "us" that Avrum is referring to here is the assimilated French Jew who has left the bosom of the Jewish community and can no longer take comfort in faith but is nonetheless unable to fully belong a national community that does not completely accept him as a Jew.

Reading this passage from our contemporary post-Holocaust standpoint, we can only regret that the protagonist's prediction did not come true; "the little one"—a Jewish adolescent who would turn fifteen the year the Nazis occupied Paris—would have faced hardships that were unimaginable to Jacob and Avrum in 1925. As this disjuncture indicates, the horrific interruption of World War II and the Holocaust meant that the process of integration and acculturation that Jewish immigrants from eastern Europe undertook in early twentieth-century France was radically cut off by forces beyond their control. It was the Jewish North Africans arriving in the postwar years who would be able to fulfill their quest—fraught though it may have been—to become both French and Parisian. Ultimately, it is this sharp historical divide that made the trajectories of Jewish immigrants who arrived in the pre- and postwar years so different. Allouche, Rubinstein, and their fellow North African Jews were able to follow a natural course toward becoming both French and Parisian that had been so cruelly denied their ill-fated brethren who came to France a generation too soon.

Notes

1. As Billy's preface indicates, his coauthor was undoubtedly a descendant of Menachem Twersky, the mid-eighteenth-century founder of the Chernobyl Hasidic dynasty, and likely the great-uncle of the American-born Hasidic rabbi and Harvard scholar, Isadore Twersky.

2. As Philippe Landau and others have so clearly demonstrated, the majority of immigrant Jews in fact evinced their patriotism at the outbreak of the war, and willingly responded when called for up for military service.

3. This fictional portrayal of the contrast between immigrant Jewish life in fin-de-siècle London and Paris reflects real differences in housing patterns in the two cities. Whereas in London (and New York), Jewish immigrants lived largely among themselves, in Paris they lived in much more mixed neighborhoods. While both the Marais and Montmartre, for example, had a high concentration of Jewish residents, at no point did Jews form the majority of the population (Malinovich, 113).

Bibliography

All translations from the Bibliography in French are my own.

Allouche, Jean-Luc. *Les Jours Innocents*. Paris: Lieu Commun, 1983.
Azria, Régine. "Sefarades et Ashkenazes en France: Un rencontre difficile." *Contemporary French and Francophone Studies* 11, no. 2 (2007): 207–16.

Billy, André, and Moïse Twersky. *L'Épopée de Ménaché Foigel.* 3 vols. Paris: Plon, 1927–28); vol. I: *Le Fléau du savoir* (1927); vol. II: *Comme dieu en France* (1928); vol. III: *Le Lion, l'ours et le serpent* (1928). This trilogy was reissued by Les Éditions de Seuil in 1956, with a preface by André Billy.

Green, Nancy. *The Pletz of Paris: Jewish Immigrant Workers in the Belle Époque.* New York: Holmes and Meier, 1986.

Hyman, Paula. *From Dreyfus to Vichy: The Remaking of French Jewry, 1906–1939.* New York, Columbia University Press, 1979.

Landau, Philippe. "Les Juifs russes à Paris pendant la Grande Guerre: cibles d'antisémitisme."*Archives Juives* 40, no. 1 (2007).

Lecache, Bernard. *Jacob.* Paris: Gallimard, 1925.

Malinovich, Nadia. *French and Jewish: Culture and the Politics of Identity in Early Twentieth-Century France.* Oxford: Littman Library of Jewish Civilization, 2008.

Michlin, Gilbert. *Of No Interest to the Nation: A Jewish Family in France, 1925–1945.* Detroit: Wayne State University Press, 2004.

Rubinstein, Katia. *Mémoire illettrée d'une fillette d'Afrique du nord à l'époque colonial.* Paris: Stock, 1979.

6

Sarah Kofman

A Strange Familiarity

HENRI RACZYMOW

Rue Ordener Rue Labat

It's a curious title for a book. I spontaneously relate it to two mathematical concepts in the Cartesian coordinate system, in which there are two axes reaching to infinity, the ordinate and the abscissa. Rue Ordener, named after a general, is obviously the ordinate (the vertical or y axis), and rue Labat, which sounds the same as the French adverb of place *là-bas* (over there), is the abscissa (the horizontal or x axis). Two streets, two axes, two mothers that do not meet at any point. Sarah Kofman herself established an imaginary play between the signifiers Ordener and Labat. Ordener was *ordinaire*, ordinary, or here; Labat was *là-bas*, elsewhere, other. Rue Labat also figures in a famous song sung by Édith Piaf that includes a nice oxymoron, "La fille de joie est triste, / Au coin d'la rue Labat" (The prostitute—literally, girl of joy—is sad / On the corner of rue Labat), the second line of which is often misheard as "au coin d'la rue là-bas" (on the corner of the street over there).

Chapter translated from the French by Phyllis Aronoff.

Thus there is, first, a Paris topography in which the second mother is named using a periphrasis: "the lady on rue Labat" (20). Sarah tells us the qualities that characterize her are beauty, gentleness, femininity: "She . . . looked very lovely to me, and she was so gentle and affectionate" (32). As well, she has blond hair and blue eyes. These are all things that the real mother lacks; she has only one virtue, that of being the real one. The dichotomy of 5 rue Ordener versus 6 rue Labat, the real mother, unnamed because unnamable, versus Mémé (Grandma), as Sarah calls "the lady on rue Labat," is the real subject of the book, the other one being the dramatic itinerary of her successive moves in Paris and the provinces during and after the war. Finally, at the center, is the figure of the father, Rabbi Bereck Kofman, and the hole left by his disappearance. Bereck Kofman is the only character whose family name is given. The mother has no name at all; Mémé, we learn from events, is called Claire. And there is a passing mention of the first names of Sarah's brothers and sisters and the French names substituted for them. Of these siblings she tells us nothing; they are but minor characters in the drama.

In a short essay published in translation in the US, I have spoken of "memory shot through with holes." For Sarah Kofman, memory does not have holes; it is intact. She is not, to use Froma Zeitlin's term, a "vicarious witness," although she does indeed have, to use another term from Zeitlin, a "belated memory." But not, as in my case, an imagined memory, what Marianne Hirsch calls a "postmemory."[1] Here is a first similarity and a first difference between Sarah Kofman and me: a belated, but firsthand, memory in her case and a postmemory for my generation and succeeding ones.

Sarah's memory is certainly not shot through with holes, but there is a hole, a gaping hole that nothing can fill, that writing tries to fill, impossibly, without success: the place of the father. It is from this hole that the writing is born. As she says on the first page of this book, a fountain pen is the only thing she still has of her father. This pen, a metonym for the father, functions not exactly as a superego that forces her to write—a terrifying injunction and an unhappy destiny—but as a draft caused by an emptiness that must be filled. To fulfill the father, in the two senses of fill and satisfy. To perpetuate his name, to rename him. Basically, to give him symbolic children. His fountain pen, kept permanently on her desk before her eyes, is like a totem—a magical, religious object, to whose magic she is subject, a thing that determines her life, that tells her, you will live for me, you will write. Your writing will be the evidence of your obedience, your submission to my command, a metaphorical way of obeying the law I have inculcated in you. It is related to what anthropologists call mana, a magical and religious power possessed by certain objects. She says of her father's pen, "it is right in front of me on my desk and makes me write, write" (3). In this repetition "write, write," I read something like a compulsion, and like a misfortune and a weariness. As if she must get to the point where it would be possible not to write anymore. At the end of writing, and of sentences and books, there would finally be deliverance; the hole would have been filled by satisfying the father. But, more precisely, with the hole filled, there is nothing left but to die. Which Sarah will do. This sentence from the first page is often quoted: "Maybe all my books have been the detours required to bring me to write about 'that'" (3). As if Sarah Kofman had taken a long, indirect path by way of philosophy to arrive at this book outside of philosophy and almost outside of literature, so much are its rhetorical effects reduced to a minimum, or virtually absent. This book that would finally say what she had to say, black on white, after which she would no longer have anything to say—which was true in a certain way, as some of her women friends, such as Françoise Armengaut, have reported her telling them.

The Cadavre, the Cadaveresque

Yet this is not Sarah Kofman's last piece of writing. There is another, unfinished one that is a commentary on a painting by Rembrandt, the famous *Anatomy Lesson of Dr. Nicolaes Tulp* (The Hague). She wrote this short piece, titled "Conjuring Death: Remarks on *The Anatomy Lesson of Doctor Nicolaes Tulp* (1632)," in the last weeks of her life (237). In it, we read, "What is most astonishing about this Lesson is that with the help of a cadaver that is fully exposed but that no gaze sees as such, the cadaveresque that each living being, already from the origin, carries within itself comes to be hidden" (239). Jacques Derrida, who was her friend, said that he was tempted to "hear in [this text] a final confidence imparted or confided to us" (8). It is a commentary on a "lesson." The cadaver in the painting by Rembrandt is that of a man who was hanged (for theft, in Leiden in 1632). Death is made unreal in it. Nobody is looking at the cadaver itself, although it is the subject of the anatomy lesson, but at the big book open at its feet. As if the book made death unimportant, kept it at a distance, took the drama out of it, made it ordinary, bracketed it off. But that was a failure.

Sarah Kofman's first book, *The Childhood of Art*, published in French in 1970, had on the cover a reproduction of Leonardo da Vinci's London cartoon of Saint Anne and Mary, the two mothers of Jesus, side by side, their bodies hardly distinguishable from each other, and the child Jesus playing with Saint John the Baptist. She dedicated this first book to Mémé as follows: "For my mémé, who, having saved my life, first enabled me to write this book. Kisses, Sarah."[2] And her last book, in 1994, speaks of Sarah's own two mothers. In it she comes back to Leonardo's image, her sole comment a long quotation from Freud's *Leonardo da Vinci and a Memory of His Childhood*. Thus, no comment. Everything has been said, it seems. But, no, everything remains to be said, namely, death itself. Death as death; death that insists and that must be conjured. However, death is never conjured. Sarah ended her life that same year, 1994, at the age of sixty, leaving this last text on Rembrandt unfinished. Her final text is unfinished, but not her body of work, which has come full circle, the last book ending where the first one began.

Two Mothers

Sarah Kofman's first book, then, speaks, among other things, of Freud's text on Leonardo da Vinci's "memory of his childhood," and in particular, of the two mothers, Saint Anne and Mary, as Leonardo depicted them in his preparatory cartoon in London and his painting in the Louvre. Sarah was very deeply interested in this painting, and I should say immediately that I, too, am deeply interested in it, although the stakes seem slightly different. Broadly speaking, it is the feeling of having had two mothers, apparently a good mother and a bad mother, but with very ambivalent feelings toward each of them. What strikes me is that, as a little girl, Sarah called "the lady on rue Labat" Mémé. Mémé, and not Tata [Auntie] or Nounou [Nursie]. A *mémé* is a grandmother. Thus, Mémé and her biological mother (rue Labat/ rue Ordener) are, in fantasy, like Saint Anne and Mary, two inextricably entangled bodies that, as Freud says, are merged in a single form. I will not here recount the personal story I have already told elsewhere—in *Le Cygne invisible* (The Invisible Swan) in 2004 (in which the narrator goes to the Louvre fourteen times by the number 39 bus, obsessively taking the same route through Paris, to confirm the extreme importance of what is said in Leonardo da Vinci's Saint Anne for his inner life and his family life, as if he were going to analytic sessions), and more explicitly in *Heinz* in 2011. A story of substitution, of maternal roles indistinct and confused, of replacement, of maternal rivalry with regard to a young man who died a deportee and his "replacement" born after the war, who was given his name.

So I share with Sarah Kofman the theme of our two mothers. The title of Sarah Kofman's last book, *Rue Ordener Rue Labat*, as we know, refers to the respective addresses of her biological mother and Mémé, "the lady on rue Labat," who took her in and loved her and was loved by her. I, too, had two mothers: Anna, my biological mother, and her own mother, Mania. Or Anne and Mary—no comment! I was the son of these two women, in reality the son of Anna and, through substitution, as a replacement, that of my grandmother.

As a child, I constantly went from rue Bisson to rue de la Mare, by way either of rue des Couronnes or rue de Belleville, in the same neighborhood where Georges Perec lived as a child, on rue Vilin, a street that no longer exists. At the center of this cast of characters was someone who had preceded me, someone I had not known, another Henri, my grandmother's real son, my mother's brother, deported to Majdanek at the age of twenty. I told that story in *Heinz* in 2011. When I began an analysis, unfortunately belatedly, it was with the clear intention of receiving an answer to the question I finally dared to ask myself: why did I always have a very bad relationship with my mother, from as far back as I can remember until her death? My mother had entrusted me to her own mother on rue Bisson, who had probably asked for me as a replacement for her son who had died five years earlier, whose name I had been given. As a result, I had the benefit of a "good mother," a "good breast," as Sarah Kofman says, and resented my real mother, the "bad breast," for abandoning me. As we see, the story can be summed up in two sentences. Yet it took me decades, and books and books, and what's more, an analysis with a shrink who, although not Jewish, was named Rabain (pronounced in French like *rabbin*, rabbi—Sarah's father's occupation) to be able to express it.

In addition to the London cartoon and the Freudian analysis of Leonardo da Vinci's childhood memory, Sarah Kofman also speaks of the 1938 Hitchcock film—which, incidentally, is far from a sheer masterpiece—*The Lady Vanishes*, a vaguely patriotic film in which Miss Froy, a "nice little old lady" in the train taking the protagonists to London, who is actually a spy working for the Foreign Office, disappears and is replaced by another woman, the horrid Madame Kummer.

Sarah Kofman says she experiences "the same visceral anguish" (65) each time she sees it. At its center is a story of substitution: one woman in place of another.

The Carrion Beetle

And so I come now to my novel *Writing the Book of Esther*. Published in 1985 as *Un cri sans voix* (A Silent Cry), it was preceded by a text of some

twenty pages, a novella titled "Le Nécrophore" (The carrion beetle), which I
wrote in 1979 and published in the *Nouvelle Revue française* in the summer
of 1980, in the same issue as many pages from *L'Ecriture du désastre* (*The
Writing of the Disaster*) by Maurice Blanchot, which was very important to
Sarah Kofman and which would be published in book form in October of
that year. My text was the matrix of the novel to come, which I was not
aware of at the time I wrote it. In it, I imagined an elder sister, a child
during the war, an extraordinary intellectual, a brilliant student, who was
seen as "crazy" in the family, a literature teacher, obsessed with the Warsaw
Ghetto, who would commit suicide, perhaps because she was unable to
write the book she had in her. Her name was Judith Szpiro. Allow me to
present a short passage from it: "I don't like Judith. Everything I think,
everything I imagine, everything I discover, every intuition, I have, she
has already thought it, already imagined it, already discovered it. She went
through the whole thing a long time ago. She is always walking ahead of
me. It's unbearable . . . Judith is my shadow, the shadow I can't overtake."[3]
The narrator, the little brother, sets out to write his sister's story,
suddenly very proud of being a writer (or of thinking himself one), rival-
rous and proud of prevailing over the sister who has crushed him with
her intellectual superiority, of achieving what she had failed to do: write.
He sees his sister's failure even in her suicide and he soon has the feeling
of usurping a role, of taking someone else's place. He says so explicitly:
"Treading on your sister's corpse. It's worse than cannibalism." Because, in
writing the book his sister was unable to write, he has the feeling of living
through usurpation, by proxy, of laying his eggs in his sister's corpse, so to
speak. And that's how the idea came to me of that insect that lays its eggs
in the corpse of another animal, which serves as food for the larvae that
will hatch. The narrator of the story is himself a teacher and he constantly
thinks about one of the girls in his class, the most intelligent one, who
reminds him of his sister at the same age. Rereading this text today, I see,
much to my surprise, that the name of the imaginary student is Edith
Kaufman. Why Kaufman? I have no idea.

In the novella "Le Nécrophore," and later, in *Writing the Book of
Esther*, the issue was substitution, writing in place of another, stealing her
book, exploiting her life and death, and a second substitution, that of the
arrest of the heroine's Aunt Esther in place of her mother, Fanny, on rue des
Couronnes in Paris. I had to write several books in order to understand, to
realize, to admit the real substitution that was the basis of these fantasies. I

would do so in 2011, with *Heinz*. It was no longer a question of *writing* in place of another, but of *living* in place of another, on behalf of that other person, with his name and his position as son and brother. This was, in fact, already present in *Writing the Book of Esther* since it is suggested that Esther has a feeling of usurpation because she bears the name of her aunt Esther, whom she did not know and who died a deportee. In short, the novel *Writing the Book of Esther* anticipates the very real basis of *Heinz*. But in *Writing the Book of Esther*, the substitution is also, quite concretely, when someone dies in place of another, or is arrested in place of another who was in principle supposed to be arrested by the French or German police but was absent at the time, by chance or not. This is what occurs in *Rue Ordener*. The father knew, on July 16, 1942, that the police were going to come and pick him up (as Sarah Kofman says). He was lying on his bed waiting. When the policeman came asking for him, the mother said he was not there. The father then came out of his room and gave himself up. He had feared, as Sarah Kofman explains, that his wife and his six children would be taken in his place. That was a real possibility.

Smothered Words

I would like to come back to Sarah Kofman now, to *Smothered Words*, a book she wrote in August 1985 and published in 1987. August 1985 was the year *Writing the Book of Esther* was published in French. The dates coincide and so do the titles, both of which refer to the impossibility of speech, yet speech nonetheless, or in other words, writing. And thus, literature nonetheless. "How can one speak of that before which all possibility of speech ceases? . . . To speak: it is necessary—*without (the) power*: without allowing language, too powerful, sovereign, to master the most aporetic situation . . . to enclose it in the clarity and happiness of daylight. And how can one not speak of it, when the wish of all those who returned . . . has been to tell, to tell endlessly. . . ." And she quotes Blanchot in *The Step Not Beyond*: "silence like a cry without words; mute, although crying endlessly" (9–11).

While Sarah Kofman's book and its title refer explicitly to Maurice Blanchot, I took the title of my novel (A silent cry) from the Hassidic tradition, from Rabbi Menahem Mendel of Vorki, who said that there are three attitudes that characterize a true Jew: upright kneeling, a silent cry, an unmoving dance. The same expression was used by the Yiddish poet

Itzhak Katzenelson in his "Song of the Murdered Jewish People," written in the French camp at Vittel before his deportation to Auschwitz in 1944.

But let us immediately note a difference: the impossibility of speaking in Blanchot and Kofman arises from a philosophical position, that of the absurdity of words in view of the unprecedented enormity of the fact of Auschwitz. In *Writing the Book of Esther*, the impossibility of speaking arises from something rather different: the feeling of usurpation of speech. Usurpation, the illegitimacy of speaking, for someone who was born after, who is neither victim nor witness (cf. "Memory Shot Through with Holes"). And who would thus be speaking in place of another, which is the subject of the novel.

But let us go back to *Smothered Words*. To speak, to write this book, Sarah Kofman seems to have to take cover behind Maurice Blanchot and Robert Antelme (in fact, she is commenting on Blanchot, who is commenting on Antelme); she cannot bring herself to speak in her own name, for she would then have to use first-person narration and say "I." A first-person narrative orders, organizes, places in causal and syntactic sequence what would otherwise be nonsense, absurdity, impossibility. Hence, at that time, her refusal of first-person narrative. She hides behind Blanchot and Antelme precisely to achieve her purpose, to say and not say, to speak "smothered words," to speak the impossibility of speaking, a double bind. For that matter, the term *gas chamber*, a metonym for the extermination of the Jews, is not used, nor is the word *Jew* (or if it is used, it is, as in the film by Alain Resnais and Jean Cayrol, in passing, as if inadvertently, among other victims); moreover, Blanchot and Antelme are not Jews. In addition, as in Resnais and Cayrol, the name Auschwitz is mentioned in *Smothered Words*, but only as that of a camp like any other.

Auschwitz designates the horror of the Nazi camps, but not the Shoah. However, it was no longer the 1950s or 1960s; it was the middle of the 1980s, which saw the release of *Shoah* by Claude Lanzmann and *The Destruction of the European Jews* by Raul Hilberg. We have known since then—those who wanted to know—that there were camps and camps, and that, precisely, a "camp" such as Treblinka was not a camp but, to use Hilberg's term, a "killing center." Yet *Smothered Words* opens with the deportation of her father to Auschwitz and even a reproduction of the page from Serge Klarsfeld's *Memorial to the Jews Deported from France, 1942–1944* on which his name appears. There is thus neither concealment nor denial. There is a lack of awareness. There is a desire to maintain a philosophical position: she is speaking of man, of humankind, of what man can do to man, of that which man is capable of, and of the shared nature of the

SS and the deportee—their common humanity. Allow me to point out that Perec, too, twenty years earlier, in 1963, had commented on Robert Antelme. But exactly, that was in 1963.

To Write about That

I quoted earlier the opening sentence of *Rue Ordener Rue Labat*: "Maybe all my books have been the detours required to bring me to write about 'that.'" As if, with this book, she was nullifying her previous books, as if this last one, in short, could take the place of all the others, making all the others pointless, or useful only as facilitators of this one. As if she knew very well that this would be her last book, not only the latest one but the final one. And that afterward, she who was destined only to obey the paternal injunction to write and write more might as well bring down the curtain and take a final bow. That is what she did; she killed herself. Somewhat like my character Esther, who commits suicide because she does not manage to write. While Sarah commits suicide because she no longer has to write, since she has now said everything, she has come to the last sentence of her last book, the last sentence, in which she speaks of Mémé's death: "I know that at her grave the priest recalled how she had saved a little Jewish girl during the war" (85). This sentence, so simple, so stark, so poignant. Sarah Kofman has finally been able to speak of "that," what she calls "that." That which cannot be named in any language, which is an intimate wound that cannot scar over or heal.

It is curious that in the sheet inserted in the review copies of the 1985 French edition of *Writing the Book of Esther*, a short text written by me, I chose to use the word *that* as follows: "Mathieu Litvak will go further in his search for the truth, going through increasingly impenetrable layers of silence, forgetting, pain, and perhaps the impossibility of speaking of 'that' [my translation]." This neuter pronoun *that* comes, I believe, from Duras, where one often encounters such expressions as "pas de mots pour dire ça" ("no words to say that") or "pas de mots pour ça" ("no words for that"). There is no correspondence between words and things, especially when the thing is literally unheard of. A comment in passing on the name Mathieu. I used it in my *Contes d'exil et d'oubli* (Tales of Exile and Forgetting) (Mathieu Schriftlich) as well as in *Writing the Book of Esther* (Mathieu Litvak). It comes from Sartre's *Roads to Freedom*, which, like Sarah Kofman, I read when I was very young, about fifteen.

What is striking in *Rue Ordener* is the simplicity of the writing, syntax, and vocabulary, and the lack of affectation in the tone. It is strangely factual, matter-of-fact. A prephilosophical language. A few psychological comments, but little more. As if, at the age of sixty, Sarah Kofman could finally say to herself what had happened in the brutal nakedness of things. In general, the positive outcome of an analysis is the ability to finally say things to oneself in an orderly way, to fill in the holes, the gaps in memory, to not leave "memory shot through with holes," to use the expression I used once—in 1986 to be exact, the year when Sarah Kofman was writing *Smothered Words*. With *Rue Ordener*, the words are freed, below or beyond all philosophy. There is no recourse here to philosophy any more, as if the philosophical words had only been a cover, a padding, a smokescreen, words of substitution (again, substitution!). For the first time, Sarah Kofman allows herself to use words that do not involve erudition, hermeneutics, or decoding, but the facts themselves in their naked horror. She authorizes herself: she becomes author. She has finally fulfilled the mission she imagines her father gave her. Mission accomplished. She can die. She has nothing more to do on earth.

I have always thought that the tragedy of the Shoah for the Jews living in occupied Europe then and their descendants until today, the third and perhaps even the fourth generation, lay in the connection of the collective tragedy and the private, intrafamilial tragedy. The conflict between Sarah and her mother, the rivalry between the two mothers, the one on rue Ordener and the one on rue Labat, and Sarah's ambivalent position between the two are echoed in my situation, the circumstances of which, while different, are comparable, it seems to me. The difference being the generations to which Sarah Kofman and I belong, she to what Susan Suleiman has called the "1.5 generation,"[4] and I to the generation after. It is not a coincidence that I used these words of Pierre Goldman as the epigraph for *Writing the Book of Esther*: "For a long time I thought that I was born and that I died on June 22, 1944. . . . I was not old enough to fight, but as soon as I saw the light of day, I was old enough to have been killed in the crematoria of Poland" (n.p.).

And Paris?

I haven't yet spoken of Paris, where I was born, where my parents were born, where my grandparents, my four grandparents, came from Poland to settle in the same period, the 1920s, in the same neighborhood, Belleville. A working-class, revolutionary area, and also an immigrant area, as it still is today. The immigrants of that time essentially aspired to become French—at any rate they wanted their children to quickly learn the language, to diligently attend the school of the Republic, and to succeed, to integrate and assimilate. A child's neighborhood is necessarily a very small area, a few blocks: the school and nearby businesses, two or three familiar Métro stations. At our house, we never went to synagogue (we called it *shul*), we did not wear the kippah, we did not keep kosher; my father was a Communist activist who read the newspaper *L'Humanité* every day and analyzed everything through a Marxist lens, as the Party taught him to. From this point of view, my family was very different from that of Sarah Kofman, which was religious. But both families had emigrated from Warsaw, from a very modest background. The way Sarah Kofman describes her Paris of the 18th arrondissement is very familiar to me, although I don't know her neighborhood well. She notes, for example, the name of the street where she went to buy her father Zig-Zag cigarette papers, rue Jean-Robert. When she speaks of the Adler family, that of a playmate she meets at her father's synagogue, she says they lived on rue Simart. Or mentions a classmate, Hélène Goldenberg, and says she lived on rue Emile-Duployé. When she speaks of a street, such as rue Duc, where her father's little synagogue was located, she indicates that it was two Métro stations from rue Ordener because on Shabbat, they would go home on foot. There is a very precise topography that could be reconstructed on a map of this Paris neighborhood, just as Robert Bober, in his film *En remontant la rue Vilin* (Going back up rue Vilin), draws the topography of the few streets that Georges Perec walked when he was a child, among them rue Vilin, which was very familiar to me because it connected rue Bisson, where my grandparents lived, and rue de la Mare, my street. Why this insistence by Sarah Kofman, but also by others, on scrupulously noting the names of the streets of childhood? I think it is a trait of childhood to check that things are in their proper places, the walls of one's bedroom, the location of one's school, the Métro station, and so on,—because a child needs this protective framework, which is a mental framework. And then, in the writer, speaking much later of his or her childhood, there is the feeling of a land lost. What is lost, precisely, is the past. Writing the names of streets, Métro stations, neighbors, classmates, and so forth, is a way of connecting one's memory to something solid and objective, something that will endure: the names of the streets of one's neighborhood.

In contrast to the words of the song sung by Joséphine Baker, "J'ai deux amours, mon pays et Paris" ("I have two loves, my country and Paris"), I have only one country, and it is Paris. It reminds me of the Vel' d'Hiv' Roundup of July 16, 1942, which saw the arrest of my paternal grandmother, Rywka, by the French police, but it also reminds me of the barricades of Victor Hugo's *Les Misérables*, and those where I found myself in May 1968, when I was twenty.

Notes

1. See in particular her analysis of my *Contes d'exil et d'oubli.*
2. The dedication was not included in the English-language edition and was translated by me.
3. All quotations from this work are my translations.
4. Suleiman writes, "By 1.5 generation, I mean child survivors of the Holocaust, too young to have had an adult understanding of what was happening to them, but old enough to have *been there* during the Nazi persecution of Jews."

Bibliography

Armengaut, Françoise. "Le Rire de Sarah." *Fusées* 16 (September 2009): 12–18.
Derrida, Jacques. "Introduction." In Sarah Kofman, *Selected Writings*, edited by Thomas Albrecht, Georgia Albert, and Elizabeth Rottenberg. Stanford, CA: Stanford University Press: 2007.
Hirsch, Marianne. *Family Frames: Photography, Narrative and Postmemory.* Cambridge, MA: Harvard University Press, 1997.
Kofman, Sarah. *The Childhood of Art: An Interpretation of Freud's Aesthetics.* Translated by Winifred Woodhull. New York: Columbia University Press, 1988.
———. *Rue Ordener Rue Labat.* Translated by Ann Smock. Lincoln, NE: University of Nebraska Press, 1996.
———. *Selected Writings.* Edited by Thomas Albrecht, Georgia Albert, and Elizabeth Rottenberg. Translated by Pascale-Anne Brault. Stanford, CA: Stanford University Press, 2007.
———. *Smothered Words.* Translated by Madeleine Dobie. Evanston, IL: Northwestern University Press, 1998.
Raczymow, Henri. *Le Cygne invisible.* Paris: Collection Melville, Éditions Léo Scheer, 2004.
———. *Heinz.* Paris: Gallimard, 2011.

———. "Memory Shot Through with Holes" Translated by Alan Astro. *Yale French Studies* 85 (1994), 98–105.

———. "Le Nécrophore." In *Nouvelle Revue Française* (July–August 1980). [All quotations from this work are my translations.]

———. *Writing the Book of Esther*. Translated by Dori Katz. New York: Holmes & Meier, 1995.

Schulte Nordholt, Annelies. "Heinz d'Henri Raczymow, une écriture du silence." In *Le Silence de l'écriture de la Shoah* [*Çédille, revista de estudios franceses, monografías* 5 (2015)].

Suleiman, Susan Rubin. "The 1.5 Generation: Thinking about Child Survivors and the Holocaust." *American Imago* 59, no. 3 (2002): 277–95.

Zeitlin, Froma. "The Vicarious Witness: Belated Memory and Authorial Presence in Recent Holocaust Literature." In *Shaping Losses*, edited by Julia Epstein and Lori Hope Lefkovitz. Urbana and Chicago: University of Illinois Press, 2001.

PART 3 AMBIVALENCES

The chapters in this section explore the feeling of haunting by nameless forces captured in the writing of Patrick Modiano and Georges Perec. Ruth Malka points out that Perec and Modiano use two diverging approaches: Perec's childhood memories are sparse and it is thus the idea of lack that dominates *W or the Memory of Childhood*. Modiano brings the time of the German occupation of Paris through an abundance of stories that precede his birth.

For Amira Bojadzija-Dan the fear of what could be uncovered through writing and the desire for the ideals that Paris represents are at the core of the ambivalence that haunts Perec and Modiano. Walking along the former seat of the Gestapo can fill a sensitive observer such as Modiano with foreboding, and cause a momentary drop into a reality of another time, and bring him closer to his Jewish origins. In contrast, for Perec, the ruins of what used to be poor quarters in the northeast of Paris where his family lived stand indifferent and empty. Writing an exhaustive inventory of Paris, the most banal aspects of its everyday life, transparent and free of affect, was a way of keeping the little memory he had of his parents alive in a changing landscape.

Maxime Decout explores the idea of a "hollow imprint" left by the Bruder family and the possibility of existence through absence and emptiness. He points out that Dora's trail, imagined by Modiano, is both a physical and symbolic route into identity, writing, and Jewishness. In Modiano's world Jewishness is not a positive identity. Rather, it is an emptiness. Instead of filling the blanks, his inquiry into Dora Bruder's destiny fails by revealing the absence. Decout argues that Modiano's failure reveals the part of emptiness proper to all human beings, its core mystery, too frequently masked and forgotten. In the case of Dora Bruder, this absence became far more precious than a successful inquiry.

7

A City of My Own

Paris and Desire in the Work of
Georges Perec and Patrick Modiano

AMIRA BOJADZIJA-DAN

If we try to imagine Paris of the 1960s, two contradictory images are likely to emerge: that of a city undergoing a profound transformation, living the *"trente glorieuses,"* thirty "glorious" years of economic growth and reconstruction following the end of the World War II, and that of a city that had not changed that much since the Occupation. The rumble of German tanks and the sound of their troops triumphantly marching down Champs Elysées painfully echoes in the hearts and minds of the Parisians, while the facades of Belleville and Le Marais conceal the emptiness of the plundered apartments and absence of their deported Jewish inhabitants.

For Georges Perec, a six-year-old torn out of his family's midst about a year later, in 1943, becoming a writer meant that he had to try to imagine and then reconstruct his life prior to this moment of complete disruption when so many lives fell apart. By becoming a writer, he had to symbolically conquer Paris as the ground of both his happiest memories and his greatest loss. Paris acts as the repository of his family memory, the background of his fiction, and the laboratory of his many literary experiments. In order to respond to the violence of recent history, Perec sought to render Paris transparent through minute observation and exhaustive description of the most mundane details of urban life.

For Patrick Modiano, postwar Paris took on the form of a vast crime scene, sheltering both petty war profiteers and real murderers tangled together in a network of corruption and crime. A neglected child, Modiano received very little affection or role modeling from his parents. At eleven, he lost his younger brother, Rudy, to leukemia. It devastated him. Writing became his way of staying close to Rudy by revisiting the childhood memories, knowing an enigmatic father, and coming to terms with a cold, selfish mother. Most often, Modiano's novels unfold in Paris, in unclear time-spaces between the past and present, echoing one another, folding in the themes of war and collaboration, the deportations of Jews, characters of uncertain origins and intentions, and autobiography.

According to Roland Barthes "On étudie ce que l'on desire ou ce que l'on craint" ("We study that which we desire or we fear"). The uncertainty and instability that marked France in the years following World War II is reflected in the restlessness of Perec's 1967 novel, *A Man Asleep*, and Modiano's *La Place de l'étoile* (1968). Perec was influenced by Barthes. His writing presents an exceptionally disciplined, exhaustive description of the subject matter, so much so that David Bellos argues that Perec trained himself to write at "degree zero" of style. Modiano was equally obsessed with style and the ways in which it produces a "concentrated reality, more violent than real life." The discomfort and the atmosphere of uncertainty that we find in Modiano's novels are produced by style; not the rhetorical style, but a sentence that produces "une musique emotionnelle," similar to Céline and Queneau. In contrast, Perec, with the notable exception of *W, or the Memory of Childhood*, produces atmosphere through attempts to exhaust and classify reality, using constrained writing, word play, and puns.

Marcel Bénamou argues that Perec rediscovered his Jewishness in the process of unearthing and re-creating the story of his childhood. It was articulated along the following axes: "writing," "writing the story of my childhood," "feeling Jewish." Modiano, as Raymond Queneau wrote, was "absolutely devastated by the idea of both being and not being Jewish." His Jewishness is inscribed in his search for origins, more uncertain than Perec's, but also not as devastating in its effects. Modiano also embraced being Jewish as an act of defiance against the antisemitism of French writers whose style he admired, such as Céline and Drieu La Rochelle. In an interview he gave in 1971, he jokingly describes feeling "insulted with lots of talent and style" by Céline and wanting to respond in kind through *La*

Place de l'étoile. For both Perec and Modiano, writing was instrumental in recovering their Jewishness. It was also a way of dealing with what Maxime Decout described as "an element" in French literature that "triggers most contradictory emotions going from hatred to empathy."

Perec's attitude toward his Jewishness in his youth was one of refusal. Although his family history was close to the Judaism of the Polish Ashkenazim, he grew up in a milieu where desire for assimilation and embrace of the ideals of the French Revolution were strong. Ideologically, Perec was attracted to the ideas of socialism and secularism. As Bénamou points out, he even went through a period in which he was "allergic" to Judaism and could accept neither Judaism's religious heritage nor Zionism's nationalist inclinations. But as minimally Jewish as Perec was, the effects of this uneasy relationship on his life were immense.

It is this particular discomfort in dealing with the experience of history and trauma that I wish to explore. How do Georges Perec and Patrick Modiano, two tireless walkers of the Paris streets that consecrated its most anonymous quarters, devoted explorers of its unrecorded history, reconcile its beauty, the unequivocal success and sometimes adoration it afforded them, with the mute horror of the lives of their fellow Jews that ended at Vel' d'Hiv', Drancy, and ultimately the death camps across eastern Europe? How are the two realities—that of historical violence and that of great beauty—reflected in the same space? How can this space be reclaimed through a literary work?

Perec spent the first six years of his life in Belleville, where the recently arrived and poor most often settled. His father was killed in the early days of the German attack in June 1940 while serving as a soldier in the French army. In October 1941, his mother, Cyrla-Cécile Szulewicz, sent little Georges on a Red Cross train to his aunt Esther and uncle David, who had escaped Paris earlier and were living in the relative safety of the so-called free zone. This was the last time he would see her. Cécile was arrested in January 1943, together with her sister and father, and sent to Drancy prison, from which she was deported and murdered in Auschwitz. After the war Esther and David Bienenfeld, his paternal aunt and her husband were granted guardianship of the young Georges and brought him up with their own children in the elegant 16th arrondissement. Concerned with the loss that Georges had suffered, his guardians ensured that he was seen early on by Françoise Dolto, one of the most prominent postwar pediatricians and psychoanalysts in France.

His literary career consisted of surprises: his first novel, *Les Choses: Une histoire des années soixante (Things, a Story of the Sixties),* was a resounding literary success; next came *Quel petit vélo au guidon chromé au fond de la cour?* (*Which Moped with Chrome-plated Handlebars at the Back of the Yard?*)—a riddle of sorts in which the principal character kept changing his name—and *Un homme qui dort* (*A Man Asleep*), a portrait of alienation. *A Void*, a novel written without the letter *e*, put Perec in a literary category of his own.

For Modiano the exploration of Paris was a search for the solution of the enigma that was his father. A Sephardic Jew from Salonika, and a possible collaborator with the German authorities, he formed an unlikely couple with Modiano's mother, a Flemish actress. Modiano's anxious sense of place in the world was built on the unlikelihood of this parental couple, Louise Colpeyn and Albert Modiano, who were brought together by the war. He spent his childhood in boarding schools and finally settled with his mother in Quai Conti, in the heart of the intellectual and artistic Paris. Nonetheless, his teenage years were marked by deprivation, as his parents failed to provide for him. Very early on, Modiano identified literature as answer to this anxiety, and the mystery of the city provided a fertile ground for his imagination and relief for a mind seeking answers. Even the titles of Modiano's novels such as *La Place de l'étoile*, *Boulevards de ceinture* (*Ring Roads*), and *Dans le Café de la jeunesse perdue* (*In the Café of Lost Youth*) powerfully evoke the Paris of a recent but now vanished past. The enumeration of street names and building numbers, the unearthing of the old newspaper articles, school registers, and city hall records conjure up the events and the atmosphere of the Occupation years and details of the lives of those who had disappeared leaving little trace of their passage.

Modiano's novels unfold as virtual histories of Paris told by the voices of the periphery, of, one might say, neglected characters not unlike himself. The circumstances of his father's survival as a Jew, explorations of the Paris *demi-monde* under the Nazi occupation, and the indifference with which Albert and Louise treated their children, are among the principal themes of Modiano's work.

Georges Perec and Patrick Modiano meet at the junction of absence and silence of postwar Paris: the absence of its Jewish population and the uncomfortable silence about the years of Nazi occupation. Perec first captured this in *A Man Asleep*, then explored the gradual degradation of what used to be the Jewish quarter, Belleville, in a variety of essays and stories about space; *Species of Spaces and Other Pieces*, *En Remontant la rue Vilin*, and other works testify to Perec's efforts to register the waning of the traces of human presence and capture the materiality of the passage of time. *A Man Asleep* focuses on the inner journey of an anguished student of sociology from disenchantment with the world to the gradual disengagement with his environment. This journey is mapped onto the streets of Paris. It starts in the Quartier Latin, which is physically, intellectually, and politically at the heart of Paris: schools, universities, and publishing houses are all located there. As the young man's inner state worsens, the narrative migrates away from the center and toward the periphery. This part of *A Man Asleep* takes its inspiration from Perec's biography; like the student in the novel, he abandoned his studies of history and sociology at the Sorbonne. Although *A Man Asleep* is considered to be a text about the effects of alienation in the consumer society, Perec was most pleased by the reviews of *A Man Asleep* that characterize it as a narrative about a rupture.

There is a moment in the book in which the young man observes his reflection in a cracked mirror, looking for the signs of his inner transformation in the reflection of his face that is distorted by a crack: "Did you never see the cracks in what, for you, takes the place of a history?" he asks (144). Bearing in mind the devastating effects of the loss of his parents on Perec's life, it is not hard to imagine that he saw his own life as a violently disrupted story. Lacan's idea of the mirror stage operates here, as the subject discovers himself within and without in the mirror's reflection: within is his subjectivity as an individual and without is his identity as a member of a community. A later text, *Ellis Island* (1980) offers a clue about the kind of rupture and alienation Perec may have had in mind when he wrote *A Man Asleep*. "Somehow," he writes, "I am a foreigner in relationship to something that is part of me; I am 'different' not from the others, but from those who are like me" (44).

Perec's first novel, *L'Attentat de Sarajevo*, may offer another clue about the nature of the rupture. In it he writes, "I am tired of being a son." At that time, he was twenty-one and had just dropped out of the history program at the Sorbonne, much like the hero of *A Man Asleep*. Tired of being a son? Tired, perhaps, of the overdetermination of being Jewish without the means that make one a Jew, that is, a culture, a language? Tired of being a descendent of two murdered parents? Tired of finding absence as the only evidence of their passage in the city that surrounds him? How does one, indeed, in order to become a man, symbolically kill a father who was murdered first literally, then symbolically, by the collective silence?

Perec's *Lieux*, texts about specific locations in Paris within the strict framework of a longitudinal study (1969–1975) of twelve locations to which he was particularly attached, reveal a similar sense of rupture and absence. His enduring anxiety regarding the instability of space is best described in *Species of Spaces*: "My spaces are fragile: time is going to wear them away, to destroy them. Nothing will any longer resemble what it was, my memories will betray me, oblivion will infiltrate my memory . . ." (91). The objective of the project was to record "the triple aging: of space, of my memories and my writing." Every month he trained himself to describe what he saw at a chosen location in the most neutral way. Then, in another text, he wrote his memories about it. Each time, the texts were sealed in an envelope, along with a photograph and sometimes a Métro or cinema ticket. The texts he wrote about rue Vilin were integrated into a documentary film, made posthumously, *En Remontant rue Vilin*. They represent a painstaking, and no doubt painful, work of reappropriation of his childhood by regular visits to the street he lived on with his parents. With time, the buildings fall into decay. Boarded windows slowly come to dominate the street. Some houses are destroyed to make place for new construction. Perec rediscovers the hairdressing salon owned by his mother. At the back is the house in which the family lived.

Over the years, life along rue Vilin slowly wanes but, paradoxically, the traces of its past residents, revealed through the writer's work of memory, come to fill the void. By writing, Perec forcefully populates the street and brings it back to life, through what he called the "ineffable joys of enumeration." So the void and absence are not simply thematized; they are, as Bénamou points out, generators of new literary genres. Perec's writing about space is unique in that it seeks to exhaust the city by writing it "to the end" as a way of keeping the memory of his family alive and reappropriating Paris through complete knowledge. This approach comes across as a poignant testimony to the uniquely Jewish anxiety over space and belonging.

Modiano's way of approaching Paris takes the shape of a walk as a kind of a red thread that, if followed from one novel to another, tells the story of an unknown Paris. I focus here solely on the Occupation Trilogy—composed of *La Place d'étoile*, *Night Watch*, and *Ring Roads*—and on *Dora Bruder*. The Trilogy and *Dora Bruder* stand at the opposite sides of the literary spectrum and on the opposite sides of Paris. The characters of the trilogy are fictional; Dora Bruder was a real person. The wealthy west of Paris sheltered its inhabitants and kept them safe from the most unpleasant aspects of the Occupation; the working-class east had to confront shortages and rationing. Many of the orders sending Jews, communists, and suspected members of the resistance to the detention center Tourette were signed at the Gestapo headquarters in rue Lauriston. For most, it was the first stop on the journey to the death camps.

The Trilogy is populated by a fauna of traitors operating in the legal gray zone of war profit in occupied Paris—criminals, collaborators, black marketeers, hate-mongers, and pamphleteers. There is no shortage here. For this set, the Occupation was one long bacchanal where every fantasy could be fulfilled. They evolve in dimly lit salons where stolen and plundered goods change hands and the champagne flows to the sound of Nazi star Zarah Leander's smoky alto. Most characters go by fake names such as Khédive, Chalva, the brothers Chapochnikoff, Rashid fon Rosenheim, Maxime de Bel-Respiro. . . . The names hint at the artifice, excess, and bad consciousness. The wealthy west of Paris, deserted by its inhabitants in the early days of war, is a playground and a treasure island for this group. The narrator of *Night Watch*, a Gestapo collaborator, tells of the Khédive and how he used to have him "raid private houses and confiscate objects of art: Second Empire *hôtels particuliers*, eighteenth century 'follies,' turn-of-the-century buildings with stained glass windows, faux-châteaux in the gothic style" (79). Modiano pushes the fantasy of absolute power felt by Maxime de Bel-Respiro to the end: "I remember long walks: Ranelagh-La Muette-Auteuil, this was my route. I'd sit on a bench in the shade of the chestnut trees. Not a soul on the streets. I could enter any house in the area. The city was mine" (81).

Dora Bruder is set in the northeast of Paris. Published in 1997, almost thirty years after *The Night Watch* and twenty-five years after *The Ring Roads*, it contains many of the elements of Modiano's earlier work, such as the juxtapositions in which the autobiography of the author—who may or may not be Modiano himself—is brought into the stories to create connections between two remote realities. Paris is visited, and revisited, obsessively, in a style different from Perec's but comparable in its obstinacy and exhaustivity. What we do not find in *Dora Bruder* are the Occupation Trilogy's elements of fantasy and atmosphere of excess.

In 1968 Modiano spent a lot of time in the area around the Place Blanche, where he waited for his mother to come from a theater where she had a role in a play. We find the seeds of *Dora Bruder* here and farther east, toward the Boulevard d'Ornano. Within this space, delineated by the Boulevard des Maréchaux in the north, we find Sarah Kofman's rue Ordener and rue Labat, and Perec's Place Clichy, where, under the rain, *A Man Asleep* ends. Modiano's search for clues in the case of Dora Bruder, a young girl whose disappearance in 1942 he learns about in an old newspaper, must proceed from the narrator's own life. To reconstruct Dora's short existence,

Modiano must superpose the winter of 1942 onto that of 1965; the story receives its full historical dimension in the 1990s when the narrator's exhaustive search for the story of the Bruder family brings forth the story of the murdered Jews who were neither wealthy industrialists, financiers, nor prominent art dealers or intellectuals of their time, but simple industrial workers—tailors, seamstresses, merchants, or community workers.

Dora's parents are foreigners. As such, they are in the most vulnerable group of those targeted by the roundups and deportation of Paris Jews in 1942. They move frequently and, as Modiano points out, leave "little trace" behind them. Thus, emptiness is the prevailing sensation in places formerly inhabited by Dora's family. To bring them back into existence Modiano has recourse to intuition: the narrator feels that he is "following someone's steps" (DB, 27). This is an approach he uses often: his narrators start from a sensation of discomfort and déjà vu to bring about a space and time, as in *L'Herbe de nuit*. In *Dora Bruder*, the narrative voice changes time lines so effortlessly that, as readers, even though we are fully aware that almost fifty years separate the events from the moment of narration, we still feel the shiver of near-encounters with Dora Bruder on the streets of Paris. The narrator's retelling of his father's arrest by the Gestapo during the Occupation is another occasion for a near-encounter with Dora: in the police car the father is sitting next to a young woman of about eighteen, who could be Dora.

Patrick Modiano's own escape from a boarding school, told by the narrator, propels the reconstruction of Dora Bruder's last days.

> What makes us decide to run away? I remember my own flight on 18 January 1960, at a period that had none of the blackness of December 1941. . . . the only point I had in common with Dora, was the season: winter. A calm, ordinary winter, not to be compared with the winter of eighteen years earlier. But it seems that the sudden urge to escape can be prompted by one of those cold, gray days that makes you more than ever aware of your solitude and intensifies your feeling that a trap is about to close. . . .
>
> It would help to know if the weather was fine on 14 December, the day of Dora's escape. Perhaps it was one of these mild sunny winter days when you have a feeling of holiday and eternity—the illusory feeling that the course of time is suspended, and that you need only to slip through this breach to escape the trap that is closing around you. (46)

Here it is the radical difference that brings two realities together. Everything separates the narrator from the subject, but similarities stem from a deeper level of the sensations and moods of two unhappy adolescents and, because of this, their encounter feels almost real.

On the first page of *Dora Bruder* is the passage: "Eight years ago, in an old copy of Paris-Soir dated 31 December 1941 a heading on page 3 caught my eye. . . . I remember Boulevard Ornano and the Boulevard Barbès deserted on a sunny afternoon in May 1958. I was in this neighborhood in the winter of 1965" (3). Even careful readers can find themselves scratching their heads at the order in which the events occurred, but it is a literary device that Modiano relishes: Paris is both the real and the imaginary city. It is a mythological city. The names of its streets conjure up places that evoke desire and an atmosphere that creates the illusion of closeness to events that have happened in the past.

Modiano's Paris is replete with mystery. As a child and later as an adolescent growing up in and around Paris, Modiano spent his formative years in the *grisaille* of its streets. He enjoyed walking and got to know the provincial quiet of some of its quarters, the danger of others, its seedy quarters, and those that the Sunday crowds favored. For Modiano, every part of Paris corresponds to a set of sensations and intuitions that he uses as starting points for infusing Paris with stories. The Right Bank corresponds to adulthood and adventure, to getting away from his father's shadow. The Left Bank is childhood, boarding school, and a failed attempt at a university education. As an adolescent, the narrator of *Dora Bruder* lives in Quai de Conti, located in the heart of Paris. His mother likes spending time with her friends—theater artists and writers—all very much part of the Paris intellectual establishment. The events of *Dora Bruder* take place on the Right Bank, between Dora's parents' apartment on Boulevard d'Ornano; her boarding school, Saint-Cœur-de-Marie; les Tourelles; the army barracks used as a detention center for women in the east; and finally outside the ring roads, toward the suburbs. Her journey ends in the northeast, in Drancy, the prison from which she was deported to Auschwitz.

Physically, the path from 15, Quai de Conti to Dora Bruder's working-class neighborhood in the northeast of Paris is not very long, but symbolically they could not be farther apart. By writing a book of mourning for Dora and her family, Modiano brought them closer together. The path from Quai Conti to Boulevard d'Ornano is also symbolic of breaking free from his parents' past. For Georges Perec, for whom the condition of being the son of murdered parents could not be changed, writing an exhaustive inventory of Paris, recording the most banal aspects of the everyday, transparent and free of affect, was the way of keeping his memories alive in a changing landscape; for Modiano, who through writing got to know his father, it was not exhausting the city, but infusing it with his story and linking it with the material traces of other lives that added reality to what must have felt like an unstable world where everything, down to his very birth, was an accident.

Bibliography

Barthes, Roland. "Leçon inaugurale au Collège de France, 1977." http://bestofmoocs. com/2015/08/25/roland-barthes-cours-au-college-de-france-1977-1980. Accessed on December 30, 2017. (My translation.)

Bellos, David. *Georges Perec: A Life in Words.* London: Harper Collins, 1993.

Benamou, Marcel. "De la Judeité à l'esthetique du manqué." http://oulipo.net/fr/ perec-de-la-judeite-a-lesthetique-du-manque. Accessed on January 30, 2017.

Bober, Robert. *En Remontant la rue Villin* (film). 1993. https://www.youtube.com/ watch?v=8HfvFHQ-j6s. Accessed on April 10, 2016.

Bourgellin, Claude. *Les Choses, un devenir roman des Mythologies?* In *Recherche et travaux* 77 (2010): 57–66.

Cosnard, Denis. http://lereseaumodiano.blogspot.ca/2012/01/raymond-queneau-patrick-modiano.html. Accessed on April 2, 2016.

Decout, Maxime. *Ecrire la judéité. Enquête sur un malaise dans la littérature française.* Ceyzérieu, France: Editions Champ Vallon, 2015.

Modiano, Patrick. *Dora Bruder.* Paris: Gallimard, 2015.

———. *L'Herbe des nuits.* Paris: Gallimard, 2012.

———. Interview with Jacques Chancel, December 31, 1971. https://itunes.apple.com/ us/album/radioscopie-%C3%A9crivains-jacques-chancel-re%C3%A7oit-patrick/ 966296786. Accessed on December 30, 2017. (My translation.)

———. "Modiano, souvenir écrin." Interview with Antoine de Gaudemar. *Libération* (April 26, 2001 2001), 1–2. (My translation.)

———. *La Ronde de nuit.* Paris: Gallimard, 2010.

Perec, Georges. *L'Attentat de Sarajevo.* Paris: Seuil, 2016.

———. *Ellis Island.* Translated by Robert Bober. New York: The New Press, 1995.

———. *Un Homme qui dort.* Paris: Gallimard, 1990.

———. *Species of Spaces.* Translated by John Sturrock. London: Penguin Books, 1997.

———. *W, or the Memory of Childhood.* Translated by David Bellos. London: Vintage Books, 2011. Translation of *W, ou le souvenir d'enfance.* Paris: Gallimard, 1993.

Queneau, Raymond. https://www.la-croix.com/Culture/Livres-Idees/Livres/Patrick-Modiano-Prix-Nobel-de-litterature-2014-2014-10-09-1218759. Accessed on December 30, 2017.

8

Patrick Modiano's *Dora Bruder*

Wandering Down Memory Lane

MAXIME DECOUT

Patrick Modiano is known as a writer of wartime Paris. The Nobel Prize emphasized this aspect of his reputation in recognizing him "for the art of memory with which he has evoked the most ungraspable human destinies and uncovered the life-world of the occupation." But very few novels by Patrick Modiano are actually set during the Occupation. Even in *La Ronde de nuit*, where the reader is sure that the story takes place during the Occupation, there are no dates or keywords that would make it a historical novel. The characters are haunted by something unknown and nameless, they are tracked, but nobody knows exactly by whom and why. The reader is left with the impression that something in the characters' past is troubled and linked to the Occupation but it is often difficult to be sure.

Most of Modiano's characters are not Jewish. Jewish identity does not seem to be a key component of the stories, and the Jewish tragedy of the Shoah is not at the heart of Modiano's work. Characters are not designated as Jewish, but may be presumed to be Jewish because of the context, because of an impression that we are seeing a scene that reminds us of the Occupation. The question for us is then: why this refusal on the part of Modiano to confirm the Jewishness of some of his characters? How do we interpret his silence, his oblique evocation of their identity?

In this respect, *Dora Bruder* is quite different from Modiano's other books because the narrative is clearly situated during the war and its characters are identified as Jewish. Yet we may wonder whether the choice of Jewish characters is linked to Modiano's desire to question his own Jewishness, or whether it is a way of investigating the period of the Occupation, which clearly consumes him, with the very emblematic figures of marginality.

Dora Bruder is a nonfiction novel or documentary narrative that tries to reconstruct the life of a young girl who vanished during the Occupation. In 1989, Modiano discovered a notice about the search for Dora in the newspaper *Paris-Soir* of December 1941.

PARIS.

Missing, a young girl, Dora Bruder, age 15, height 1,55 m., oval-shaped face, gray-brown eyes, gray sports jacket, maroon pullover, navy blue skirt and hat, brown gym shoes. Address all information to M. and Mme Bruder, 41 Boulevard Ornano, Paris. (3)

The notice first led Modiano to write a fictional version of Dora's story in 1990, titled *Voyage de Noces*, but the fiction failed to encompass the reality of the missing young girl. Modiano then decided to rewrite the book by investigating the real Dora Bruder.

Like other novels by Modiano, *Dora Bruder* presents an obsessive interest in places, in particular urban and Parisian places. The detailed locations, street names, and precise urban geography of the capital are as much a feature of this novel as they are of the rest of Modiano's work. But places are not only meant to situate the plot, to be used as setting for the protagonists, and to produce an "effect of reality," as Roland Barthes said. Rather, they are the clues in the texts, always constructed as detective novels, much like Georges Simenon's novels.

Modiano's inquiries are not often successful as they investigate missing persons. They are based on three problematic elements: people, dates, and places. Modiano destabilizes all three elements—the identity, the temporal context, and the spatial markers—so that they become inseparable and all of them subjected to uncertainty. He has varied the narrative means to explore the uncharted through perspective, perception, and place with his characters' difficulties with identity.

Modiano's places are often deserted, marginal parts of Paris outside of the tourist circuits that limit themselves to the landmarks emblematic of the capital. They are places of everyday life more than symbolic places: streets, buildings, cafés, garages, run-down hotels, seedy nightclubs, squares, Métro stations, and the outskirts of the city. Modiano's characters often walk a lot through the city and sit in cafés to converse with other people, or simply to look around. The melancholy atmosphere of these places combines with the conundrum of the vanishing or the apparition of some characters for no obvious reason. Modiano never tries to consider the places from a sociological point of view, as Georges Perec does. He prefers to speak about them as "neutral zones," separated from the rest of the city by the invisible frontiers that look like no-man's lands. More precisely, places are the main operators of the haunting, bizarre, and melancholy atmosphere of Modiano's novels in which the reader becomes immersed, glimpsing characters as though through a mist, where they change, lose, or recover their identities. Modiano creates a Parisian geography of the mind that, like a palimpsest, is superimposed with lost pasts, memories, and identities, in which he tries to follow the trace of somebody's existence. Places in Modiano's novels are full of memories. Modiano chooses to build a common memory for Jews under the Occupation in *Dora Bruder* through the places Dora and her family visited, where they lived, in some neighborhoods, streets, buildings, schools, or boarding schools. With these places, Modiano reconstructs an individual memory that is also a collective memory.

A Topographical Inquiry

In *Dora Bruder*, as in other novels by Modiano, places are more often named than described. The narrator frequently needs to give the complete addresses as if they were some magic words able to revive the places.

> I wrote to ask if her name was to be found on the school registers, addressing my letter to the head of each:
> 8 Rue Ferdinand-Flocon,
> 20 Rue Hermel.
> 7 Rue Championnet.
> 61 Rue de Clignancourt. (9–10)

Description, when present, is short. It never achieves the meticulousness and the exhaustiveness of the Balzacian description. Instead, Modiano's descriptions are fragmented, they aim to capture a fugitive aspect only. Descriptions are meant to simply attest to the fragile existence of things;

they are not realistic in that they do not seek to capture the wholeness of
the thing depicted. Because there is always something missing in Modiano's
descriptions, the hidden and secret parts of things and places, it is frequently
enough to name a place. Lists often replace descriptions.

> The Boulevard Mortier is a hill. It slopes southward. On my way
> there, that Sunday of 28 April 1996, I took the following route:
> Rue des Archives, Rue de Bretagne. Rue des Filles-du-Calvaire.
> Then the hill of the Rue Oberkampf, where Hena had lived.
>   To the right, the Rue des Pyrénées, offering a vista of trees.
> Rue de Ménilmontant. The apartment blocks at number 140
> lay deserted in the glare of the sun. (108)

Description is a more static approach to space, whereas naming
embodies a dynamic relationship that reflects not only the movement of the
narrator and of the characters, but also the uncertainty of places. Modiano
is a topographer rather than a painter of the real. He is a stroller, like the
Baudelairian narrator of the *Paris Spleen*. He likes to report the details of
his walks through Paris, looking for the places where Dora went. We can
observe two kinds of relations to space: the wandering, where the walk has
no precise goal, and the investigation, in which the movement is oriented by
a task and dedicated to a precise search. Constant walking in *Dora Bruder*
helps the narrator find clues for his investigation about Dora and imagine
the experience that Dora lived. Places are used to reconstruct itineraries that
are more important than the places themselves.

These perpetual walks through Paris sometimes have to be extended
by looking at maps. For instance, a map is substituted for a missing photo
of Saint-Cœur-de-Marie's boarding school. The text describes the map, but
it seems to be a description of the place with qualifications such as "on
the same pavement" (33) that turns the narrator looking at the map into
a direct spectator of a place he has never been. Modiano approaches the
subway map in the same way: "I look at the plan of the métro and try to
retrace her route in my mind. The simplest, avoiding too many changes, is
to take a train for Nation" (37). Moreover, Modiano rereads the fifth and
sixth volumes of Victor Hugo's *Les Misérables* that describe the nocturnal
escape of Cosette and Jean Valjean, tracked by Javert (41). It dawns on the
narrator of *Dora Bruder* that as Hugo's characters flee down actual streets of
Paris, they suddenly stumble into a fictional neighborhood and find refuge

in an imaginary convent. Although Modiano himself neither comments on this reading, nor draws any explicit parallels, this intertext mirrors Dora's flight and creates a kinship between the two couples, the fictional Jean Valjean and Cosette and the real Modiano and Dora Bruder. Through the reference to Jean Valjean guiding Cosette, Modiano makes himself into a paternal and protective figure for Dora: the implicit identification with a fictional protagonist is the way for him to participate in Dora's story, to go with her and help her.

Through maps and intertextual itineraries, Modiano extends his survey of the city even when he does not move, so as to leave his present and his habits, and live in the past with Dora. Writing about *Honeymoon* (Voyage de noces), he points out that the only moment in *Dora Bruder* when, without knowing it, he approached Dora, was when he invented a subway trip to the real places where Dora went (42).

However, the main difficulty for the detective is that Dora and her family had to remove all traces of their existence in an attempt to escape the French authorities. The only marks to be used are thus spatial marks: "It is said that premises retain some stamps, however faint, of their previous inhabitants. Stamp: an imprint, hollow or in relief. Hollow, I should say, in the case of Ernest and Cécile Bruder, of Dora. I have a sense of absence, of emptiness, whenever I find myself in a place where they have lived" (21). Spatial marks are fragile and hollow, and the reader has to learn to look differently in order to catch sight of them. It is all the more important that Dora and her family merge with the places through which they passed: "The list of their names is always associated with the same streets. And the street-names and house-numbers no longer correspond to anything." Human beings are intimately linked with places that are not only uncertain (because we do not know exactly where Dora and her family went) but also erased by the passage of time. "They are the sort of people who leave few traces. Virtually anonymous. Inseparable from those Paris streets, those suburban landscapes where, by chance, I discovered that they had lived. Often, what I know about them amounts to no more than a simple address. And such topographical precision contrasts with what we shall never know about their life—this blank, this mute block of the unknown" (20).

To follow Dora's trail is therefore to accept that people also exist through absence. Modiano's Parisian itineraries highlight the core mystery of human beings. In *Dora Bruder*, searching all over Paris teaches the reader that a void can be more precious than a successful inquiry. The riddle of

Dora incarnates the riddle of being human, a fragile piece of mystery that neither French authorities nor Modiano could pierce; it is the reason why the failure of the writer's investigation is finally a kind of success.

From Biography to Autobiography:
An Excursion into Jewish Identity

Strolls through Paris and studies of Dora's itineraries are thus unconscious means to move toward the young girl, to travel into the past so intensely, that it becomes difficult for the narrator to distinguish his own memories from Dora's life.

> From day to day. With the passage of time, I find, perspectives become blurred, one winter merging into another. That of 1965 and that of 1942.
> In 1965, I knew nothing about Dora Bruder. But now, thirty years on, it seems to me that those long waits in the cafés at the Ornano crossroads, those invarying itineraries—the rue du Mont-Cenis took me back to some hotel on the Butte Montmartre: the Roma or the Alsina or the Terrass, rue Caulaincourt—and the fleeting impressions I have retained, . . . all that was not simply due to chance. Perhaps, though not yet fully aware of it, I was following the traces of Dora Bruder and her parents. Already, below the surface, they were there. (6)

Suddenly, the search for Dora gives meaning to what made no sense in the narrator's past, to his old aimless wanderings in Paris. Dora is what the narrator looked for without knowing it. Modiano's past is thus reread as an unconscious pursuit of Dora, as if she had always been a ghostly presence beside him when he was strolling through Paris: "She would have got out at Simplon, just opposite the cinema and the hotel. Twenty years later, I often took the métro at Simplon. . . . Late on Sunday afternoons, she too would have returned by the same route" (37). In addition, places from Modiano's childhood and his past correspond to the places where Dora lived, such as Clignancourt or the Boulevard Ornano. Describing the neighborhood around the rue Sancerre, Modiano writes: "twenty-five years ago, in June 1971, I spent an entire day walking around there, I found it unchanged. . . . That afternoon, without knowing what, I had the impression of walking in another's footsteps" (39). The reader thus does not know exactly whether it is the search for Dora that brings back memories, or whether his own personal memories attract Modiano to these places to look for Dora. As a result, the narration in *Dora Bruder* is constructed around three temporal layers that alternate and merge: the narrator-detective's present and his inquiry; the reconstructed past of Dora and the history of the Jews under the Occupation; the narrator's past, his childhood, undetermined reminiscences of walks through Paris, of the time when he, like Dora, ran away from boarding school, and memories about his father. But the links between these layers are not always explicit. This structure allows a lot of subtle games of reflections, with tacit comparisons and differences.

Dora Bruder is both a reconstructed but incomplete biography and an indirect autobiography. Investigating a young girl's disappearance and narrating the history of the Jews under the Occupation by copying archives, decrees, ordinances, letters, sometimes without any commentary, is how Modiano reconnoiters his own problematic Jewish identity. Not only does his Jewishness derive patrilineally rather than matrilineally (the traditional way that Jewishness is deemed to be passed along according to Jewish law), but his father is a "non-Jewish Jew," to use the term coined by Isaac Deutscher, who was in league with collaborators during the Occupation. Consequently, all the implicit parallels between Modiano's father and Dora aim to counterbalance the father's negative image. The first analogy that can be traced between Modiano's father and Dora is their similar status as missing persons. For example, when Modiano learns that his father, whom he has not seen since adolescence, is in a hospital, he remembers looking for him and not finding him. The episode is symptomatic of the father's absence. His son has to look for him, and continue to investigate, even if he does not find him. The unconscious reasoning is that if Dora is worth looking for, the father may also be worth looking for.

We see another connection between Dora and his father as Modiano imagines that when his father was picked up by the Jewish Affairs police and meets a young girl in the police van, she may have been Dora. "Perhaps it was that I wanted them to have met, she and my father, in that winter of 1942. Utterly different though they were, one from the other, both, that winter, had been classed in the same category, as outlaws. My father, too, had missed the census in October 1940 and, like Dora Bruder, had no 'Jewish dossier' number" (51–52). From Modiano's perspective, being categorized as an outlaw establishes a kinship between Dora and his father, which adds a surplus of Jewishness to his father. Under the Occupation, being Jewish meant being branded as a marginal, a fugitive, a figure incarnating otherness. This situation of exclusion, harassment, persecutions, and deportation for Jews is certainly part of the reason for Modiano's choice to write explicitly about the Jewish people. But Dora and his father are doubly marginalized: they are Jewish and they refused to be identified as such during the census by receiving a number. They fully embody the figure of the outsider and the otherness that echoes Modiano's fascination with outlaws.

The resemblance between Dora and the father is blurred in the episode in which the young Modiano is arrested for domestic disturbance and is driven, with his father, in a Black Maria to the police station. The reader may wonder if Modiano is not drawing an implicit analogy between himself, Dora, and his father. As in Perec's *W, ou le souvenir d'enfance*, when the child's escape to the Vercors is implicitly compared to the mother's deportation, the arrest in the Black Maria allows Modiano to experience something that is not exactly the arrest of somebody because he is Jewish, but something that resembles it, a kind of a substitute.

Moreover, for Modiano, writing itself is linked with his father. Modiano explains why he wrote *La Place de l'étoile*, his first novel, and the only one that is explicitly devoted to Jewishness, with an ambiguous narrator who is also sometimes antisemitic. Jewishness as the principal issue practically disappears from Modiano's work until *Dora Bruder*. The narrator of *La Place de l'étoile* adopts all the possible images of the Jew that literature, philosophy, society, history, antisemitism, and philosemitism have given to Jewish people. *La Place de l'étoile* deals with the impossibility of being Jewish in the face of such conflicting definitions. And it is not a coincidence that Modiano refers twice to this novel in *Dora Bruder*. From his point of view, *La Place de l'étoile* was written following a discovery, in the paternal library, of antisemitic texts that drew a heinous portrait of the Jews. And Modiano needed to put himself in the place of his father reading those texts. "I can well imagine his surprise at the portrayal of this imaginary, phantasmagoric monster with clawlike hands and hooked nose whose shadow flitted across the walls, this creature corrupted by every vice, responsible for every evil, guilty of every crime. As for me, I wanted my first book to be a riposte to all those people whose insults wounded me because of my father" (58). *La Place de l'étoile* was a vengeful answer to those writers. It was also a means for Modiano to atone for his father, to express what his father would or should have said or thought.

Because this first book can be misinterpreted as antisemitic, *Dora Bruder* corrects those misinterpretations. If one looks at the contrast between the excessive depiction of the Jewish identity in *La Place de l'étoile,* and the contrasting discretion in *Dora Bruder,* it becomes clear that *La Place de l'étoile* corresponds to the "imprint in relief" of Jewish identity while *Dora Bruder* is its "hollow imprint." From the first book to the book of 1996, Jewishness is lived in a more pacified way. Becoming more silent after *La Place de l'étoile,* Jewishness is more easily linked to a kind of mystery and lived as a conundrum. Although a great number of parallels can be drawn between Dora, Modiano's father, and Modiano, still these three people remain very different. Modiano's father is neither the equivalent of Dora nor of Dora's father: he abandons his son while Dora's father did everything possible to find his daughter. The negative aura of Modiano's father is not suppressed, it is only softened.

Paris itineraries are thus absolutely necessary for Modiano to follow Dora. They allow Dora to be more than just a name in a newspaper. But because Modiano does not want to speak for her, to invent what she thought or felt, he can only give her a life through her travels in Paris. Topography more than history brings the dead back to life. At the same time, since memories of his father are intimately associated with Dora, investigation and itineraries also become a way to appropriate a Jewish identity felt as unknown and unreachable. For Modiano, writing about the quest for Dora Bruder means thus questioning his own problematic belongings and origins by wandering down memory lane. It is a physical route and a symbolic route into identity, writing, and Jewishness, a concrete inquiry and a symbolic inquiry where nothing is settled and where everything moves. Instead of filling the blanks, the inquiry, which fails, reveals absence. In Modiano's world, Jewishness is not exactly a positive identity: it reveals the part of emptiness that is proper to human beings but is too frequently masked and forgotten because it is too disquieting.

Bibliography

Bem, Jeanne. "*Dora Bruder* ou la biographie déplacée de Modiano." *Cahiers de l'Association internationale des études françaises* 52, no. 1 (2000): 221–32.

Decout, Maxime. *Écrire la judéité. Enquête sur un malaise dans la littérature française.* Seyssel, France: Champ Vallon, 2015, 246–55.

Higgins Lynn. "Lieux de mémoire et géographie imaginaire dans *Dora Bruder.*" In *Le Roman français au tournant du XXIe siècle,* edited by Bruno Blanckeman, Aline Mura-Brunel, and Marc Dambre. Paris: Presses de la Sorbonne Nouvelle, 2004, 397–405.

Khalifa, Samuel. "The Mirror of Memory: Patrick Modiano's *La Place de l'étoile* and *Dora Bruder*." In *The Holocaust and the Text: Speaking the Unspeakable*, edited by Andrew Leak and Georges Paizis. New York: St. Martin's Press, 2000, 159–73.

Modiano, Patrick. *Dora Bruder*. Translated by Joanna Kilmartin. Berkeley: University of California Press, 1999.

———. Nobel Prize reception speech. http://www.lemonde.fr/prix-nobel/article/2014/ 12/07/verbatim-le-discours-de-reception-du-prix-nobel-de-patrick-modiano_ 4536162_1772031.html.

"The Nobel Prize in Literature 2014. Press Release." Nobelprize.org. Nobel Media AB 2014. http://www.nobelprize.org/nobel_prizes/ literature/laureates/2014/ press.html. Accessed on August 31, 2016.

Sheringham, Michaël. "Le dispositif *Voyages de noces-Dora Bruder*." In *Lectures de Modiano*, edited by Roger-Yves Roche. Nantes: Éditions Cécile Defaut, 2009, 243–66.

9

"Paris of Days Gone By"

The Quest for Memory in a Postwar Haunted City—
A Case Study of Georges Perec's and Patrick Modiano's Novels

RUTH MALKA

"I have no childhood memories" (6) is the opening line of the autobiograph-ical part of Georges Perec's *W, or the Memory of Childhood.* "My memory preceded my birth" (96) writes Patrick Modiano in his first autofiction, *Livret de famille.* These authors express contrasting relationships with mem-ory: Perec declares a lack of childhood memory while Modiano suggests that his memory is filled with stories older than him. Both, however, are writing about the same period of time: the late 1930s and the early 1940s.

"A different history, History with a capital *H,* had answered the ques-tion in my stead. the war, the camps" (6), explains Perec. Born in Paris in 1936, the author has been orphaned at young age: his father, Icek Peretz, has been killed in 1940 during the Battle of France and his mother, Cyrla Szulewicz, has been murdered in Auschwitz in 1943. Whereas, to Perec, World War II symbolizes the graveyard of childhood memories involving his parents, to Modiano it represents his origins. Born in 1945, right after the Liberation, Modiano explains in his second autofiction, *Pedigree,* that only a period of time as obscure as the Occupation could have brought together his Flemish mother, Louisa Colpeyn, and his Jewish father, Albert Modiano.

123

In spite of Albert Modiano being Jewish, Patrick Modiano's autofictions portray his father as having been close to the Gestapo and taking part in the black market during the war. The author depicts himself as having grown up surrounded by parents and family friends who belonged to the collaborator side of the underworld during the Occupation of Paris. Even though he himself never experienced the shady times of World War II, Patrick Modiano's literary work is haunted by what he considers to be his family's story and thus constantly deals with the questions of collaboration, guilt, responsibility, and betrayal. Georges Perec, on the contrary, orphaned at the age of seven, wrote books in which the themes of absence, missing people, and lack of memory are omnipresent.

Despite these two authors dealing with opposite problems—Perec being the son of victims of World War II and of the Holocaust, and Modiano being the son of a man who collaborated with the persecutors—both pursue their respective quests for memory through their literary works. After the war, each of them uses the act of writing as a way to look back at their families' stories and investigate their respective origins and identities.

Perec's and Modiano's literary quests for memory and identity are bound up in their respective representations of the city of Paris. In both their works, particular districts, streets, and buildings of Paris are almost always involved in the narrators' or characters' investigations into their identities. Modiano's novels mostly take place in the 16th arrondissement of Paris where the French Gestapo headquarters were located during the Occupation, whereas Perec focuses on the 20th arrondissement where his parents use to live.

Even though Perec's and Modiano's traumas are rooted in different arrondissements, the French capital left similar marks on their fictional works: both Perec, who affirms that he does not remember the late 1930s and early 1940s, and Modiano, who was not born yet at the time of World War II, are haunted, years later, by the Paris of days gone by and constantly write about the same areas.

For both Perec and Modiano, their personal traumas are deeply connected to the city of Paris: in both cases, when they took up their pens, the city is the only remaining witness to their parents' past lives. Since the two writers cannot be witnesses themselves—Perec was too young while Modiano was not yet born—neither of them is able to write autobiographically about their families' lives during the Occupation. Nevertheless, because their personal traumas are so different, not only do Perec and Modiano carry out their investigations in discrete Parisian places, but they also use dissimilar writing approaches to follow their respective quests for their own or their parents' memories in the city.

In the tenth chapter of *W, or the Memory of Childhood*, Perec explains that even though he knew he lived on the 24 rue Vilin with his parents as an infant, by the age of twenty-five he did not know how to locate this street on the map of Paris: "In those years I would not have been able to say where the street was and I would more likely have put it near Belleville or Ménilmontant metro stations than around Couronnes" (48). Moreover, after crossing the street by chance in 1961 or 1962 when he visited friends who lived nearby, Perec notices the structure of the building and writes that he does not know which apartment was his parents': "The building at number 24 is made up of several modest, one- and two-storey constructions around a small and distinctly squalid courtyard. I don't know which is the part I lived in. I haven't attempted to go inside any of the dwellings, which are inhabited nowadays mostly by Portuguese and African immigrant workers, since I am in any case convinced that it would do nothing to revive my memories" (48).

Even though the 24 rue Vilin is an essential place to Perec—the tenth chapter, the only one out of the thirty-seven chapters of *W, or the Memory of Childhood* to have a title, is titled "Rue Vilin" (47)—he writes that going "inside any of the dwellings [. . .] would do nothing to revive [his] memories." His childhood home, impossible to find on a map and not reminding him of anything, symbolizes his loss: he is unable to remember.

Contrary to Perec, whose issue is forgetting his own past, Modiano vividly imagines the period of time preceding his birth. Despite being born in 1945, he declares in *Livret de famille*: "I was sure . . . I lived in Occupied Paris, since I could remember some characters from this time period, some small and disturbing details, the kind of memories that no history books would have mentioned" (96). Modiano's haunting imaginary memory, certainly partly inherited from what he knew, guessed, or invented about his father's life story, led him to constantly write about World War II; the 2014 Nobel Prize committee granted him the literary award "for the art of memory with which he has evoked the most ungraspable human destinies and uncovered the life-world of the Occupation."

Except for *Dora Bruder*, most of Modiano's "human destinies" are simultaneously related to both the victims and the persecutors of World War II, as was Modiano's own father figure. This duality is rooted in Paris, shaping a map of the city in which specific areas are linked to one of the two aspects of the characters' identity. The narrator of *The Night Watch*, for instance, a twenty-year-old man who plays the role of double agent for both a unit of the French Resistance organized by "the Lieutenant Dominique" and a group of collaborators led by two characters named "the Khedive" and "Monsieur Philibert," associates each of these factions with the address of their headquarters: "The metro slowed as it approached the Pont de Passy. Sèvres-Lecourbe–Cambronne–La-Motte-Piquet–Dupleix–Grenelle–Passy. In the morning, I would take the opposite route, from Passy to Sèvres-Lecourbe. From Cimarosa Square in the 16th arrondissement to rue Boisrobert in the 15th. From the Lieutenant to the Khedive. From the Khedive to the Lieutenant. The swinging pendulum of a double agent. Exhausting. Breathless" (90–91).

As far as the group of collaborators is concerned, Modiano's novel echoes French history. The French Gestapo, called "the Bonny-Lafont gang" after its two criminal leaders, settled its headquarters in the 16th arrondissement of Paris, close to the Nazi Gestapo offices that were mainly located on avenue Foch, rue de la Pompe, and the Champs-Elysées. The establishment of the French Resistance unit in the 15th arrondissement, however, is fictional. Thus Modiano (re)-creates a half-historical, half-fictional map of Paris in which the 16th arrondissement is associated with "thugs" (39) and the 15th with the idealized "Goodness, Freedom and Moral Standards" (85). Torn between the two parties of the internal underworld French war, the narrator's identity changes as he goes from the 16th arrondissement to the 15th: "spy, turncoat, killer" (29) on the collaborators' side, "tempted to shout out loud just what [he is]: an informer" when "faced with the frank stare" of the Resistance "heroes" (37).

Both the 16th and the 15th arrondissements are located in the west end of Paris and are accessible by the Métro line number 6, which already existed in its current form during the Occupation. All the metro stops mentioned by the narrator—Sèvres-Lecourbe–Cambronne–La-Motte-Piquet–Dupleix–Grenelle–Passy—are close to the western end of the line leading to Place de l'Étoile. Also the title of Modiano's first novel, La Place de l'Étoile similarly expresses at the same time the victims and the persecutors of World War II since it refers to both the yellow star on the Jews' chests and to the headquarters of the Oberkommando der Wehrmacht, which was situated at this Métro stop.

Whereas Modiano turns the west of Paris into the symbol of occupied Paris, he transforms the eastern end of Métro line number 6 into a possible way out. Torn between the French Gestapo and the French Resistance, the narrator ends up first revealing the addresses of the "heroes" to the collab-

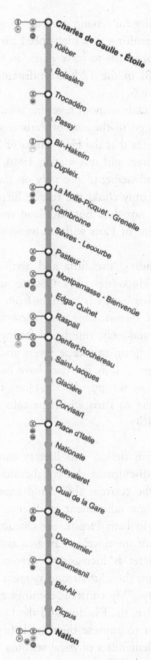

Figure 9.1. Map of Paris Métro line 6. (*Source*: RATP [régie autonaume des transports parisiens])

orators. Then, feeling guilty for having caused a good haul, he attempts to shoot at "the Khedive," resulting in a high-speed car chase. To escape from certain death, the narrator wants to leave Paris "to the east" (127), driving by "Quai de Bercy" (128) in the 12th arrondissement at the eastern end of the Métro line number 6.

Although the novel ends without revealing who survived the car chase, the narrator's decision to go to the east of Paris is a meaningful detail. In *Dora Bruder*, Modiano notes that the Holy Heart of Mary Catholic residential school, where the teenage girl was sent in 1940, was located in "rue de Picpus, in the 12th arrondissement," precisely on the route of the narrator of *The Night Watch*. Not only could the rue de Picpus have been a shelter to Dora Bruder had she not fled, but Modiano reinforces the association of the 12th arrondissement of Paris with an imaginary haven.

> I have been re-reading the fifth and sixth volumes of *Les Misérables*. Victor Hugo describes Cosette and Jean Valjean, tracked by Javert, crossing Paris by night from the Saint-Jacques tollgate to the Petit Picpus. One can follow their itinerary on a map. [. . .] And suddenly, one has a feeling of vertigo, as if Cosette and Jean Valjean, to escape Javert and his police, have taken a leap into space: thus far, they have been following real Paris streets, and now, abruptly, Victor Hugo thrusts them into the imaginary district of Paris which he calls the Petit Picpus. (*Dora Bruder*, 45–46)

Merging history with fiction and literary intertextuality, Modiano's imagined map of Paris disculpates the collaborator-resistant character of *The Night Watch*. Since the convent that could have rescued Dora Bruder was located in the 12th arrondissement, and since Colette and Jean Valjean escaped from Javert in Petit Picpus, the character of *The Night Watch* finds himself, at the end of the novel, in an area associated with the saving of innocents. This character is increasingly presented as a victim as his back-and-forth travels from the 15th arrondissement to the 16th make him unsure of his own identity: "My constant comings and goings between the Lieutenant and the Khedive, the Khedive and the Lieutenant, are beginning to wear me down. I want to appease them both (so they'll spare my life), and this double-dealing demands a physical stamina I don't have. Suddenly, I feel the urge to cry. My indifference gives way to what English Jews call *a nervous breakdown*" (55).

Illustrating the idea that to betray one's country and to collaborate with the enemy are not always rationally made decisions, Modiano attempts to morally rehabilitate his father's behavior during the Occupation. Whereas Modiano's imagined memory that "precedes [his] birth" (*Livret de famille*, 96) leads him to feature in *The Night Watch* a fictional character who, like his father, is neither completely corrupted nor a stereotypical villain, Perec, who has "no childhood memory" (*W, or the Memory of Childhood*, 6), is unable to fictionalize his family story in the very city symbolizing the loss of his parents.

W, or the Memory of Childhood alternates autobiographical chapters dealing with Perec's childhood and fictional chapters recounting a detective story. Since Perec does not remember the past, the autobiographical texts of *W, or the Memory of Childhood* consist of factual information about his parents provided to the author either by pictures or by family members who survived the war. On the other hand, the fictional chapters feature an adult character named Gaspard Winckler who, looking for the missing boy whose identity he uses, ends up observing the imaginary island of W where athletes compete to survive. Drawing a parallel between the contents of the two narratives, the structure of the book turns the island of W into an allegory of Auschwitz, where Perec's mother was murdered.

Even though every second chapter of *W, or the Memory of Childhood* is invented, Perec's fiction is dissimilar from Modiano's transposition in *The Night Watch*. Contrary to Modiano, Perec neither creates characters inspired by his parents nor sets his fiction in places where his family lived or died: Gaspard Winckler is an avatar of no one but Perec himself and the imaginary island of W is located in Tierra del Fuego, far away from Paris and Auschwitz. Thus, when Perec invents, he creates a dystopic Neverland rather than fictionalizing his parents.

In the biographical chapters of *W, or the Memory of Childhood*, which are visually separated from the fictional ones, Perec aims to describe his former life with his parents as precisely as possible. When he is not sure about a detail and falls into using his imagination, Perec always makes sure to make that clear, while still maintaining an emotionless realism. "I think that when I was very little the street had wooden paving. Perhaps there was even a great heap, somewhere, of nice cubic wooden paving blocks with which, like the characters in Charles Vildrac's *L'Île rose*, we built castle and cars" (47).

Whereas Modiano fictionalizes his father's past life in Paris, merging historical places with fictional events and shaping a map of the city where particular districts and cardinal points are associated to specific atmospheres, Perec prefers neutral descriptions of pictures.

> Two photographs. The first was taken by Photodefer, 47 Boule-
> vard de Belleville, Paris XI. I think it dates from 1938. It shows
> me and my mother in close-up. Mother and child make a picture
> of happiness, enhanced by the photographer's shading. I am in
> my mother's arms. Our temples touch. My mother's hair is dark,
> brushed up at the front and falling in curls over the nape of
> her neck. She is wearing a flowered-printed bodice, perhaps held
> by a brooch. Her eyes are darker than mine and have a slightly
> wider shape. Her eyebrows are very fine and sharply delineated.
> Her face is oval, her cheeks well defined. (49)

Since he lacks childhood memories, Perec substitutes these descriptions of pictures for his reminiscences of events. The absence of recollections, however, entails the neutrality of his tone, as no emotion can be added to the depiction of the picture. Instead of focusing on feelings he is unable to remember, Perec focuses on reliable data such as portraits and places. Indeed, while he is unsure about dates—"I think it dates from 1938"—the location of the photographer is certain, so he knows that his mother definitely went to "47 Boulevard de Belleville, Paris XI" to get the picture taken. Unlike Perec, who writes about his parents, the lone occurrence of such a factual investigation in Modiano's work is found in *Dora Bruder*, which is the only text that does not deal with its author's own family story.

Among the places mentioned by Perec, the 24 rue Vilin is the most important one. Even though he could not locate the rue Vilin on the map of Paris, from the moment Perec walked back there, this street became the focus of his attention. "Since 1969 I have been to Rue Vilin once a year in connection with a book I am writing, currently entitled *Les Lieux* ("Places"), in which I try to describe what happened over twelve years to a dozen places in Paris to which I am particularly attached for one reason or another" (48).

In spite of the fact that Perec left *Les Lieux* unfinished, the project of describing his childhood home over the course of several years is meaningful. To the survivor, whose mother never had a grave, going back to the 24 rue Vilin every year is similar to a graveyard pilgrimage. Unfortunately, and at the same time so symbolically, the course of history made Perec the witness of the dismantling of the rue Vilin. "Today, Rue Vilin has been three-quarters demolished. More than half the houses have been razed, leaving waste ground, piling up with rubbish, with old cookers and wrecked cars; most of the houses still standing are boarded up" (47).

Thus, Modiano and Perec's different second-generation traumas entail contrary ways to haunt Paris in their respective literary quests for memory. On the one hand, Modiano's *The Night Watch* fictionalizes the story of the author's father through a symbolic map of Paris where significant districts are associated with particular emotions. On the other hand, Perec's *W, or the Memory of Childhood* shows the author both unable to develop Parisian characters inspired by his parents and stuck in neutrally describing his childhood home in the 20th arrondissement.

Nevertheless, in both cases, the city of Paris is deeply associated with Modiano's and Perec's personal wounds. The aim of the previous analysis of *The Night Watch* and of *W, or the Memory of Childhood* was to illuminate the Parisian sites that are so key to these authors. Whereas it seems expected that the 16th arrondissement would be associated with collaboration in a novel transposing Modiano's father's life and that the 20th arrondissement would capture the loss of Perec's parents in a biographical text, the following comparative analysis of *Quartier perdu* and *A Man Asleep* intends to illustrate that Modiano's and Perec's different key Parisian locations leave similar marks on fictional works that do not, at first glance, seem to be related to the author's families stories.

Both Modiano's *Quartier perdu* and Perec's *A Man Asleep* recount the stories of men haunting Paris. The hero of Perec's second-person narrative, a twenty-five-year-old male student, decides one day to extricate himself from the world, and to neither write his examinations nor open the door to his friends. This decision to become indifferent to life leads the young man to walk in the streets of Paris.

> Now you wander up and down Boulevard Saint-Michel, without recognizing anything, not seeing the shop windows, not seen by the streams of students who pass by you. You no longer enter the cafés, checking all the tables with a worried expression on your face, going into the back room in search of you no longer know whom. You no longer look for anyone in the queues which form every two hours outside the seven cinemas outside Rue Champollion. No longer do you wander like a lost soul in the great courtyard of the Sorbonne, or pace up and down the long corridors waiting for the lecture-rooms to empty, or

go off to solicit greetings, smiles or sign of recognition in the
library. (163)

This excerpt from the beginning of the narrative illustrates that the
character attempts to specifically separate himself from the rest of humanity.
Whereas the Boulevard Saint-Michel, the rue Champollion, and the Sorbonne are part of the Latin Quarter, Perec's hero "wander[s] up and down"
and "enter[s] the cafés" neither looking at, nor looking for, fellow students.
Disregarding Parisians, the young man turns himself into a "ghost" (187)
and haunts a city reduced to buildings, streets, and places: "You are a tireless
walker: every evening you emerge from the black hole of your room, from
your rotting staircase, your silent courtyard, to criss-cross Paris; beyond the
great pools of noise and light: Opéra, the Boulevards, the Champs Elysées,
Saint-Germain, Montparnasse, you head out towards the dead city, towards
Pereire or Saint-Antoine, towards Rue de Longchamp, Boulevard de l'Hôpital, Rue Oberkampf, Rue Vercingétorix" (187–88).

Similarly, the narrator of Modiano's *Quartier perdu* also defines himself as a "ghost" (11) haunting Paris. This first-person novel is a detective
story told by a narrator who is himself a whodunit writer. Introducing
himself as British writer Ambrose Guise, the narrator flies from London to
Paris to meet with his Japanese publisher. Once he arrives in the French
capital, the narrator reveals that, up until twenty years ago, he used to be
a French citizen whose birth name was Jean Dekker. Bit by bit, the reader
gets to understand that the narrator changed name and citizenship because
of a murder he has been associated with but did not commit. Originally
undertaken under the pretext of the whodunit's Japanese publication, the
Paris journey turns into the narrator's quest for memory. "And yet, since
I left Paris twenty years ago, thinking that I would never come back, my
life became so consistent, so clear, so sound. . . . No grey areas anymore,
no quicksands anymore. . . . Motionless, keeping my eyes open, I gradually
cast aside the British writer shell I created to hide myself for twenty years.
Let's stand still. Let's wait for the past to come back to me, as if I para-
chuted down time. Let's return to Paris of days gone by. Let's visit the ruins
and attempt to find a trace of myself. Let's try to answer all outstanding
issues" (29–31). Ambrose Guise/Jean Dekker looks back at his past life in
Paris. He first recalls the people he used to consider his mentors: the more
senior members of an underworld gang he was proud of belonging to. Then,
he decides to go back to the places where the gang used to hang out. "I
slowly walked up and down Avenue des Champs-Elysées. I strolled along

Le Lido's arcades and I went to Sinfonia. I walked for hours without taking notice of time and I certainly crossed every single street in the area" (110).

Thus, the wanderings of both the "man asleep" and the detective-story writer are linked to their respective quests for identity. Perec's student decides to "drift around the streets" (176) to "withdraw his affections" and "detach [himself] from everything" (177): "You are invisible, limpid, transparent. You no longer exist: across the passing hours, the succession of days, the procession of seasons, the flow of time, you survive, without joy and without sadness, without a future and without a past, just like that: simply, self-evidently, like a drop of water forming on a drinking tap on landing, like six socks soaking in a pink plastic bowl, like a fly or a mollusc, like a cow or a snail, like a child or an old man, like a rat (177). Even though he is twenty-five years old, Perec's character defines himself as someone "without a future and without a past." The structure of this nominal group, stating first the "future" and second the "past," indicates that the young man is unable to conceive of any upcoming plan because he ignores where he comes from. The parallelism between Perec's life story and his character's behavior is reinforced by the enumeration beginning with "a drop of water," mentioning "six socks," "a fly or a mollusc," "a cow or a snail," "a child or an old man," and ending up with "a rat." This catalog refers first to a natural element, second to things created by humans, then to insects and animals, and, instead of culminating the list with the mention of human beings, it finishes with "a rat." The particularity of this rodent is that Nazi propaganda used it to symbolize the Jews. Interestingly, the "man asleep" also identifies himself with "rats," defined as "the exiles, the banished, the pariahs, the wearers of invisible stars" (201).

Not only do the absence of a "past" and the mention of "a rat" refer to Perec's Jewish mother lost in Auschwitz, but the places the "man asleep" does not haunt are also significant. As the map on the next page reveals, indicating each place mentioned in the narrative, Perec's character wanders in every single arrondissement of Paris but the 20th. Nevertheless, in the autobiographical parts of *W, or the Memory of Childhood*, Perec points out that the intersection between rue Vilin, rue du Transvaal and rue Olivier Metra "is one of the last street-level points from which you still have a view over the whole of Paris, and it is where Bernard Queysanne and [he] filmed the closing shot" (47) of the movie adaptation of *A Man Asleep*. Both the absence of the 20th arrondissement in the narrative and the lone presence of the rue Vilin in one of the very last scenes of the movie provide an explanation to the attitude of the "man asleep": haunting Paris in

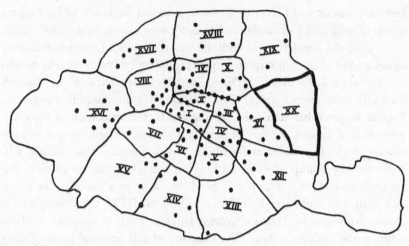

Figure 9.2. The Paris arrondissements and locations from the narrative where Perec's "man asleep" wanders; the "absent" 20th arrondissement is highlighted. (*illustration by Ruth Malka*)

an attempt to "no longer exist" (177) and associating himself with "rats" illustrates the character's desire to sacrifice himself because of the death of Perec's mother. Only at the very end of the narrative, corresponding to the final movie scene set in the 20th arrondissement, does the character realize that he is "not dead" (217) and that he shall live.

The wanderings of Modiano's main character in *Quartier perdu* are similarly meaningful. As the map on the facing page illustrates, while Ambrose Guise/Jean Dekker returns to the areas where the gang used to spend time together, most of the addresses he mentions are located in the 16th, 17th, and 8th Parisian arrondissements. Avenue de Wagram (28), rue de la Pompe (53), rue Troyon (83), avenue Victor-Hugo (124), and avenue Rodin (134), to name a few of the places, refer to streets and avenues where the Nazi Gestapo and the French collaborators historically occupied townhouses during World War II.

Even though the reading scheme of *Quartier perdu* does not take place during the Occupation, the omnipresence of the western Parisian arrondissements is not the only reference to this time period. Despite being one generation younger than the other members of the gang and, therefore, despite not having been around during World War II, the character knows that his friends, who still belong to the "underworld" (31), used to be involved in suspicious activities at the time when "Paris [was . . .] fun" (132).

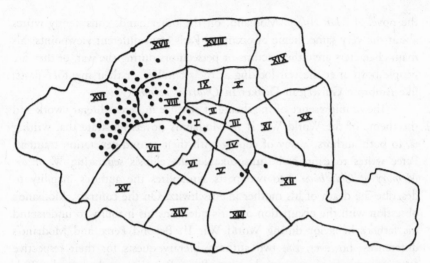

Figure 9.3. Map showing the wanderings of Modiano's Ambrose Guise/Jean Dekker in *Quartier perdu*. (*illustration by Ruth Malka*)

Whereas Modiano fictionalizes his father's war experience in *The Night Watch*, *Quartier perdu* focuses on the implications of dubious activities for the second generation. Even though he was innocent, Jean Dekker has been associated, years later, with the crimes committed by his gang. Not only did he have to change his name and citizenship to save his life, but this time period continues to haunt him: "as from today, I don't want to remember anything" (184) is the closing line of the novel. The only option for Ambrose Guise/Jean Dekker to live a full life would be to forget the past.

Thus, even though *A Man Asleep* and *Quartier perdu* contain no direct references to World War II, both novels echo the respective authors' second-generation trauma. Perec's character decides, at first, to act as if he did not belong to the world of the living and Modiano's protagonist is preoccupied by his mentors' past. In both cases, the characters succeed in living their lives only after haunting Paris: since the city is the sole witness of the past, Perec's "man asleep" awakes in the 20th arrondissement and Modiano's detective-story writer roams around the western arrondissements.

Although Perec's and Modiano's characters prove capable, at the very end of both *A Man Asleep* and *Quartier perdu*, to live fully, this is not the case for the authors themselves. There is always something missing in Perec's stories—for example, the presence of an ellipsis in the heart of *W, or the Memory of Childhood* and the absence of the 20th arrondissement of the novel *A Man Asleep*. Modiano, on the other hand, consistently writes about the very same theme of occupied Paris from different viewpoints: his main characters are either victims or persecutors during the war, or they are people born after the war looking at their families' or their mentors' pasts, like Ambrose Guise/Jean Dekker in *Quartier perdu*.

The omnipresence of the theme of absence in Perec's literary work and the theme of the World War II in Modiano's novels illustrate that writing is, to both authors, a way of coping with their second-generation traumas. Perec writes to express the unspeakable: the ellipsis separating *W, or the Memory of Childhood* into two parts symbolizes the author's inability to describe the death of his mother in Auschwitz. On the contrary, Modiano's obsession with the occupation of Paris questions his inability to understand his father's behavior during World War II. Beyond Perec and Modiano's differences, however, the two authors' literary quests for their respective families' memories are carried out in Paris: Perec is attached to the 20th arrondissement and Modiano is obsessed with the 16th arrondissement.

Even though the two authors deal with contrasting issues, and even though their respective key Parisian places are different, the representation of Paris in both Perec's and Modiano's literary works has an analogous function: questioning the past. Nevertheless, although neither Perec nor Modiano found satisfying answers in their respective quests, the city of Paris did give each of them a response. While Modiano fictionalized life in Paris during the Occupation, there are now commemorative plaques in the 16th arrondissement exhorting passersby not to forget French collaboration. And while there is no longer any rue Vilin to symbolize Perec's lost memory, there is today a rue Georges Perec in the 20th arrondissement.

Bibliography

"All Nobel Prizes in Literature." Nobelprize.org. Nobel Media AB 2014. http://www.nobelprize.org/nobel_prizes/literature/laureates/index.html. Accessed October 2016.

Modiano, Patrick. *Dora Bruder*. Paris: Gallimard, 2015.

———. *Livret de famille*. Paris: Gallimard, 1977. Print. (The translations of quotations from *Livret de famille* are mine.)

———. *The Night Watch*. Translated by P. Wolf; revised by F. Wynne. London: Bloomsbury, 2015. Translation of *La Ronde de nuit*. Paris: Gallimard, 1969.

———. *Quartier perdu*. Paris: Gallimard, 1988. Print. (The translations of quotations from *Quartier perdu* are mine.)

———. *La Ronde de nuit.* Paris: Gallimard, 2010.

———. *The Search Warrant.* Translated by J. Kilmartin. London: Harvill Secker, 2014. Translation of *Dora Bruder.* Paris: Gallimard, 1999.

Perec, Georges. *Things: A Story of the Sixties.* Translated by D. Bellos. Published with *A Man Asleep.* Translated by A. Leak. London: Vintage Books, 2011. Translation of *Les Choses, une histoire des années soixante.* Paris: Pocket, 1990; and of *Un homme qui dort.* Paris: Gallimard, 1990.

———. *Un homme qui dort.* Paris: Gallimard, 2016.

———. *W, or The Memory of Childhood.* Translated by D. Bellos. London: Vintage Books, 2011. Translation of *W, ou le souvenir d'enfance.* Paris Gallimard, 1993.

———. *W, ou le souvenir d'enfance.* Paris: Gallimard, 2007.

PART 4 ABSENCE

The chapters chosen for this section grapple with the idea of the "work of memory." Scott Lerner suggests that the experience of remembering offered in Sarah Kofman's memoir is, in the Freudian sense, a work of memory. This "work" belongs, directly, to the subject-narrator of each memoir, and, indirectly, to the reader. It is doubly painful as it revives not only the lost object, but also the painful experience of the loss of that object. A Holocaust memoir represents a creative merger of the search for memory and the work of mourning: a work of memory. It is always imperfect and its perspective is ongoing, repeated through the creative act.

Thomas Nolden explores the difficulties that Jewish writers experience in paying tribute to their love for Paris as the *locus amabilis*, the birthplace of human rights and the capital of the European Republic of Letters. Indeed: how can a Jewish writer describe the City of Light during the so-called *années obscures*, its dark years? How to claim one's place among the cultural elite alongside openly antisemitic writers such as Louis-Ferdinand Céline? How to write about a past that, for decades, the city had tried to repress?

Sarah Hammerschlag argues that the current attitudes toward the Holocaust can be understood only if we take into consideration the later historical events. Hammerschlag looks at the sites evoked in post-Shoah writing, pointing out how, during the Algerian War (1954–1962), symbols of World War II were consistently deployed by the political dissidents in order to portray France as a persecutor not unlike Nazi Germany. She argues that the returning specter of state-sponsored violence sparked the emergence of the Shoah in public discourse.

PART 4 · ABSENCE

10

Past Imperfect

Mourning and the Work of Memory in Holocaust Memoirs

L. SCOTT LERNER

What is the aim of memory in *W, or the Memory of Childhood*; *Rue Ordener Rue Labat*; and *Dora Bruder*? Any activity of memory, and especially of the kind that serves the writing of a memoir, is an operation of restitution. When we remember we seek the return of something we no longer possess. In its etymological sense, "to remember" means to recall intensely (Latin *re*) to mindfulness (*memor*). Today we would speak of a return to conscious awareness: as I remember, a piece of my past is restored to me, if only in consciousness. In Holocaust memoirs, this operation of memory becomes decidedly more complex. Here, the thing recalled, the object of memory, is itself an experience of profound loss, whether of parents, of extended family members, of "childhood," of identity and community, or of some combination of these. The very thing that memory seeks to restore is the experience of being robbed of something or someone we intensely loved. In such a case, the aim of memory—in the sense of the purpose and also the directionality of memory—becomes paradoxical. On the one hand, the object of memory moves toward us, as a return; on the other hand, it abandons us, as a loss.

Perhaps this is the paradox of any operation of memory. Perhaps this is memory's false promise: to bring back—to the present, to mindfulness, to the real—that which is definitively gone. This paradox becomes infinitely more acute when the object of memory was not only lost to consciousness, like any experience that is forgotten or put out of mind, but rather constituted a traumatic rupture endured in real life. As we shall see, it is this paradox that characterizes *W, or the Memory of Childhood*; *Rue Ordener Rue Labat*; and *Dora Bruder*, and the Holocaust memoir in general. To remember the object of loss is to recall to existence (to consciousness) the loved one who ceases to exist. In the deeply personal manner of these memoirs, the aim of memory corresponds to the search for the return of that which, by definition, is being taken away. I say "is being taken away" and not "has been taken away" because the recall of the lost object restores its presence to conscious awareness. In so doing, it revives not only the lost object, but the painful experience of the loss of the object. In such cases, memory becomes a work of mourning.

Freud had a great deal to say about both trauma and mourning but tended to keep the two separate. His essay "Mourning and Melancholia" makes no mention of trauma, just as *Beyond the Pleasure Principle* never refers to mourning. In contrast, Freud's combined work on mourning and traumatic neurosis, including the concept of repetition compulsion, proved extremely influential in subsequent trauma theory, particularly in the work of Dominick LaCapra. Mourning and trauma theory have likewise converged when psychoanalysis has been extrapolated from the realm of the individual subject to that of a society. In his study of postwar France, for example, Henry Rousso in *The Vichy Syndrome* describes the relationship of the French toward their national past under the Nazi occupation and the Vichy government in a way that explicitly combines repressed memory and mourning. With respect to postwar Germany, Jean-François Lyotard argues that the long silence about the Nazi atrocities constituted a failure to remember, work through, and successfully mourn ("Ticket"; *Postmodern Condition*). Eric Santner's *Stranded Objects* and Jean-Philippe Mathy's *Melancholy Politics*, among others, have brought memory and mourning together in their analyses of contemporary societies.

At the level of the individual subject, Freud's own conceptions of (trauma-induced) repression and "the work of mourning" (*Trauerarbeit*) and Freudian trauma theory, with its notions of repression and the return of the repressed, do not generally converge because they are understood as applying to dissimilar situations. Indeed, the role of memory in trauma would appear to be the reverse of the role of memory in mourning. A trauma is understood as an experience that overwhelms the normal defenses of the ego, causing the painful experience to be pushed out of consciousness—repressed—and forgotten, until such time that it is triggered and returns, unbidden. In mourning, however, memories that bind the subject to the person who has been lost are cut loose. In "Mourning and Melancholia" Freud characterizes mourning as the painful process by which a subject "works through" the loss of a loved one. When this process is successful, and the subject eventually succeeds in accepting and, in a sense, surviving, the loss, Freud calls it "mourning"; when the subject fails to overcome the loss Freud refers to it as pathological and a form of melancholia or depression. The mark of successful mourning is to become detached from the lost object and from each of the "memories and expectations" that bound the object to the mourner, so that the ego becomes "free and uninhibited again" and able to form a new attachment ("Mourning and Melancholia," 244, 245).

What we find, then, is that the relationship between the function of memory in trauma and its counterpart in mourning parallels the paradoxical memory of the Holocaust memoir. In each case, an operation of return runs counter to an operation of rupture. These dynamics, moreover, should not be understood as being restricted to the subjectivity of the narrator. It is the particular quality of the Holocaust memoir to cause personal losses to merge with the collective tragedy of the Holocaust. What is remembered is not only the loss individually endured, but also the one endured by others within the same collective experience. Readers who have not participated directly in the experiences recounted and may have no direct experience with Holocaust loss can also come to identify with this loss by indirect means. Susan Suleiman has shown how Patrick Modiano performs a similar kind of indirect identification in relation to Dora Bruder, who died before Modiano was born. Suleiman calls this identification "empathetic" rather than "appropriative," arguing that it leads to an "ethical consciousness" and a type of mourning that is both individual and collective ("Oneself," 334, 343). Unable to encounter Dora's story directly, both because it took place before he was born and because the story remains, in large measure, unknowable, Modiano nonetheless identifies with it empathetically as he assembles those elements he is able to gather and, speculatively filling in some gaps, writes her story, or her nonstory. Our own encounter with Dora's story, as Modiano gives it to us, is similarly indirect. In this sense, Modiano's creative-investigative "reading" of Dora's story mirrors our own reading of

Dora Bruder and of Holocaust memoirs in general. To the extent that we readers, living in the shadow of what Perec calls the *grande hache* (great ax/capital *H*) of History (*W*, 6), are able to identify with the subjective narrators of the memoirs, their memory and their mourning become ours.

Memory and the Work of Mourning: The *Work of Memory*

The question that interests me is how memory—the memoir—and the work of mourning become elided in these works by Perec, Kofman, and Modiano, creating what we might call a "work of memory." By adopting this term, I am suggesting that the experience of remembering offered by the memoirs effectively becomes an activity—in the Freudian sense, a *work*—of mourning. This "work of memory" belongs, directly, to the subject-narrator of each memoir, and indirectly to readers. In order to see how this work is performed, we need to examine how traumatic memory and the work of mourning merge in these memoirs. Along the way it will be important to look briefly at how certain of these major tenets of classical Freudian psychoanalysis have been reevaluated in the light of recent scholarship in social psychology and neuroscience.

One of the first things we notice when reading these texts is that all three represent memory as a search, an uncovering and voicing of something that has become obscured, buried, hidden, guarded, or forgotten. "Maybe all my books have been the detours required to bring me to write about 'that,'" writes Sarah Kofman (*Rue Ordener*, 3). "It takes time for what has been erased to resurface," observes Patrick Modiano. "[All] this auto-biographical work has been organized around a unique memory that, for me, was profoundly buried and in a certain sense denied," asserts Georges Perec (*Je suis né*, 83). Modiano casts the city of Paris as a collective psyche with a repressed memory, its bureaucratic organs standing guard over memory-secrets: "Traces survive in registers, and nobody knows where these registers are hidden, and who has custody of them, and whether or not these custodians are willing to let you see them" (*Dora Bruder*, 9). Perec evokes "the wall of ready-made memories" that psychoanalytic treatment has enabled him to take down (*Thoughts of Sorts*, 52). These brief examples are characteristic of the language each memoirist uses in speaking about memory and loss. They illustrate the degree to which all three authors adopt a perspective that is indebted to Freud's conception of repression as a force that pushes disturbing memories out of consciousness and compels them to remain unconscious (*Five Lectures*, 48). The theory of repressed memories, and their return, would thus appear to occupy a central place in Perec's, Kofman's, and Modiano's work of memory.

The repetitions that mark each of the narratives, moreover, lend themselves to interpretation in the light of Freud's theory of repetition-compulsion. Just as, in Freud's theory, the compulsive repetition of experiences that cause pain without bringing pleasure can provide a means of gaining mastery over the traumatic situation, so the repetitions of past traumatic events may allow the subject of the memoir to come to terms with traumatic loss. Indeed, one finds a striking parallel between the *fort-da* game that Freud describes as an illustration of his theory of repetition-compulsion and what I have described as the "aim of memory" in Holocaust memoirs. In this well-known passage from *Beyond the Pleasure Principle*, Freud describes how he once observed his grandson playing with a spool on a string, exclaiming "gone" ("*fort*") *as* he throws it from him and "there" ("*da*") as he reeled it back in. For Freud, the toy symbolized the boy's mother, whose departure from the home caused him pain. By compulsively repeating her act of separation from him, the child gained a degree of control over his loss. The back-and-forth movements of the of the toy present a visual parallel to the movement of the object of memory in Holocaust memoirs, which I have described as moving toward us, as a return, and also moving away from us, as a loss. Produced in a culture steeped in Freudian ideas, the memoirs by Perec, Kofman, and Modiano, therefore, open themselves to interpretation both in relation to the theory of repetition-compulsion and to the general theory of repression on which repetition-compulsion depends.

Repression under Review

In the past few decades, however, the validity of repressed memories, and the Freudian theory underpinning them, have come under sharp attack in empirical studies on traumatic memory, especially those related to childhood sexual abuse (Loftus, McNally). In 2008, Yakov Rofé, writing in the *Review of General Psychology*, the journal of the American Psychological Association, undertook a broader review of the theory of repression, examining three areas: traumatic memory, patient adjustment, and the unconscious. "This comprehensive evaluation," Rofé declared, "reveals little empirical justification for maintaining the psychoanalytic concept of repression" (63). Notably, Rofé introduced as evidence a paper by the neo-Freudian psychoanalyst Peter Fonagy, who had asserted that positive therapeutic results were not the consequence of the lifting of repression or the recovery of memory; those who continued to make this claim only damaged the field (Rofé, 74; Fonagy, 215). Rofé was not advocating that "rival theories of psychopathology, such as behavioral, cognitive, or biological models" should replace psychoanalysis, for these, too, lacked sufficient empirical evidence of their viability (76). Consequently, a new theory of psychopathology, "perhaps a new theory of repression," was needed in order to shed light on the underlying causes of certain disorders. For Rofé, however, the need for a theory could not justify maintaining a theory—the Freudian theory of repression—that so clearly had failed to stand up to empirical scrutiny.

Most recently, research in the young field of social neuroscience has started to draw a higher-resolution picture of how human memory works. Notably, non-Freudian investigators conducting experimental scholarship in this field have reaffirmed the concept of the unconscious popularized by Freud and long debunked by his detractors (even though they sometimes take pains to distinguish the unconscious revealed by cognitive science from Freud's dynamic unconscious). In this general—yet crucial—sense, Freud's understanding of the unconscious is supported by experimental scholarship: no more than a minuscule portion of our total memory is conscious memory. This research has continued to challenge the theory of repression, however. It has drawn attention to the significance of the gaps, holes, and inaccuracies of memory while rejecting the claim that these are symptoms of repression. Summarizing these findings, one author observes: "The inaccessibility of the new unconscious is not considered to be a defense mechanism. . . . It's normal" (Mlodinow, 17). According to the view that emerges from this body of research, traumatic events, on the one hand, are more rather than less likely to be remembered. On the other hand, the brain, having retained in conscious memory only a minute fraction of the vast quantity of stimuli to which it is exposed, unconsciously smooths out narratives and fills in the gaps of conscious memory, such that what we think of as memories are not only recorded and recalled, but filled in, smoothed out, and invented. In a word, a great deal of our work of remembering consists in unconsciously making things up.

On the basis of this research, should we thus reject the representation of memory in the memoirs as inaccurate because it is reliant on the theory of repression? I do not think so. The reason is that when all three authors speak about the work of memory—like the work of therapy—as the attempt to recover hidden (repressed) memory, they do so in metaphorical rather than theoretical terms. Writing elsewhere on "Freud and the Photographic Apparatus," Kofman explicitly draws attention to the *metaphor* of repression: "The metaphor here is that of the watchman, the censor, present at the entrance of the dark antechamber, forbidding certain drives from entering into the clear room of consciousness" (*Camera obscura*, 22). Commenting here on Freud's own use of a metaphor—the camera obscura—she describes defenses in Freud's writing yet stops short of making assertions in her own name. Perec also adopts metaphorical language when, referring to the end of his psychoanalysis, he says that his "story/history" has exited "this underground terrain," and come together "like a memory returned to its space" (*Thoughts of Sorts*, 52, 53).

Similarly, when Modiano searches for the traces of Dora in the civil records of the city of Paris, he refers to unhelpful civil servants of the Mairie of the 12th arrondissement as "sentinels of oblivion whose role is to guard a shameful secret" (11). This language is best read metaphorically rather than as suggesting that the search for the past in *Dora Bruder* involves a weakening of psychic defenses and a return of the repressed—any more than the topography of repressed memories—the city of Paris—is truly akin to a human psyche. Modiano explicitly dramatizes the search for Dora's past as a journey into the inner sanctum of repressed memory when he describes his visit to the Palais de Justice. The purpose of this visit is ostensibly a bureaucratic errand: as a nonrelative of Dora, he will apply for a special exemption to obtain her records. Yet it becomes much more than this. Located on the Île de le Cité, the Palais de Justice stands on the site of the former Palais de la Cité that served as the residence and the seat of power for the kings of France from the tenth to the fourteenth centuries. The surviving jewel of the former royal palace is the Sainte-Chapelle (Holy Chapel) with its extraordinary stained glass windows. It turns out that the Palais de Justice and the Sainte-Chapelle share an entrance, and Modiano recounts, step-by-step, how in his search for the memory of Dora he passes through the "big iron gates" and crosses the courtyard, and "[penetrates]" a large room (*Dora Bruder*, 11, 12 trans. modified). It is as though his search for the past has taken him into the Holy of Holies of repressed memory. Representing memory figuratively, these writers do not so much tie themselves to the scientific theory of repression as they demonstrate that creative writing can be the cousin of the creative remembering described by social neuroscience.

The Primary Mourning of Lost Parents

If the aim of memory is only metaphorically to enter the Sainte-Chapelle of repressed memory, then what is it? In *W*, *Dora Bruder*, and *Rue Ordener*, we find not only that memory is thematized as a search for something hidden or inaccessible, but also that this search inevitably leads to the principal object of loss. For Perec and Kofman, this is the lost parent, and the work of memory is performed, in the first instance, by the *child* survivor. Perec and Kofman are child survivors both because they survived the Holocaust as children and because their principal loss to the Holocaust was the loss of their parents. Modiano's case is more complex. Insofar as he was born after the war ended and lost no one, directly, to either the war or the Holocaust, he would appear to have no place in this classification of child survivors. And yet the narrative of his troubled relationship with his father, interwoven with the story of Dora, points toward an unresolved personal loss, of the father, that precedes, accompanies, and underlies the obsessive search for Dora.

Modiano's memoir of his own childhood provides numerous examples of his "loss" of both parents, up to and including the moment when his father cut off all ties with him. Its title, *A Pedigree*, alludes ironically to precisely this condition of lacking, or having lost, one's parents: "I'm a dog who pretends to have a pedigree," Modiano declares at the outset (5). He later recounts how he preserved a teddy bear his mother gave him when he was born "as a talisman and my only souvenir of an absent mother" (13). Patrick and his brother, Rudy, were baptized "without my parents being present" (29) and, in this tale of his "pedigree" the individuals who gave him life have no importance: "[a]part from my brother, Rudy, his death, I don't believe that anything I'll relate here truly matters to me" (41). At one point, while in England, Patrick is geographically separated from both parents, with "no word" from his mother and certain that "it suits" his father for him to remain abroad (57). Implicitly, he is relating his journey, as a young man, toward the realization that his absence from his parents' lives was more than temporary and circumstantial. Rather, to be absent from the lives of his mother and father, and therefore to be in a state of loss of one's parents, corresponded to his existential condition. This fate was sealed when his father wrote him a letter, permanently severing their relationship. The letter's finality conveys an extraordinary brutality.

> ALBERT RODOLPHE MODIANO 15 QUAI DE CONTI Paris VI, August 9, 1966. I've received your letter of August 4th, addressed not to your father but to 'Dear Sir,' in whom I must recognize myself. Your bad faith and hypocrisy have gone too far. It's the Bordeaux business all over again. My decision regarding your enlistment in the military in November was not made lightly. I considered it indispensable not only that you get a change of scenery, but also that you conduct your life by discipline rather than whimsy. Your insolence is contemptible. Your decision has been duly noted. ALBERT MODIANO. (126–27)

Following the letter, Patrick Modiano simply states: "I never saw him again." Despite the date of this letter (1966), this loss of the father was a loss *to* the war, for the father, whether portrayed in real or symbolic terms, as so many of Modiano's narratives make clear, was a figure who could not be dissociated from the experience of the Occupation. In Modiano's case, although this loss of the father to the war was not a loss by death (Albert Modiano died much later), and although their rupture also occurred much later, it was nonetheless a complete loss. On its deepest level, it thus seems apparent that Modiano's empathetic identification with Dora follows the path laid out by his own self-image as a child who lost his father to the war.

From the point of view of psychoanalysis, especially object relations theory, all mourning is a repetition of one or more earlier losses experienced by the subject. These earlier losses take the form of the young (pre-Oedipal) child's separation from the loved object (the mother, the primary caregiver, or the breast), and the means employed by this young subject to cope with such a loss serve as the basis for the process of mourning later in life. From this psychoanalytic point of view, we might then say that mourning is by definition the work of child survivors.

The position of Perec and Kofman, who both survived the Holocaust as children and lost parents to the Holocaust, adds an additional stratum of real experience to this situation of the mourner as a child survivor. Indeed, their position as writers who are also child survivors of the Holocaust, becomes exemplary of the process of grieving generally, as understood within psychoanalysis. In a still different sense, Modiano's narrative of loss, in which the real and the symbolic already fused, provides its own type of exemplum of mourning. All of this is not, of course, to say that mourning, whether conceived in symbolic or real terms, is limited to parents; clearly it is not.

The *bruder*, Modiano's brother, Rudy, is mourned; the victims of the deportations and the gas chambers are mourned. All these acts of mourning extend from what we might think of as a primary mourning of lost parents.

In each of these works the aim of memory thus becomes the continual search for and preservation of the lost parent. The mapping of memory onto the topography of Paris stages this search. The relation to the parent is represented as a story of locations, movement, events, and associations attached to the city of Paris, its streets, archives, and places (*lieux*). When Modiano's search for the traces of Dora Bruder takes him to the Palais de Justice, for example, his admittance to the Holy Chapel of Dora's hidden past merges inexorably with the search for his own father. "Twenty years before I had a similar experience. I had learned that my father was in hospital, in the Pitié-Salpêtrière. I hadn't seen him since the end of my adolescent years. . . . I found my way into ancient buildings, into communal wards lined with beds, I questioned nurses who gave me contradictory directions. I came to doubt my father's existence, passing and repassing that majestic church, and those spectral buildings. . . . I tramped the paved courtyards till dusk (*jusqu'à ce que le soir tombe*)" (12, 13). The final word, "tombe," is here used as a verb: "le soir tombe"—"night falls"—but its visual and aural evocation of the tomb (*tombeau*) is crucial. The sentences that follow underwrite the entire episode as being driven by the relation to the "lost" father: "It was impossible to find my father. I never saw him again."

Similarly, the urban topoi in Kofman's text, constituted by streets, channels of movement, are associated with the lost parents of the tale. The father belongs to the once ordinary and familiar world represented by the rue Ordener; Mémé resides at a place removed from the world of the father, on the rue Labat, the street *là-bas—over there*. The rue Marcadet connects these two worlds, providing a possible route from one to the other and back again. It is a traumatic avenue of transition, a terrifying counterpart to the road not taken to Drancy and Auschwitz. "[It] seemed endless to me," Sarah recounts, "and I vomited the whole way" (31).

The rue Marcadet will reappear as the site of the battle for possession of Sarah. Having been granted custody of Sarah by the court, Mémé declares triumphantly: " 'We won. I'm keeping my little girl!' " while Sarah feels "neither triumphant nor completely happy nor altogether secure" (60). Finally, for the postwar Sarah, the address of the biological mother is signaled by yet another Parisian street, an *impasse*: "So I had to return to my mother's apartment, on the Impasse Langlois" (82).

Among the sites (*lieux*) included in *W*, I will mention only Georges Perec's early childhood home at 24 rue Vilin. The site constitutes a *non-lieu* (non-place/dismissal) more than a *lieu*, as the writer uses the term elsewhere: "it's the very image of this point of no-return, the awareness of a radical rupture. What I wanted to question, to put into question, to put to the test, was my own rootedness in this nonplace (*non-lieu*), this absence . . ." (*Je suis né*, 101, 102). Perec has little recollection of his family life in the apartment at 24 rue Vilin because he lived there when he was very young, yet the place, or nonplace, retains its value for him as a concrete link to his past and to his parents. The apartment, however, is simultaneously a link and a nonlink, a door to the past that opens to nothing, to no memory. In his remarkable film documentary, *En remontant la rue Vilin* (Walking Back Up the Rue Vilin), Perec's friend the filmmaker Robert Bober uncovers the many layers of what, borrowing from Pierre Nora, we might call this *non-lieu* of memory.

Preserving the Bond through Memoir-Writing

If the search is only metaphorical insofar as it applies to hidden or repressed memory, it may correspond to a psychological reality when it merges with the search for the lost parent.

The key characteristic of such a search and the one represented, I believe, in each of the memoirs, is not that it ultimately leads to a discovery, but rather that, as a work of mourning, the search continues. In recent years the classical Freudian view of mourning (in contrast to melancholia) as coming to an end has been challenged, leading to reconceptions of mourning as, potentially, permanently incomplete. Incomplete mourning may be susceptible to reactivation, for example, when triggered by links to the one who has been lost. The conventional notion of mourning implies a kind of forgetting of the lost object, whereas the memoir does just the opposite. Instead of releasing the object, the work of mourning represented in the memoirs strives to remember and retain it. It feeds the mouth of grief while ensuring that the appetite is insatiable.

My own understanding of the work of mourning, based especially on my reading of Marcel Proust's *In Search of Lost Time*, has similarly led me to question whether the unconscious aim of mourning is to become "complete": whether the subject in mourning unconsciously seeks to *finish* the work or simply to engage in it (Lerner). To endure the loss of the loved object is always to struggle for survival against the threat of self-annihilation. The question (which I am not alone in asking) is whether the aim of mourning is to give up the lost love object or preserve it. From a somewhat different starting point, Judith Butler reaches a similar conclusion: "Melancholic identification," Butler writes, "permits the loss of the object in the external world precisely because it finds a way to *preserve* the object as part of the ego and, hence, to avert the loss as a complete loss" (134). If you look at the representations of loss and mourning in Proust's fiction, especially in his representation of Marcel's "belated" mourning of his grandmother, I believe you will find that the mental attacks on the lost loved one serve the purpose of producing guilt, which in turn becomes the source of self-punishment. Such self-punishment, or masochism, is secondary rather than originary; ultimately it serves as a means of resisting the relinquishment of the lost love object. By preserving the object, the bond with the lost other, in this guilt-laden and extremely painful way, the subject ensures his or her own self-preservation.

What, then, of the "work of memory"? Just as the aim of mourning is not the end of mourning but its work, the aim of memory, in *W, Rue Ordener* and *Dora Bruder*, is not memory itself, but its work. According to this hypothesis, memory-writing preserves an ongoing attachment to the lost parent by means of a complex, conscious, and unconscious dynamic. First, the mourning subject, the writer, attacks the loved object either directly or by representing him or her in a way that invites condemnation. Then, these attacks—consciously or unconsciously—provoke remorse and feelings of guilt. Finally, this guilt leads to new attacks directed back on the subject. The intensity of this self-punishment serves to keep alive the bond with lost loved one, who is not given up but preserved.

And here I want to return to the conception of memory that has emerged in social neuroscience according to which missing pieces are unconsciously added and rough edges are unconsciously smoothed in our "recalled" narratives. The work of memory also adds, invents, and plays with narrative gaps. When Perec declares, "I have no childhood memories" (6), he underscores not the total lack of memories of childhood but the fact that the determinant event, the loss of his mother, her deportation and death at Auschwitz, took place beyond the limits of his direct experience. The most significant event to be recalled of his childhood is thus not *his* to remember because he was absent from it. *I have no childhood memories.* He thus came to perceive it as a rupture and a gap, a lack that would be filled first by a "phantasme," as he calls the early story and images of *W,* and later by *W, or The Memory of Childhood.* According to his biographer, Perec rarely sought concrete information about his mother, although such information was available (Bellos, 367–68). Instead, he preferred to preserve her image as one of absence: the break in the *fils* (threads) that once connected him to her and that left him a child survivor and *fils de personne* (nobody's boy; *W,* 12). From *W* to *La Disparition* (*A Void*)—an adventure novel written without the letter *e*—and many other writings, a great portion of Perec's activity as a writer could be considered an imagined or imagined-remembered "act of disappearance" that mirrored his mother's official *Acte de Disparition* (certificate of disappearance; Bellos, 168–69).

Fired by the unconscious guilt of the child who failed to care for his mother and punishes himself for her loss, Perec's intermittent mourning of his mother, and of his father with and through her, depends on a divorce between the original event and its memory. Like all of us, only more extremely in relation to his work of mourning, Perec fills in the gaps and dynamically extends the memory narrative. His obsession with lack of memories, roots, of being without an attic, and therefore of being *inengendré*—not engendered (*W,* 12; translation modified)—is an outgrowth of his conscious and unconscious determination to pursue the memory of his mother as a pure gap, which thus opens the opportunity for a creative filling-in. His painful work of memory, a combination of masochistic punishment and creative production, enables him to preserve, and not fully give up, his lost parents.

Patrick Modiano's quest to remember the real loss, removal from Paris, and annihilation of a girl he never knew similarly emerges from the symbolic struggle to preserve the father he hardly knew. The contrast between Kofman's aggressive treatment of her mother in *Rue Ordener* with Modiano's understated defense of his father in *Dora Bruder* is striking: "Yet I was surprised that, after all he had been through during the Occupation, my father should have offered not the slightest objection to my being taken away in a Black Maria" (57). Unlike Kofman, Modiano delivers no accusation.

I bore him no grudge. (58)

[He] ignored me as if I had the plague. (57)

[He] hid my call-up papers as a ruse to have me carted off by force to the Reuilly army barracks. I never saw him again after that. (59)

How does one mourn such a father? How does one mourn when one claims to harbor no resentment? In the absence of internalized attacks on the lost father, what will generate the guilt and self-punishment that permit the son to continue to preserve the bond with his father, rather than giving him up and forgetting him? The answer, I think we have to presume, is that such a son feels deserving of the sadism that the father unleashed on him, and he internalizes it, thus enabling himself to preserve the "good" father by endlessly seeking to remember the "crimes" of the Occupation and the losses they created.

Sarah Kofman has designed her memoir quite differently, as a journey along the road to betrayal. As we have seen, the opening of *Rue Ordener Rue Labat* establishes a symbolic attachment to the lost father by means of the fountain pen he left behind, which Sarah has taken from her mother. The idyllic memories that follow of the young girl's life under the welcome law of the father, in his home, his *vie ordinaire* (ordinary life), reinforce this picture of an attachment to the father, his household, family, religion, culture, and people. When the war and the Shoah intervene, and the father is lost in the roundup, Sarah initially remains fiercely loyal to him, observing his kosher law and clinging to her mother. Maintaining the bond with his law and her mother, who carries on in his absence, she remains inseparable from him. When the second knock at the door sends mother and daughter fleeing the family home along the rue Marcadet, back there (*là-bas/Labat*) toward Mémé, Sarah has landed on the road toward betrayal of the father. To a large degree this betrayal will be the work of Mémé, the "savior" who imposes on mother and daughter, as a tacit condition of survival, the forgetting of the law of the father and the erosion of the bond with the mother. (At times, the law of the rabbi-father is even more fiercely defended by the mother, just as the bond with the mother also preserves the connection to the father.) Yet as we know Sarah will also become an accomplice in the betrayal. When she looks at Mémé as an object of desire, when she forgets the father, when she prefers Mémé to her mother, she becomes complicit. On the level of her unconscious guilt, it is as though she, not the Nazis, has annihilated the father. As Federica Clementi aptly puts it, "*Rue Ordener, rue Labat* is the memory of this crime" (124).

Kofman could hardly be more explicit in framing this story of two mothers' "struggle over her soul" (Suleiman, "Orphans," 128) in relation to the loss of her father. Without denying the reader interpretive freedom of movement, while stopping short of providing sure answers to the question of a physical relation with Mémé, for example, Kofman's narrative nonetheless imposes this obligatory lens—of the memory and loss of her father—on the mothers' tale that will become the dominant theme of the memoir. In order to become readers of her account of the struggle over her soul, we must already have consumed the tale of her father. Her reference to a career of scholarly writing with, or along with, her father's pen, reinforces this framing effect.

Much like the early, boldfaced autobiographical texts incorporated by Perec in his *Memory of Childhood* (27–33), Sarah's account of her existence during her father's lifetime contains several errors and inaccuracies (Stanislawski, 157). This section, and the memoir as a whole, also contain important gaps. I want briefly to mention two of these gaps. The first is literally the central gap of the memoir between "*rue Ordener*" and "*rue Labat.*" Only the comma of the title signals its absence, like the ellipsis at the center of *W, or The Memory of Childhood*. Now, as we know, it is rue Marcadet, in the city of Paris as in the memoir, that connects rue Ordener to the rue Labat. And the *mar* of "Marcadet" summons the nightmare (*cauchemar*): the knock at the door, the *oiseau du malheur* (bird of misfortune), the *mala hora* (cursed hour), and the Lillit figure, *Maredewitchale*, that her mother invoked to terrify and punish Sarah as a girl (*Comment s'en sortir*, 109–12). The *Maredewitchale* makes its loathsome return after the war as the *martinet* (small whip) that the mother uses to beat Sarah and that Sarah eventually buries in a hole (*Rue Ordener*, 75).

How is it that we readers apprehend the full horror, for Sarah Kofman, produced by this "ghostly and terrifying figure" (73)? For this purpose she provides a novel literary device adopted from the genre of academic scholarship: a pair of footnotes referencing two of her other publications. It is thus that the product of the father's pen becomes manifest in concrete terms and that Sarah's claim that her scholarly works were "the detours required to bring me to write about 'that'" is validated (3). Here as elsewhere the memoir both leaves the gaps and, in a fascinating simulacrum of unconscious memory work, calls on the reader to fill them in. For we readers are the ones undertaking the task of filling in the gaps and smoothing the rough edges as we seek to understand the memoir. The text invites us to perform the very tasks that the unconscious mind performs in the operation of memory. Perhaps *Rue Ordener Rue Labat* even makes us collaborators, accomplices, in its work of memory. Ominously, for readers who are aware that Sarah Kofman took her own life a few months after completing the memoir, the text of one of the footnotes explains that the root, *mer*, leads to "all sorts of evocative words for death, and more specifically for slow death—by suffocation or being eaten alive" (73, n. 2).

The second gap obliquely serves to establish the connection of this work of memory to the work of mourning. On an unconscious level, to write the mother is sadistically to attack her. It is to attack her as the cause of feelings of shame ("'That's my daughter! That's my daughter!' I was ashamed," 77). It is to attack her by calling her out as the instrument of aggression directed against her daughter ("My mother welcomes me with shouts and blows [*à coups de martinet*]," 73). And it is to attack her as the impediment to access to desired cultures and surrogates: an *impasse*. By provoking unconscious feelings of guilt ("Deep down I was relieved," 61) and the masochistic attacks that accompany them, this treatment of the mother may also serve as its own required detour, as a way of preserving the bond with the lost object: with the mother and through her with the father.

Of the three parent figures—the father, the biological mother, and Mémé—only the mother's death is not recounted in its own right. Rather, it is mentioned only indirectly in relation to the memory of the father, as part of the story of the card he sent from the camp in Drancy. Written in the handwriting and language of someone else, the card was Sarah's last surviving link to him while he was alive and she implicitly blames her mother for losing it: "When my mother died, it wasn't possible to find that card, which I had reread so often and wanted to save. It was as if I had lost my father a second time. From then on nothing was left, not even that lone card that he hadn't even written [by his own hand]" (9).

If we, as reader-participants in Kofman's memoir, fill in the gaps—by which I mean, in this case, *inserting* gaps into the narrative through acts of elimination, using a Perec-like ellipsis—we obtain: "When my mother died . . . It was as if I had lost my father a second time." It may be that the act of writing the memoir and all the writing that preceded served to feed this sadism directed toward her mother. Fueled by guilt for having chosen Mémé, and for having survived, this sadism, and the masochistic suffering it became, enabled an ongoing melancholic identification with both parents, perhaps until the pain that ensured their preservation became too great to bear.

What, therefore, is the aim of memory in *W, Dora Bruder,* and *Rue Ordener*? It is not the return of the repressed, although repression is a central trope in each text. Instead, it is a creative merger of the search for memory and the work of mourning: a work of memory. All mourning begins, in a sense, with separation from parents. Child survivors are those who, paradigmatically, endure the loss of parents. They mourn parents by writing their loss, and such mourning can, from lost parents, extend to others: a brother, a girl, the multitude of those lost to the Shoah. When we think about the work of memory, like the work of mourning, it is more useful to focus on the process than the product. An analogy that comes to mind comes from grammar: we should focus not on the perfect tense, with its emphasis on the completed action, but on the imperfect and its perspective of ongoing, repeated, and in this case highly creative acts. Maybe we should call it the past imperfect.

Bibliography

Bellos, David. *Georges Perec: A Life in Words*. Boston: David R. Godine, 1993.

Bober, Robert. *En remontant la rue Vilin* [Walking Back up the Rue Vilin]. VF Films Production, 1992.

Butler, Judith. *The Psychic Life of Power: Theories in Subjection*. Stanford, CA: Stanford University Press, 1997.

Clementi, Federica K. *Holocaust Mothers and Daughters: Family, History, and Trauma*. Waltham, MA: Brandeis University Press, 2013.

Fonagy, Peter. "Memory and Therapeutic Action." *International Journal of Psychoanalysis* 80 (1999): 215–23.

Freud, Sigmund. *Beyond the Pleasure Principle*. In *The Standard Edition of the Complete Psychological Works of Sigmund Freud*, edited by James Strachey. London: Hogarth Press, 1957. Vol. 18, 7–23.

———. "Five Lectures on Psycho-Analysis." In *The Standard Edition of the Complete Psychological Works of Sigmund Freud*, edited by James Strachey. London: Hogarth Press, 1957. Vol. 11, 9–55.

———. "Mourning and Melancholia." In *The Standard Edition of the Complete Psychological Works of Sigmund Freud*, edited by James Strachey. London: Hogarth Press, 1957. Vol. 14, 237–58.

Kofman, Sarah. *Camera obscura: de l'idéologie*. Paris: Galilée, 1973.

———. *Camera obscura: Of Ideology*. Translated by Will Straw. Ithaca, NY: Cornell University Press, 1999.

———. *Comment s'en sortir*. Paris: Galilée, 1983.

———. *Rue Ordener Rue Labat*. Paris: Galilée, 2005.

———. *Rue Ordener Rue Labat*. Translated by Ann Smock. Lincoln, NE and London: University of Nebraska Press, 1996.

LaCapra, Dominick. *Representing the Holocaust: History, Theory, Trauma*. Ithaca, NY: Cornell University Press, 1994.

Lerner, L. Scott. "Mourning and Subjectivity: From Bersani to Proust, Klein, and Freud." *Diacritics* 37, no. 1 (2008): 41–53.

Loftus, Elizabeth and K. Ketcham. *The Myth of Repressed Memory*. New York: St. Martin's Press, 1994.

158   L. Scott Lerner

Lyotard, Jean-François. *La Condition postmoderne: rapport sur le savoir.* Paris: Minuit, 2013.
———. *The Postmodern Condition: A Report on Knowledge.* Translated by Geoff Bennington and Brian Massumi. Minneapolis: University of Minnesota Press, 1984.
———. "Ticket to a New Decor." Translated by Brian Massumi and W. G. J. Niesluchowski. *Copyright* 1 (1987): 14–16.
Mathy, Jean-Philippe. *Melancholy Politics: Loss, Mourning and Memory in Late Modern France.* State College: Pennsylvania State University Press, 2011.
McNally, Richard J. *Remembering Trauma.* Cambridge, MA: Harvard University Press, 2003.
Mlodinaw, Leonard. *Subliminal: How Your Unconscious Mind Rules Your Behavior.* New York: Vintage, 2012.
Modiano, Patrick. *Dora Bruder.* Paris: Gallimard, Coll. Folio, 1999.
———. *Dora Bruder.* Translated by Joanna Kilmartin. Berkeley: University of California Press, 1999.
———. *Pedigree: A Memoir.* Translated by Mark Polizzotti. New Haven, CT and London: Yale University Press, 2015.
———. *Realms of Memory: The Construction of the French Past.* Edited in English by Lawrence D. Kritzman. Translated by Arthur Goldhammer. 3 vols. New York: Columbia University Press, 1996–98.
———. *Rethinking France: Les Lieux de mémoire.* Translated by Mary Trouille. 4 vols. Chicago: University of Chicago Press, 2001–10.
Nora, Pierre, ed. *Les Lieux de mémoire.* Paris: Gallimard, 1984–1992.
Perec, Georges. *Je suis né.* Paris: Seuil, 1990.
———. *Penser/classer.* Paris: Seuil, 2003.
———. *Thoughts of Sorts.* Translated by David Bellos. Boston, MA: Godine, 2009.
———. *W, or The Memory of Childhood.* Translated by David Bellos. Boston, MA: Godine, 1988.
———. *W, ou le souvenir d'enfance.* Paris: Denoël, 2015.
Rofé, Yakov. "Does Repression Exist? Memory, Pathogenic, Unconscious and Clinical Evidence." *Review of General Psychology* 12, no. 1 (2008): 63–85.
Rousso, Henry. *Le Syndrome de Vichy de 1944 à nos jours.* Paris: Seuil, 1987.
———. *The Vichy Syndrome: History and Memory in France since 1944.* Cambridge, MA: Harvard University Press, 1994.
Santner, Eric. *Stranded Objects: Mourning, Memory, and Film in Postwar Germany.* Ithaca, NY: Cornell University Press, 1990.
Stanislawski, Michael. *Autobiographical Jews: Essays in Jewish Self-Fashioning.* Seattle: University of Washington Press, 2004.
Suleiman, Susan Rubin. "Oneself as Another: Identification and Mourning in Patrick Modiano's *Dora Bruder.*" *Studies in 20th & 21st Century Literature* 31, no. 2 (2007): 325–50.

————. "Orphans of the Shoah and Jewish Identity in Post-Holocaust France: From the Individual to the Collective." In *Post-Holocaust France and the Jews, 1945–1955*, edited by Seán Hand and Steven T. Katz. New York: New York University Press, 2015, 118–38.

11

Paris Obscur

THOMAS NOLDEN

The experience of the *galut*, of exile, is certainly one of the most fundamental in Jewish history. It is not surprising then to see that space emerging in Jewish writing in a most powerful way. Jewish diasporic history is reflected and refracted in innumerous narratives that trace the many trajectories of the Jewish people since biblical times. Jewish literature is, first and foremost, a literature of dispersion that over the course of the centuries of its existence has had to add chapter to chapter, telling of new experiences of dislocation and deportation, of internment and displacement. It is the merit of this volume to focus our attention on a concrete space—Paris—and the ways that Jewish writers dealt with this extraordinary city as the site of the rather ordinary tale of first being permitted to enter it and then being pushed to leave it.

To be sure, Jewish writing by no means simply reflects the diasporic existence. Authors do retell the pains of being forced to leave a place or redraw the maps to capture the itineraries and the entailed vicissitudes of their forebears. But what is just as important to discern in this literature are the narrative modes that authors have conceived to articulate the experiences of displacement and deportation, of resettlement and return as fundamental notions of existential disruption. It goes without saying that the event of the Shoah and the series of acts of forced displacements preceding the annihilation of the European Jews have challenged authors to devise a language capable of at least pointing to the most extreme pain associated with the human condition. Most of the authors discussed in this volume are immigrants to France or the children of immigrants—a notion that hovers in the back of their narratives as a second layer of displaced experience, as a palimpsest that refers to the intersection of space and time characteristic of the Jewish experience. Their stories re-create the trajectories of Jewish lives whose point of departure was outside of France, often in the eastern parts of Europe; stories in which their families' arrival and settling in France, in Paris, can no longer be presented as the climactic point of their families' flight from antisemitism and persecution in the East. As Pierre Goldman (1944–1979) writes in his autobiographical account, *Souvenirs obscurs d'un juif polonais né en France* (Dim Memories of a Polish Jew Born in France, 1975): "My father was born (in 1909) into a poor family of Polish Jews. . . . At the age of fifteen he fled from antisemitism and poverty. He came to France because he had read a book by Victor Hugo, *Ninety-three*, translated into Yiddish. When he arrived in France, he was disappointed: it was not a country that really conformed to the ideals of 1789 and racism was still alive there" (Goldman, 1).

In the accounts of the authors covered in this volume, Paris—the birthplace of human rights and religious emancipation—no longer figures as the *locus amabilis* (place of delight) of a secular form of Judaism, a "Vilna on the Seine," as the capital of the European Republic of Letters, a city which—according to literary historian Pascale Casanova—has "neither borders nor boundaries, a universal homeland exempt from all professions of patriotism, a kingdom of literature set up in opposition to the ordinary laws of states, a transnational realm whose sole imperatives are those of art and literature: the universal republic of letters" (29).

French Jewish authors before the Shoah needed to understand that the flip side—or the dark side—of the French capital's universalism had long fueled a dynamic that didn't necessarily make it easier for Jewish authors to find their works accepted in a literary marketplace. The imperative of universalism tended to devalue—if not discredit—any accentuation of ethnic or religious particularism. They needed to learn that to become celebrated in this capital of cultural and literary emancipation, the Jewish immigrant writer might be allowed to enter as an immigrant, but hardly as a Jew who was not ready to pay the self-effacing price for Jewish emancipation. After the Shoah, Jewish authors had to tackle yet another difficulty of Jewish life in Paris, the City of Light, the City of Love: how does one describe *Paris, La Ville Lumière*, during the so-called *années obscures*, the dark years? Despite one's love for it, how does one pay tribute to a place that had expelled one's parents, grandparents, friends, and neighbors? How does one document in writing a memory that, for many decades, the city had tried to expel and to keep, as it were, outside of its own walls?

We find a preliminary answer to these queries in the work of Georges Perec (1936–1982), whose preoccupation with the notion of space expressed itself in a continuous series of experimental texts. According to the critic Derek Schilling, the very fact that Perec had never experienced a place that he could have called a family home led to his literary "multiplications" (Schilling, 130) of spaces he had—or may have—inhabited and that he scans, catalogs, locates, and lists in a futile attempt to ground his childhood and youth spatially. Before the deportation of his mother, Perec spent the first six years of his life in the 20th arrondissement, in an apartment in rue Vilin whose exact location Perec does not remember. His frequent returns to the street in the years after the war are motivated by his hope to return missing memories (Perec, 49), though he is "in any case convinced that it would do nothing to revive my memories" (48).

Perec's revisitations to the childhood home that he was not able to pinpoint exactly were part of a larger project titled *Les Lieux* (Places) in which he tried "to describe what happens over twelve years to a dozen places in Paris to which I am particularly attached for one reason or another" (48). His obsession with Parisian locales would eventually generate books and essays the very titles of which—*Lieux où j'ai dormi* (Places I Have Slept), *Tentative d'épuisement d'un lieu parisien* (Attempt at Exhausting a Place in Paris), *Journal d'un usager de l'espace* (Journal of a User of Space), *Les Espèces d'espaces* (Species of Spaces)—give away the hopelessness of finding in the city what had been lost in his memory: a space where his family could have established roots. Perec was sent away from Paris with a Red Cross convoy when he was six and his mother was murdered by the Nazis when he was nine. "My mother" he writes, "has no grave" (41).

Patrick Modiano shares Perec's insistence that the Jewish writer cannot "let go" of the need to scan the streets of Paris in search for the quotidian traces of her Jewish inhabitants. In *Dora Bruder*, Modiano describes the end of 1941 as "those dying weeks of the year [that] were the blackest, most claustrophobic period that Paris had experienced" (Modiano, 44). Modiano's formulation may serve as a good vantage point for my reading of the spatial dimensions with which authors such as Georges Perec, Patrick Modiano, Sarah Kofman, and Henri Raczymow inform their works. Modiano's words show that the so-called darkening of Paris is experienced spatially, a claustrophobic experience that reveals how the city—once open to everybody—was closing in on the Jews. Racist policies transformed the city into an *Umschlagplatz*, a holding place, that for her Jewish inhabitants soon turned into a "trap that is closing around you" amid "the feeling that the course of time is suspended" (48).

In the works of these authors, the tradition of French Jewish writing has come not to a screeching but a silent halt as Paris now is revealed as but another stopover in the itinerant experience of her Jewish denizens. In *Dora Bruder*, the Jewish writer feels as though he is "alone in making the link between Paris then and Paris now, alone in remembering all these details," remembering then-Paris as a site construed of "dark walls, themselves engulfed by the darkness of the curfew" (40).

To be sure, this observation must be read as a reference to the hiatus within the history of France and Paris, but in addition it needs to be understood as a comment on how Modiano's disruptive take figures as the solitary act of the Jewish writer who is alone in pointing to the "link between Paris then and Paris now." In this regard, Modiano's book emerges to challenge what the French cultural historian Henri Rousso has called the "Vichy syndrome"—France's difficulties in the postwar decades in properly addressing the period of collaboration by obscuring the memory of the victims of the Vichy regime.

Paris, for the biographer of Dora Bruder, can no longer be the cityscape that allows for the flâneur's encounter with the quotidian. The Jewish German philosopher Walter Benjamin, who in 1939 in the *Bibliothèque Nationale* was at work on his monumental *Arcades Project* [*Das Passagen-Werk*], had situated the figure of the flâneur in Paris of the nineteenth century. For Benjamin, the flâneur is the man of leisure who engages with the urban spaces of emerging capitalism (the Arcades standing as the temples of consumerism), acutely experiencing—like the poet Charles Baudelaire—its fragmentation and commodification. Modern urban experience provides a cacophony of discontinuous stimuli that the flâneur is capable of rendering aesthetically: the strolling artist succeeds in rendering the shock of the banal in aesthetic-eternal form.

While Baudelaire's shock may mark the beginning of modernity, the shock of the authors who search the city for the traces of their compatriots after the roundups points to a dimension of modernity that some of Benjamin's friends and critics have discussed as modernity's very extreme, others as its alter ego.

In any case, Modiano's Paris no longer is a place that can be strolled with the perceptive apparatus of the nineteenth century. Instead, it needs to be read, scanned, and mapped by the author as cartographer, detective, and historical researcher. Thus, the English-language editor of Modiano's book pushes its logic to one of its conclusions by printing the maps of the 12th and 18th arrondissements in the front matter of the translation, although the maps are but illusory aids as only a palimpsestic overlay of them would yield an understanding of the erasures in the city's urban memory.

> For the rupture of the Shoah has left its mark on the city: I remember experiencing for the first time that sense of emptiness that comes with the knowledge of what has been destroyed, razed to the ground. As yet, I was ignorant of the existence of Dora Bruder. Perhaps—in fact, I'm sure of it—she explored this zone that, for me, evokes secret lovers' trysts, pitiful moments of lost happiness. Here, reminders of the countryside still surfaced in the street names: Allée du Puits. Allée du Métro. Allée des Peupliers. Impasse des Chiens. (29)

The act of remembering the victims disrupts the evocations of quintessential Parisian tropes. Put differently, writing about Paris's antisemitic past constitutes a break in French literary history.

Walter Benjamin coined the term *"raumgewordene Vergangenheit"* (a past become space) (871) in one of his autobiographical texts that all bear the name of the city he called home in their titles: *Berlin Chronicle* and *Berlin Childhood around 1900*. The notion of a past turned into space was meant to capture how memories correspond with the topography of the places, the cities, that are associated with these memories. If places are storage containers of our memories, recollecting cannot be severed from the spatial: the memories of Dora Bruder can be found only in the streets, the places, and the buildings of Paris. The flâneur has been replaced by the archeologist who has to

> conduct himself like a man digging. Above all, he must not be afraid to return again and again to the same matter; to scatter it as one scatters earth, to turn it over as one turns over soil. For the "matter itself" is no more than the strata which yield their long-sought secrets only to the most meticulous investigation.

That is to say, they yield those images that, severed from all earlier associations, reside as treasures in the sober rooms of our later insights—like torsos in a collector's gallery. It is undoubtedly useful to plan excavations methodically. Yet no less indispensable is the cautious probing of the spade in the dark loam. And the man who merely makes an inventory of his findings, while failing to establish the exact location of where in today's ground the ancient treasures have been stored up, cheats himself of his richest prize. In this sense, for authentic memories, it is far less important that the investigator report on them than that he mark, quite precisely, the site where he gained possession of them. (*Dora Bruder*, 611)

Modiano's topographical obsession, the repetitive trajectories that lead so many of his books back to the same places of his upbringing as well as the associative rather than methodological manner with which he scans the Paris of the present for traces of the past are features that attest to the impossibility of severing the story of Dora from the story of the city that expelled her. *Dora Bruder* is first of all an acknowledgment that writing about the past needs to establish an accurate record for which "topographical precision" is tantamount. Modiano introduces his remarks on Cécile and Ernest Bruder's arrival in Paris in the following way:

Were Cécile and Ernest Bruder already living in the Avenue Liégard, Sevran, at the time of their marriage? Or in a hotel in Paris?

They are the sort of people who leave few traces. Virtually anonymous. Inseparable from those Paris streets, those suburban landscapes where, by chance, I discovered that they had lived. Often, what I know about them amounts to no more than a simple address. And such topographical precision contrasts with what we shall never know about their life—this blank, this mute block of the unknown. (20)

Topographical precision at times is the only narrative tool available to those telling the lost stories of the victims—hence Modiano's incessant insistence on locating addresses and listing street names. Street addresses abound in this and many others of his works though Modiano understands very well the futility of trying to geographically locate on the map of Paris the traces of people who vanished. His notion of literary realism is almost empiricist in nature. In his novel *Accident nocturne* (translated as *Paris Nocturne*), he has his narrator declare self-critically, "I probably attach too much importance to topography" (37). It is, however, rooted in the hope that the material, the physical world may provide testimony to the spiritual one: "It is said that premises retain some stamp, however faint, of their previous inhabitants" (21).

This reliance on physical coordinates goes hand in hand with what could be called a refusal of the psychological in *Dora Bruder*, as the narrator eschews the temptation to create psychological portraits about his subjects in the venerable tradition of French literary realism. "The children with Polish or Russian or Rumanian names who were forced to wear the yellow star, were so Parisian that they merged effortlessly into the facades, the apartment blocks, the sidewalks, the infinite shades of grey that belong to Paris alone" (114). With their disappearance, the narrator is left with the task of turning and returning to the sites of the city in which they used to dwell. The formulation of the "infinite shades of grey that belong to Paris alone" seems cast in the legacy of the Paris novel, a phrase one may expect to find, let's say, in Rainer Maria Rilke's *Notebooks of Malte Laurids Brigge* (1910). It is one of the few stamps, "however faint," of the topological tropes to which Modiano alludes, as if he wanted to remind his readers of the urban experiences that his victims did not live to enjoy.

The absence, the deportation, the annihilation of Jews changes the city—and their deaths estrange the survivor from it as well—which he now experiences as a dystopian site, a place that one might just as well call *Paris, la morte*:

> The city was deserted, as if to mark Dora's absence.
>
> Ever since, the Paris wherein I have tried to retrace her steps has remained as silent and deserted as it was on that day. I walk through empty streets. For me, they are always empty, even at dusk, during the rush-hour, when the crowds are hurrying towards the mouths of the metro. I think of her in spite of myself, sensing an echo of her presence in this neighborhood or that. The other evening, it was near the Gare du Nord. (119)

Modiano tries to trace the transient experiences of his subject against the backdrop of the changes in the urban topography whose spatial features, landmarks, and architectural characteristics the author presents toward the very end in the form of a catalogue: "The facades are rectangular, the windows square, the concrete the color of amnesia. The streetlamps throw out a cold light. Here and there, a decorative touch, some artificial flowers: a bench, a square, some trees. They have not been content with putting up a sign like that on the wall of Tourelles barracks: 'No filming or photography.' They have obliterated everything in order to build a sort of Swiss village in order that nobody, ever again, would question its neutrality" (113). This is one of the rare moments when the narrator's voice takes on an accusatory tone: Modiano tends to avoid both the sharp rhetoric of Émile Zola's *J'accuse* (I accuse, 1898) and the gripping lamentation by Albert Cohen's *Ô vous, frères humains* (Oh Human Brothers, 1972), as he does not consider these to be appropriate stylistic means of rendering the harrowing events he is narrating. The passage quoted above dryly posits a "they"—the ubiquitous pronoun standing in for the anonymous, faceless "Other" who is responsible for the willful erasure of anything that could point to their complicity in the genocide. "Amnesia" is a conceptual term introduced to a narrative that otherwise stays away from explanatory modes, whereas the image of the erection of "a sort of Swiss village" is very much part of the pattern that we have been discerning throughout Modiano's work, if not his oeuvre. The rebuilding of the area is anything but a normal part of urban rejuvenation; instead it is exhibited by Modiano as part of a strategy of spatially obliterating the past.

The "Swiss village" is a facade that distorts and displaces the previous stages of the site in order to conceal the traumata related to it. The gentrification of the street described by Modiano shows the city's psychic forces at work, rendering its past incomprehensible. One can discern in this process the power of a mechanism that Sigmund Freud called "screen memories"—the psyche's ability to hide traumatic experiences by creating memories in which the painful past has been displaced by more manageable figments of the past. Sarah Kofman deals with this defense mechanism from her very first book, *L'enfance de l'art: Une interprétation de l'esthétique freudienne* (*The Childhood of Art: An Interpretation of Freud's Aesthetics*), in which she offers an explanation that one can read as a direct reference to the municipal gentrification to which Modiano alludes when he comments on the fake Swiss facades that now conceal the city's horrific past: "Generally speaking, screen memories function as counterinvestments intended to maintain repression" (59). It may be worth mentioning as an aside that Kofman's reluctance to engage in the project of autobiographical writing goes back to her insight into the repressive force with which screen memories displace painful childhood memories. Critics have wondered whether important passages in her 1994 autobiographical story, *Rue Ordener Rue Labat*, that address the young Sarah's relationship to Mémé, the proselytizing Catholic surrogate mother, aren't precisely that: surrogate memories.

Georges Perec, too, is painfully aware of the fallacies involved in the remembrance of childhood memories and thus pushes himself to act as a scrutinizing editor of his own memories that he proofreads and annotates by adding, for example, footnotes to his autobiographical notes. Self-critiquing the only three memories he can produce about his early school experience in *W, or The Memory of Childhood*, he detects that one of them is simply false: "I wonder if this memory does not in fact conceal its precise opposite: not the memory of a medal torn off, but the memory of a star pinned on" (54).

The ability of screen memories to conceal their opposites is an irritant to the project of autobiographical writing precisely because it can serve as the catalyst for fiction. As such, it is complicit in the creation of a narrative form that generates overlapping images that at times are so stark they obscure underlying ones or of palimpsest in which the traces of the concealed image remains visible to the scrutinizing mind of the writer and, possibly, to the alert eye of the reader. Literary history and criticism offers the term *contaminatio* to help unlock some of the textual notions at work in these forms of superimposition. As a literary practice, *contaminatio* goes very far back in literary history and is associated with the works of the Roman dramatist Terence, who was accused by some of his contemporaries of "defiling" his plays by incorporating "foreign" literary materials and sources into his plays, thus "soiling" a standard and tradition celebrated as pure.

Interpreted as the grafting of parts of one's own texts by using features and quotations derived from other texts, *contaminatio* is at play in Modiano's first novel, *La Place de l'étoile*, in which Modiano uses the voices of some of the most repugnant antisemitic authors to sharpen the grotesque world of wartime and postwar Paris. Indeed, many a critic looked at Modiano's first novel as a kind of defilement of Jewish literature, a transgression of a literary *contrat social* that Modiano himself seems to have regretted in retrospect. *Contaminatio* is evident in *Dora Bruder* when he superimposes the fictitious path that the criminal Jean Valjean and his ward Cosette follow in Victor Hugo's *Les Misérables* onto the real cityscape of Paris of the early 1940s. Modiano pursues the imaginary trajectory outlined in one of the canonical pieces of French belles lettres to have it converge with the one researched by Modiano; they meet in a concrete space, the Saint-Cœur-de Marie school where Dora was a border (42). Documentary space appears superimposed onto imaginary space that in itself is a contamination of fictitious and real topographies. Bruno Chaouat has analyzed in considerable detail how Modiano superimposes Victor Hugo's *Les Misérables* onto his own *recherche du temps perdu*, a search for a time lost long ago. It thus suffices here to acknowledge yet another literary allusion that Modiano creates when referencing Edgar Allan Poe's "The Fall of the House of Usher," conjuring up a morbid setting of unspoken crimes that keep haunting a site the physical integrity of which has been deformed by what had happened within it.

There is yet another aspect of *Dora Bruder* that critics have difficulties explaining, yet make sense if seen as part of the larger dynamics of *contamination*: pushing this technique even further into the realm of the literary, Modiano populates, as it were, his account of his search with memorials to several non-Jewish German writers, such as Friedo Lampe and Felix Hartlaub. Their appearance in Modiano's account of the disappearance of the Jewish girl is part of a narrative move that interweaves texts—and authors—into a "memoryscape" (Sanyal) that—like the city of Paris—is host to what the Jewish philosopher Ernst Bloch once called the "simultaneity of the non-simultaneous." Modiano here applies *contaminatio* by pushing Bloch's concept from the temporal realm into the spatial one when he incorporates the memories of non-Jewish German writers whose disappearance from literary history Modiano acknowledges.

Although he explores various forms of intertextuality, Modiano seems to be aware that literary history provides little assistance in creating viable models for a text that sets out to articulate the horrors with which he is dealing. Neither the vernacular of Romanticism (Hugo) nor of the Gothic (Poe) can provide the language or the stylistics to capture the abyss of the Shoah. In this regard, Modiano's turn away from the provocative grotesque of his first novel, *La Place de l'étoile*, is an acknowledgment that a radical critique of the canon of forms and stylistic devices is needed to create a literature capable of rendering what pre-Shoah literary imagination could not even fathom.

To return to the multiple—or in Freud's term, *overdetermined*—meaning of the notion of *contamination*: aside from employing the literary mode of intertextuality, we see that the writers' portraits of wartime Paris reveal a space thoroughly contaminated by antisemitism. In Georges Perec's anti-autobiography, *W, or the Memory of Childhood*, while the author attempts to sort the figments and fragments of his childhood memories growing up in Paris by stating at the outset, "I have no childhood memories" (6), he curiously injects his biographical account with the "careful reconstruction of

a childhood fantasy about a land in thrall of the Olympic ideal"—a dystopian narrative of place that at the end of the book becomes discernible as
"the site of W. Pinochet's Fascists" (164) located in Tierra del Fuego. The
fragmented account of the author's wartime upbringing and the narrative
of the pandemonic community of sportsmanship turned totalitarian are,
according to Perec, "inextricably bound up with each other, as though neither could exist on its own, as though it was only their coming together,
the distant light they cast on each other, that could make apparent what
is never quite said in one, never quite said in the other, but said only in
their fragile overlapping" (n.p.).

Whereas Perec overlaps in the account of his *éducation juive* an imaginary space with a real, Parisian one, in his *Un cri sans voix*, Henri Raczymow
conceives of postwar Paris as a contaminated setting into which the past
of the Warsaw ghetto casts a dark and, in the end lethal, shadow. Where
the persecuted were once unable to find refuge, their children now live to
experience Paris as kind of "City of Usher."

Mathieu, the narrator, chronicles the life of his sister, Esther, against
the backdrop of a city that has been erasing the quarters once populated
by Jewish immigrants: "Those people had vanished, maybe into the smoke
of the gas chambers, or maybe into wealthier neighborhoods" (138). Won-
dering what Jewish life during the war may have looked like, he states, "In
those days you entered the café on rue Bisson. The tenants of the building
thought of the owners as their friends. All the tenants were Jews, because the
street was Jewish, as was the neighborhood, like in Warsaw. But the owners
of the café were French, 'real' French. During the war, as soon as the curfew
was enforced, Jews in the building would gather in the café behind closed
doors and play cards or dominoes. Like in Warsaw" (139). This refrain-like
phrase "Like in Warsaw" punctuates the life of Mathieu's sister, Esther, who
experiences postwar Paris as a site so contaminated by the antisemitic past
that it leaves her no space to live. Whereas Esther gets caught in the layers
of the past to a degree that she loses sight of the present, Mathieu does
the work of Walter Benjamin's archeologist, digging through the present to
find traces of the past: "But we were in Paris, not in Warsaw. In the long
run, the result was the same. But not in the same manner. Right, note the
manner. No question but that it was more neatly done in France" (149).

Intriguingly, at the very outset of his novel Raczymow explores how
the superimposition of a place of the past onto a site of the present has
also been employed as a strategy of antisemitism when he refers to the
media's treatment of Israel's 1982 Lebanon War. His narrator first recounts

the media reports, then Raczymow has him switch his tone to end his account on a note of sarcasm: "But one day the dead woman resurfaced. It was in the summer of 1982. The summer the Israeli defense army invaded southern Lebanon, engaged the Palestinian army in a merciless battle, and occupied West Beirut. The campaign was called 'Peace in Galilee.' Shortly afterward, the newspaper informed us that West Beirut was the exact replica of the Warsaw Ghetto. In the fall, however, the newspaper said that they had been slightly mistaken. There had been no genocide. And West Beirut had no connection to the Warsaw Ghetto between 1940 and 1943. None whatsoever. So sorry" (2). Later in the book, a whole section is devoted to the tenuous equation between "West Beirut—Warsaw Ghetto" (100), accentuating the sarcastic note on which the introductory passage ends even further.

> Well, the newspapers are very cultured! They know their history. Beirut, where the PLO army was entrenched, was like the Warsaw Ghetto. That's obvious, indeed. Soon they refined it: they stopped saying "like." They eliminated the "like." Beirut was the Warsaw Ghetto. Not like. Was.
>
> Esther was dead, and Mathieu realized it that summer when the Israeli army went into Lebanon. And when the newspaper spoke of the ghetto. There were even Jews who spoke of the ghetto. Who omitted *like*. That was the most unbearable part, these Jews serving as handle for the steel as, that same ax that would strike them, that already was striking them that summer, and meanwhile they yelled with the others, Israel = Nazi! (100)

This admonition is uttered in no uncertain terms; what in the first instance looked like a sarcastic detection of antisemitism in the guise of anti-Israelism here appears as a strong critique of failure: even some Jews appear to have given into what the narrator identifies as anti-Zionist propaganda.

What is of interest to us here is the author's narrative stance against contaminative fallacies that would continue a pattern of spatial superimpositions that have prevented Esther from finding, from living in her own "place" (201).

I can only sketch out in this context how Modiano—in *La Place de l'étoile*—pushes the narrative potential of *contaminatio* to an extreme by going far beyond the numerous allusions to the writings of French antisemitic authors. Modiano's radical move superimposes wartime Paris onto postwar Tel Aviv that looks very much like Nazi Germany. Tel Aviv features "penal kibbutz" (104) where Jews of European background are being disciplined and where their literary canon is being burned. Clad in concentration camp–like garb, they are summoned to a replica of Paris's central Gestapo office at 93 rue Lauriston.

To conclude my reading, I would like to return to Henri Raczymow's novel *Un Cri Sans Voix*. The choice of words that the narrator uses at the very end to express his hope for the future of his own son points once more, one last time, to the perils associated with the tendency of conflating spaces that ought to remain separate. Standing between his son and the war, between the offspring and his ancestors, the narrator postulates, will be "an interval of space that could protect him as from a horrible taint" (204).

In referencing the biblical narrative of Esther, Raczymow demonstrably "contaminates" his secular text with references to Hebrew Scripture. Yet, the reader will close his book with the impression of resignation that Gershom Scholem gathered when reading the great writer S. J. Agnon: "The light of the Torah does not suffice to warm a frozen heart" (106, my translation).

Bibliography

Benjamin, Walter. "Berlin Chronicle." In *Selected Writings*. Vol. 2, edited by Michael W. Jennings. Translated by Rodney Livingstone et al. Cambridge, MA: Belknap Press of Harvard University Press, 1999.

———. "Arcades." In *The Arcades Project*, translated by Howard Eiland and Kevin McLaughlin. Cambridge, MA: Belknap Press of Harvard University Press, 2002.

Casanova, Pascale. *The World Republic of Letters*. Translated by M. B. DeBevoise. Cambridge, MA: Harvard University Press, 2004.

Chaouat, Bruno. "Urban and Literary Palimpsests in *Dora* and *Un cri sans voix*." Paris in Post-war Jewish Literary Memory: International Symposium, 24 May 2016, York University, Toronto. Unpublished symposium paper.

Cohen, Albert. *Ô vous, frères humains*. Paris: Gallimard, 1972.

Goldman, Pierre. *Dim Memories of a Polish Jew Born in France*. Translated by Joan Pinkham. New York: Viking Press, 1977.

Hugo, Victor. *Les Misérables*. Translated by Christine Donougher. London: Penguin, 2013.

Kofman, Sarah. *The Childhood of Art: An Interpretation of Freud's Aesthetics*. Translated by Winifred Woodhall. New York: Columbia Press, 1988.

———. *Rue Ordener Rue Labat*. Translated by Ann Smock. Lincoln, NE: University of Nebraska Press, 1994.

Modiano, Patrick. *Dora Bruder.* Translated by Joanna Kilmartin. Berkeley: University of California Press, 1999.

————. *Paris Nocturne.* Translated by Phoebe Weston-Evans. New Haven: Yale University Press, 2015.

————. *La Place de l'étoile.* In *The Occupation Trilogy.* Translated by Frank Wynne. New York and London: Bloomsbury, 2015.

Perec, Georges, *W, or the Memory of Childhood.* Translated by David Bellos. Boston: Godine, 1988.

Raczymow, Henri. *Writing the Book of Esther.* Translated by Dori Katz. New York: Holmes & Meier, 1995.

Rilke, Rainer Maria. *Notebooks of Malte Laurids Brigge.* Translated by Michael Hulse. London: Penguin, 2009.

Rousso, Henri. *The Vichy Syndrome: History and Memory in France since 1944.* Translated by Arthur Goldhammer. Cambridge, MA: Harvard University Press, 1994.

Sanyal, Debarati. *Memory and Complicity: Migrations of Holocaust Remembrance.* New York: Fordham University Press, 2015.

Schilling, Derek. *Mémoires du quotidien: Les Lieux de Perec.* Villeneuve-d'Ascq: Presses Universitaires du Septentrion, 2006.

Scholem, Gershom. "S. J. Agnon: Der letzte hebräische Klassiker?" *Judaica* 2 (1970).

12

Algerian Echoes in Modiano's and Perec's Cityscapes of Holocaust Memory

SARAH HAMMERSCHLAG

Given its shattering impact on our conception of the twentieth century, it is not surprising that the iconic images, moral categories, and political labels of World War II resonated across France's later conflicts and colored the representation and moral and political judgments of these events.

During the Algerian War (1954–1962), symbols of the World War II conflict were consistently recycled to reference the later conflict. Already in 1956, the anticolonial activist André Mandouze pointed to the ironic parallels and the "unlearned Nazi lessons of the past." The irony was particularly acute in the discussions surrounding the French army's use of torture and excessive force against the Front de Libération Nationale, the leading force of Algeria's revolutionary opposition, and those who aided its cause. Sartre, responding to Henri Alleg's 1958 book on French paratroopers' use of torture in Algeria, *The Question*, wrote in his essay "Une Victoire" that, "Fifteen years were enough to turn the victims into executioners." The term *fascist* was used not only to refer to the L'Organization Armée Secrete, the right-wing French paramilitary offshoot willing to go to any lengths to prevent Algeria's independence from France, but as a diagnosis of France's conduct in the war. The rhetorical force of the term in these conflicts cannot be divorced from its ability to conjure up the resonance of the 1930s and

1940s. The Algerian War, in its power to reverse the moral status of the French from victim to aggressor, at once remobilized the overly simplistic and monolithic heroic images of France as a nation of resistance and highlighted the instability of the mythology of good and evil already building up around the conflict. The Algerian War, Sartre wrote in 1958, revealed France's capacity to be seized in the "grip of violent and anonymous hatred": "Hitler was only a forerunner."

At the same time, the deployment of the moral categories of World War II to conceptualize the colonial conflicts of the 1950s and 1960s troubled some Jewish intellectuals. The French Jewish philosopher Emmanuel Levinas, for example, voiced his concerns in 1961 that the underdeveloped "hordes" from Africa and Asia were pushing Jews and Christians to the margins of history. Even as he published heavily on political matters during the years of the conflict, he notoriously resisted addressing the plight of the Algerians. Their conflict appears only by oblique reference and as a site of contrast with the Jews, who, unlike victims of racism and imperialism, he writes, were "without a world." Such attitudes were part of a nascent anxiety to protect the uniqueness of the Holocaust, to resist comparison, and sometimes even historical explanation. Claude Lanzmann referred to the Holocaust as "an abyss that will never be bridged," and others such as Elie Wiesel and Emil Fackenheim constructed theologies to reflect on its mystery and incomprehensibility, treating the event itself with the kind of awe traditionally reserved for the divine.

In both cases—the case of those who used the imagery to point to ironic parallels and the case of those who insisted on emphasizing the contrast—the symbolic status of World War II was already in play a decade after it had ended, even if the Holocaust had not yet developed the cultural status that it would in later decades. By now we can largely concede that its invocation in relation to later conflicts often serves a kind of mythologizing function, a means to judge these events against the backdrop of pure political evil.

Thus, the Holocaust becomes the standard by which other events are judged. As a number of scholars have noted, in these cases and also in arguments for the uniqueness of the Holocaust, the Holocaust and the events surrounding it develop a quasi-religious status. But memory doesn't only operate in one direction. Michael Rothberg's concept of multidirectional memory, a concept he develops to counter the competitive streak in Holocaust memorialization, reminds us that to think about the relationship between the Holocaust and later historical events, we must consider the impact of these later events on our memorialization of the Holocaust, and see how its emergence is sparked by the returning specter of state-sponsored violence. For Rothberg, the nexus between the Algerian War and Holocaust memory is particularly fruitful because of the coincidence between the conflict and a shift in the memorialization of World War II in France brought on by the proliferation of media representations that focused attention first on the Nazi concentration camps with the release of *Night and Fog* (*Nuit et brouillard*) in 1956 and then, in particular, on the genocide of the Jews with the television broadcast of the Eichmann trial in 1961. Rothberg himself effectively shows, particularly through an analysis of Charlotte Delbo's works *Les Belles lettres* in 1961 and *Auschwitz and After* in 1965, that the juxtaposition of the Algerian War with the emergence of Holocaust memory can be read as a kind of dialogue in texts from the era, with each informing the representation of the other.

It would hardly be surprising then if in the works of memory we are considering in this volume, most written by authors who came of age during the Algerian conflict, there were traces of the impact of the later conflict in their representations, especially when, for so many, the act of writing an account of the impact of the war on their own lives means finding a way to narrate its inaccessibility. And yet references to the Algerian conflict in these volumes are so few that they might seem easy enough to dismiss. And yet I want to suggest that their lack of explicit presence is not in fact a sign of their insignificance. For those writers of the 1.5 generation, as Susan Suleiman has dubbed them, or second-generation writers, later events nonetheless inflect and alter our perception of the earlier one. The very spatialization of memory in all of these works, for which Paris is a privileged locus, allows for the inflection of the colonial conflict onto France's World War II involvement. Space, as Modiano shows in *Dora Bruder* and elsewhere, often serves that very purpose for memory, allowing for the constellation of multiple historical moments whose spatial coincidence provides a means of linkage. This is not to suggest that the Algerian War is necessarily the privileged reference point for any of the texts considered in this volume, but, as a later military conflict, in at least the two texts I consider in this chapter, Modiano's *Dora Bruder* and Georges Perec's *W*, images and events of the Algerian War directly impact the narrators of our texts, inflecting their own efforts at memorialization in a manner opposed to the examples with which I opened.

To put this in the most concrete of terms: there are no Nazis in either text but there are still army barracks and militarized zones. In neighborhoods where Jews once lived there are now Portuguese and African immigrant workers, new displaced persons, new stories of immigration, struggle, and survival. The effects of these displacements and remainders are not only that the past weighs on the present, but also that the writers' present frames and colors their access to the past and thus ours as readers.

Modiano

In *Dora Bruder* the constellation between Algeria and the wartime story of Dora's disappearance shows up only in the first couple of pages, sandwiched between memories that the address of Dora's residence invokes for Modiano: the memory of traveling to the flea market at La Porte de Clignancourt, and a later one, from January 1965, of frequenting a nearby café and the neighboring cinema because of a girlfriend who lives in the neighborhood. In between these snapshots Modiano describes seeing "*les gardes mobiles*" (riot police), "because of the situation in Algeria" at the corner of Bruder's address in May 1958 (4). At the moment of the military coup in Algiers that brought De Gaulle back to power, these guards were in Paris to suppress French demonstrations. While it is a fleeting image, one that is not explicitly re-invoked elsewhere in the book, it introduces an important theme that repeatedly reemerges in the work: sites of our quotidian activity, where we might one day enjoy a meal or see a movie, are at the same time locations of unseen or forgotten violence. Additional references to France's colonial history and power populate the work, references that invoke the Algerian war by way of France's colonial past. There are the images of the Clignacourt barracks, right down the street from Bruder's apartment—buildings, which Modiano reports, housed colonial troops. This colonial history is also connected to the Bruders, as Ernest Bruder was a serviceman in a colonial conflict, fighting in Morocco in the 1920s to suppress native rebellion.

Then there are the colonial infantry barracks in which Dora is herself held, near Porte de Lilas, at 11 Boulevard Mortier, Tourelles, that served as an internment camp during the war. These barracks communicate their military history but not their wartime role as an internment camp for Jews. The plaque on the external wall reads, "Military Zone, Filming or Photography Prohibited" (109). The empty barracks are explicitly a symbol for Modiano of forgetting and emptiness, present but incommunicative, a faint magnetic field, but with no pendulum, he writes, to indicate their significance. At the same time these military edifices are one of the very concrete means by which Modiano is connected to Bruder's experience.

Born in 1945, Modiano is too young, unlike Perec, to have actually participated in the Algerian war, but as the opening reference to the military police reveals, the images of this later conflict are the war images to which he is most proximately connected, the reference for which the fear of army barracks is most intimately tied. The military and police that Modiano witnessed, whether on television or via the antiriot police in Paris, were French.

They were also French for Dora Bruder herself as the text reveals as it uncovers layer after layer of constraint that impacted her. From her first escape from Saint-Cœur de Marie to her internment at Tourelles, the path that she took was mediated by French institutions, French procedures, and French functionaries. One of the striking features of the research that Modiano conducts is that it is largely through the record of such policies and the reports of such institutions that Modiano is able to locate her shifting whereabouts. The very forces of her constraint are the means of his access to her story. For Modiano these are ironically also the means by which she is protected from view and thus one source of her mystery. She can only be seized and known by the records of the institutions that detained her, the forces that left her personhood untouched, even as they were capable of destroying her life. In their pairing, both the regulatory forces and the secrecy of what they cannot touch, provide the site of alliance between her experience and his.

One of the most personal stories that Modiano tells in *Dora Bruder* concerns the threat of his military conscription. But even in its telling we learn almost nothing about Modiano, almost nothing of his resentments or his internal conflicts, almost nothing but the facts. What he remembers of his ride to the police station is the path through Paris's streets. The streets are evoked clearly enough to produce a map, but, of his own emotion, we hear only of his surprise that his father showed no reticence to his being taken in a "Black Maria," a police van the French term for which, *panier à salade*, evokes its barred windows (51). That this is Modiano's story rather than Dora Bruder's seems to provide us no further access. Here, too, the image of the barracks returns. The last time that Modiano ever saw his father, he tells us, is when he hid his son's military papers to try to have him carted off to the barracks of Reuilly. The Algerian War had ended, but only the previous year.

By the book's end, military barracks have been evoked nearly twenty times. And in their recurring image the distinction between perpetrator and victim of violence, army officer and camp detainee, seems less important than the form of the barracks themselves, the edifice as a symbol of the cold hard mechanisms of violence the presence of which Modiano encounters as the gravity of a past that remains inaccessible but leaves its locations charged. The barracks serve as a spatial means, a constellating device to reveal the echo and refraction of force across time.

Unlike the function of the references to World War II that serve to index other conflicts by the war's almost mythological coordinates of good and evil, in Modiano's text, the spatialization of memory functions also to introduce a reverse vector of influence, so that the representation of World War II is mediated by the later French conflict. Instead of a temporal axis, organized by a before and after in which an invocation of the resistance can serve as an ideal, the standard by which other actions can be judged, in this text we have the representation of networks of force through space, a technique that allows multiple events in time to signify simultaneously. Consequently, the issue of motive and responsibility seems no longer to be the key question.

There are no heroes in Modiano's book but there are also no perpetrators. If one of the functions of the invocation of World War II during the Algerian War was to make clear who played what role, who was the bad guy and who the good, this black-and-white picture is complicated in Modiano's work. In his overlaying of historical moments tied together by a spatial overlap, what appears is a topographical map in which the hills and valleys demarcate sites inflected by violence. Although their coordinates may be buried, military zones are revealed and their effects radiate outward, not only via the signs on the buildings but in the behavior of the actors— even as these actors are neither characters nor agents. This is not to say that their humanity is in question, only that for those like Dora, or even Modiano's father, the language of either motive or responsibility cannot be invoked. Modiano has managed to construct an account of his search for both figures—one directly and the other obliquely—such that the language by which we normally assess character, language usually so instrumental to narrative, seems, if not irrelevant, then utterly inaccessible.

Perec

In Perec's novel, *W*, if a novel is indeed what we can call it, space is an issue as well, but not geographic space as much as that of Perec's own mind, a space that like Modiano's has the capacity to reorganize our temporal framework, to disregard the logic of before and after, fiction and nonfiction, truth and illusion. In *W, or the Memory of Childhood*, the name Algeria appears only once and it is in the context of a fiction, not the fiction of his own narrative but a description of Alexander Dumas's *Twenty Years After*. The place name appears merely as the location in which the character Raoul falls (144). Nonetheless, even when not invoked by name, the conflict in Algeria is present as a kind of spectral hinge connecting the fictional account of Tierra del Fuego, the island of Olympiads, Gaspard Winkler's tale, with the accounts of Perec's own childhood.

Of the concrete details we know about Winkler, one of the most prominent is that he was in the army and deserted. As the image of the letter *W* reminds us, there is a doubling *and* a conjunction between the two narratives, and the conjunction emerges explicitly in the details that Winkler and Perec are both orphaned and both served in the military, details that are themselves linked. While the time frame of Winkler's service is obscure, Perec's military service, we know, was during the Algerian War. Winkler, Perec's alter ego, deserts the army. It is for this reason that, when he receives the letter from Otto Apfelstahl demanding a meeting, he is fearful that the matter concerns repercussions for this act, which it does, though not as he anticipated. In the initial telling we are not told explicitly that Winkler took an assumed identity when he deserted. Once he receives the letter, Winkler reports that those who helped him did not know his original name. Apfelstahl's account suggests moreover that his taking of a new identity is directly linked to the story of the real Gaspard Winkler, whose shipwreck has motivated their meeting and thus motivates Winkler's journey to the isles of Tierra del Fuego.

Of Perec we know more concretely that in 1958, "by chance, military service briefly made a parachutist of me" (55). The date alone situates him within the time frame of active duty in Algeria. But this is not relayed as a key insight for Perec's story. While in Winkler's tale his military service and desertion is the event that puts his story in motion, in the autobiographical section of *W* the detail of Perec's career as a paratrooper is given only in the service of decoding his own memory of his evacuation from Paris during the war. "A triple theme runs through this memory: parachute, arm in a sling, hernia bandage: it suggests suspension, support, almost artificial limbs," he writes (55). The prosthetic, it turns out, is the falsified memory itself. The parachute appears in the image of Charlie Chaplin from an issue of *Charlie* that he remembers his mother having bought him for the journey; on the cover Chaplin is depicted jumping with a parachute. In Perec's memory he, Perec, has his arm in a sling, pretending to be wounded because he was being evacuated and the Red Cross evacuated the wounded. He also associates this memory with bandages and an operation. According to his aunt Esther, these are both fabrications. He was evacuated by the Red Cross because he was a war orphan, son of a soldier who died in service. As for the operation, this seems to be a transposition from either later or earlier. Perec includes the fact of his own experience as a paratrooper to explain that these details may have functioned metaphorically to describe the experience of free fall and suspension. The later experience clarifies for him what it was to be "plunged into nothingness, all the threads broken." What he leaves out is the way in which his own military experience repeated the theme of exemption and thus the possibility that the prosthetic memory does not concern the falsified injury but perhaps the image of the parachuting Charlie. David Bellos has in fact shown that the issue of *Charlie* must have been an imposition, for not only were images of Charlie Chaplin banned in Nazi-occupied Europe after the 1940 release of *The Great Dictator*, the image, which does exist, is from a 1935 copy of the magazine that wasn't re-released until 1945 (Bellos, 58).

From David Bellos's biography we also know that there is more of an analogy between the story of Perec's military experience and the story of his evacuation from Paris than *W* itself reveals. Perec, Bellos reports, was spared the reality of active combat in Algeria as a consequence—*once again*—of his own father's death in the service of France. There is thus something of a palimpsest in the very image that Perec attributes to his childhood memory, two moments in which his own father's death spared him a similar fate. Not only is the image of the parachuting Charlie a much later addition, it layers his own experience of missing military combat, merely playing at being a soldier, onto the childhood experience of evacuation. Knowledge of Perec's own biography allows us to consider the possibility that Perec himself is the parachuting Charlie in that image, a caricatured depiction of military engagement, an actor playing the part of the soldier. At the time that the exemption came through in 1958 Perec wrote, "I am in despair . . . I am the executioner" (185). The guilt of surviving the first time passes over onto the guilt of surviving a second time. The irony is that by being spared active duty, he does not have to be an executioner, yet the very experience of being spared lays on him the experience of guilt.

That said, life in training nonetheless gave him some insight into life in the barracks, even, perhaps into the world he imagined for the Olympiads "at the end of the world." As Bellos reports, for eight weeks "he was made to run, crawl, jump and clamber over obstacles, carry stones from one end of the camp to another and then back again" (185). And although he did not desert, at the moment when it seemed that the paratroopers would support pro-Gaullist insurgents, he declared, "if it is a civil war, I'll desert" (188). But this reality too he was spared.

To say that in 1958—at the moment of a major political crisis in France, at the center of the Algerian War—we have a kind of hinge between Perec's two accounts, between the fiction and the autobiography, is itself perhaps too simplistic. But in this moment we have both a clear site of proximity between Winkler and Perec, an experience that might even seem to serve as the navel for both accounts, in which Perec was once again spared the fate of his father by virtue of his father's death, a moment in which Perec had referred to himself as an executioner, and the site, coming just at the end of part 1, where the very distinction between fiction and autobiography begins to collapse.

From this point forward in the "autobiography," the memories that Perec shares become increasingly suspect, "fleeting, persistent, trivial, burdensome—but there is nothing that binds them together" (68). A few pages later the story of Gaspard Winkler gives way to the ethnographic account of the island of Olympiads, a fantasy that proves consonant with the reality of the concentrationary universe.

Bellos reports that in writing *W*, Perec wanted to write a book that unraveled but worked nonetheless (550). We have seen how its pretensions fray and how the untold story of Perec's own experience as a paratrooper may even function as a knot in its unraveling, but it remains to be said how the text works. It is compelling to argue that the book's "work" is a kind of psychoanalytic memory work. Perec's guilt for having avoided active military service on account of his father produces the spectral reproduction of a fantasy of what he had been spared, in the description of the Olympiad Island produced from the standpoint of the witness. But for the text to "work," it must also function rhetorically, must work on the expectations of the reader. Here again I want to consider how the work done in this text can be contrasted with the version of overlap between the war in Algeria and World War II with which we commenced.

In the two cases with which I opened, I considered two forms by which World War II served as an index for later events, in particular for the war in Algeria. In one version, its vocabulary and images become a means for invoking the specter of evil and the danger of its repetition. In the other, the danger itself is in comparison, in losing the singularity of the genocide of the Jews by virtue of its serving a comparative function. In the case of Modiano's text, I argued for an account of memory that avoids both these temptations—providing instead a spatialization of memory that in its capacity to layer events in one setting, into a kind of palimpsest, shifts the moral function from one of motive and responsibility to one that demands of both Modiano and the reader a practice of attention in which both writer and reader learn to see the impact of force in the mundane and also to recognize their complicity in these forces, even as they serve as the source of access to Bruder's story. In *W* Perec manages something similar though by very different means, that is to say he implicates the reader in the violence described but eschews the form of historical comparison just as he refuses to fully distinguish between historical events that belong to one period versus another or to make clear the lines between fantasy and reality.

As a setting produced by the insistent layering of restrictions, the Island of Olympiads is the strange counterpart to his own missed encounter with death as a consequence of his father's own death, a childhood fantasy in which the specter of death is pervasive, in which the imagination produces an uncanny rendering of reality. The Island of Olympiads, like Perec's novel *La Disparition*, written entirely without the letter e, is an experiment in thinking through the consequences of restraint, multiplied exponentially. As the account of the Olympiads progresses, there is no narrative, no temporal horizon at all, rather it proceeds not by telling a story but by detailing the camp's restrictions, that is to say, by adding rules to the play. As a consequence, if there is a progression, it is in the perception of the reader as she progresses from curiosity and interest in this land of athletic contests and festivals toward a recognition of the horror entailed in these games. It is a passage that by virtue of its unfolding creates a sense of complicity between the reader and the horrors described as she realizes that they have been there all along, undergirding the entertaining and delightful features of the island but tacitly. This account becomes uncanny as the increase in horror coincides with a claim for its pervasive logic. One cannot explain the life of the Olympiads to the novice, Perec writes, because it is not

> a nightmare, not something he will suddenly wake up from. . . .
> How can you explain that this is life, real life, this is what there'll
> be every day, this is what there is, and nothing else, that it's
> pointless to believe in something else, that it's not even worth
> your time pretending to believe there must be something behind

it, or beneath it, or above it. That's what there is, and that's all. There are competitions every day, where you Win or Lose. You have to fight to live. There is no alternative. It is not possible to close your eyes to it, it is not possible to say no. . . . There is this, there's what you've seen and now and again it will be less horrible than what you've seen and now and again it will be much more horrible than what you've seen. But wherever you turn your eyes, that's what you'll see, you will not see anything else, and that is the only thing that will turn out to be true. (139)

Like Jorge Luis Borges's story "The Babylonian Lottery" in which the increase in conditions for playing the lottery erodes the distinction between the contest and everyday life, in Perec's novel the mechanism of the Olympiad Island is shown not only to be a reproduction of the concentrationary universe, as Perec himself reveals, but a fantasy that in its structure, if not its magnitude, reveals something about the very nature of civilized life in its multiplication of rules and restrictions that distinguish one group from another. These rules produce the "natural" privilege of one group over another and then reinforce the distinctions, weakening the disadvantaged and strengthening the advantaged, producing a surface reality of health and hygiene undergirded by a law that parcels out suffering and in so doing produces concepts of natural advantage and disadvantage, success and failure.

To put it another way, the description of the Olympiad Island functions as a parable that allows us to conceive of civilized life itself by the very terms of the concentrationary universe.

The book then "works" by telling two stories. One story works on a historical axis, in which the absent father appears only as a site of unrecoverable loss, which at the same time exempts Perec from the concentrationary universe, yet renders him unable to develop the story of his own past, leaving him without a grammar for assembling it into order. The other is on a spatial or structural axis in which order is all that he has, a code, a set of rules out of which he produces a timeless parable, in which the Holocaust casts a ubiquitous shadow. It is produced itself from the symbolic universe that pervaded his childhood, but also one that is universal, out of the very

sign of multiplication and sorting (the X axis), the sign of the mathematical unknown and finally the starting point for a geometrical fantasy, whose basic figure is the double V, and whose complex convolutions trace out the major symbols of my childhood: two Vs joined tip to tip make the shape of an X; by extending the branches of the X by perpendicular segments of equal length, you obtain the swastika . . . placing two pairs of Vs head to tail produces a figure (XX) whose branches only need to be joined horizontally to make a star of David. . . . In the same line of thinking, I remember being struck by the fact that Charlie Chaplin, in *The Great Dictator*, replaced the swastika with a figure that was identical, in terms of its segments, having the shape of a pair of overlapping Xs. (77)

A figure of a parody, Charlie's Xs are perhaps closest to Perec's *W*. Both use the symbolic elements that make up both the Star of David and the swastika and make of it an alternative symbol, whose symbolic refractions are both historically specific and universal. The consonance between these two configurations adds another layer of meaning to the image of the parachuting Charlie on the day of Perec's evacuation. We can now see in this image another palimpsest or an instance of condensation, to use the Freudian term for the dream function in which a single image can carry multiple and variant symbolic content—a memory/fantasy in which the young child carries with him an image of his later self as parody of a soldier, a paratrooper whose performance is occasioned by his exclusion from military action. We might even read that copy of *Charlie* as a stand-in for *W* itself, in which case the boy is carrying a symbol of his own later literary production, a production occasioned by the irretrievable loss of the father. That image then becomes the navel for the work itself.

I want to suggest, in closing, that despite vast differences in style and method, what Perec's and Modiano's literary works share in common is an approach to Holocaust memory that manages to evoke the loss and the violence of the war and to implicate us in its horrors. Each allows us to sense its refractions across later historical conflicts. Yet through a focus on the spatiality of memory, a form that itself troubles our notions of linear time and thus the very concepts of responsibility and blame consistent with such a concept of time, these literary works allow us to think about the significance of the catastrophe in conjunction with France's later colonial conflict in ways that transcend the forms of repetition and competition, those frames that have so consistently dominated our sense of what it means to remember the Holocaust and to compare it to other events.

Bibliography

Azouvi, François. *Le Mythe du Grand Silence: Auschwitz, les Francais, la mémoire.* Paris: Fayard, 2012.

Bellos, David. *Georges Perec: A Life in Words.* New York: Random House, 2010.

Kritzman, Lawrence, ed. *Auschwitz and After: Race, Culture and "the Jewish Question" in France.* New York: Routledge, 1995.

Le Sueur, James D. *Uncivil War: Intellectuals and Identity Politics during the Decolonialization of Algeria.* Philadelphia: University of Pennsylvania Press, 2001.

Perec, Georges. *A Void.* Translated by Gilbert Adair. Jaffrey: David Godine, 2005.

Rothberg, Michael. *Multidirectional Memory: Remembering the Holocaust in the Age of Decolonialization.* Stanford, CA: Stanford University Press, 2009.

Sartre, Jean-Paul. Introduction to Henri Alleg, *La Question.* Paris: Minuit, 1958.

———. "Une Victoire." *L'Express* (March 6, 1958).

Suleiman, Susan. *Crises of Memory and the Second World War.* Cambridge: Harvard University Press, 2006.

Tufail, Burhan. "Oulipian Grammatology: La règle du Jeu." In *The French Connections of Jacques Derrida,* edited by Julian Wolfreys, John Brannigan, and Ruth Robbins. Albany: State University of New York Press, 1999.

PART 5   PAST IMPERFECT

The last section of this collection of essays, "Past Imperfect," is a play on words that echoes the idea that the past as such is irretrievably lost, but that the history of France remains an unfinished business. Nelly Wolf offers a reading of Perec's *W, or the Childhood Memory* and *En Remontant la rue Vilin* as expressions of a feeling of radical loss. Neither Perec's returning to places that once were home to his family, nor his intense scrutiny of his own memory can bring a reliable version of his story. Wolf argues that the feeling of loss is so profound that Perec's obsession with the past translates into his other novels: thus in *Things: A Story of the Sixties* the main characters do not follow the flow of consumerism but rather tirelessly curate an artful version of the past. In both cases, the city is as indifferent and as empty as it probably appeared to little Georges when, on returning to Paris in 1944, he found out that his entire family was gone.

Sara Horowitz explores postwar Paris as not only the home of the French Jewish intelligentsia but also, fleetingly, as a hub for the Yiddish belles lettres. In her analysis of Abraham Sutzkever's poetry, Horowitz contemplates his encounter with Paris, his hopes for the future, and his yearning for home. For Horowitz, Sutzkever's generation of Jewish exiles was very different from that of Benjamin's flâneur; their presence in Paris was the result of historically unprecedented violence that all but obliterated the Jews of Europe, the majority of whom spoke Yiddish. Yet, in the 1950s, Jews are still described in terms of the trope of indelible otherness that characterizes a strain of European discourse. Yiddish, then, comes to represent textually the unassimilable. It is the symbol for the endurance of the traumatic past, the instability of home, and the unspeakability of the deportation and genocide of the Jews, which could be brought into public discourse only decades after the war.

With Susan Suleiman's consideration of the familial legacy of Irène Némirovsky's *Suite française* we come full circle. In "The Afterlife of Irène Némirovsky's *Suite française*," Suleiman probes the effect of Némirovsky's life and literary legacy on her daughters, Denise Epstein Dauplé and Elisabeth Gille, and their children. The novel points back to the dark years of the German Occupation of Paris, while its posthumous publication and complicated reception evokes long-standing questions about Frenchness, Jewishness, secularity, ethics, and belonging in postwar Paris. Although Némirovsky's novel spans only the first year of the Nazi invasion, as ordinary Parisians contend with the challenges of occupation, the author's diminished circumstances as a Jewish, foreign-born writer, the ambiguities of her choices, and her eventual murder at Auschwitz, bring the Holocaust into later readings of the work.

13

Perec's Ghost City

NELLY WOLF

Georges Perec was born on March 7, 1936, in Paris, on rue de l'Atlas, in the 19th arrondissement. Until the age of six he lived with his family on rue Vilin, in the 20th arrondissement, a district also known as Belleville. Perec's mother, Cyrla, had arrived in Paris as a child with her family in 1922. Perec's father, Icek, born in 1909, came to Paris as a young man in 1926, a few months before his parents, David and Rosa, and five years after his elder sister, Esther, who was already living there with her husband, David Bienenfeld. Both sides of the family had emigrated from Poland.

Belleville in the 1930s was a kind of *shtetl*, and it remained so even after the war until the end of the 1950s, when the Jewish Ashkenazi population was progressively replaced by Sephardic Jews fleeing from Algeria and other North African countries, and by Arab, African, and Asian migrants. In Belleville's often miserable and overcrowded tenements gathered working-class Jews, Jewish craftsmen and shopkeepers, and poor Jews from eastern Europe who had emigrated in search of a better life. A large part of the district has been classified as *îlot insalubre*, an unhealthy (insalubrious) neighborhood, by the city authorities as early as the beginning of the twentieth century. It was nevertheless not a ghetto in the sense of being a Jewish monocultural neighborhood, as Ivan Jablonka points out in his *History of the Grandparents I Never Had.*

Even though the 20th arrondissement was one of the most Jewish areas of Paris in the 1930s, right up there with the 18th (8,500 Jews) but behind the 11th (more than 13,000), the Belleville-Ménilmontant neighborhood was nothing like a ghetto; rather, it was a patchwork of ethnicities, a tower of Babel spread over three square miles. Born-and-bred Parisians rubbed shoulders with freshly arrived provincials, such as our hotel owner from Aveyron, over on Rue des Couronnes; but also North Africans, sub-Saharan Africans, foreigners both legal and undocumented, refugees, Italians, Czechs, Romanians, Poles, Jews, Turks, Armenians, all of them working to turn raw materials into finished goods, either at a shop or at home; they strolled along the boulevard, sipped coffee at an outdoor café, stood in line at the butcher's and crossed paths in their stairwells. (108)

All this vibrant life and activity is erased from the picture Perec draws of his childhood neighborhood in *W, or The Memory of Childhood*. The neutral, blank style he usually adopts in his narrative turns the description of the city into a topographical survey more in keeping with a tourist guidebook or a geography textbook, exemplified by these few lines that open chapter 10, dedicated to rue Vilin: "It's a shortish, roughly S-shaped street that leads uphill from Rue des Couronnes to some steep steps giving on Rue du Transvaal and rue Olivier Metra" (47).

Chapter 10 of Perec's autobiography is devoted to evoking rue Vilin, where not only he and his parents lived, but also his maternal grandparents and his aunt Fanny, at 24 and 1 rue Vilin. Perec mentions when and under what circumstances he came back to this place in which he had spent the first six years of his life and which he had left in 1942 in order to escape the Nazi persecution. In 1946, he went back for the first time to rue Vilin with his aunt Esther. The second return took place in "1961 or 1962" while he was visiting friends living not far away. In 1969, he started going to this street once a year because he was writing a book, *Lieux* (Places), in which he intended to depict, over twelve years, twelve places with which he had particular ties.

In 1946, when he returned for the first time since the war, his entire family was dead, except his grandmother Rose, who, by chance, had been staying at a neighbor's house when the police came to arrest her at the family home. His father had been killed on the battlefield in 1940, while his mother, his grandfathers, and his aunt Fanny had been rounded up and murdered in Auschwitz. But their absence is not Perec's subject matter, at least, not directly. He does not write, "When I came back after the war, the house and the street which were so full of their presence and of their warmth was empty and I missed them terribly." Instead, gathering together the memories of the child and the observations of the grown adult, he builds an image of a devastated and a depopulated street that looks like a metaphor or an outside projection of his own mental scenery. Three observations are particularly salient in this respect.

Perec's visits to Belleville at the end of the 1960s and at the beginning of the 1970s coincide with an urban plan of renewal, typical of the "thirty glorious years" that targeted Belleville in general and the district around rue Vilin in particular. The rubble leads Perec to associate Paris under renewal with wartime scenes and an overall feeling of destruction: "Today, Rue Vilin has been three-quarters demolished. More than half the houses have been razed, leaving waste grounds, piling up with rubbish, with old cookers and wrecked cars; most of the houses still standing are boarded up" (47). Related to this warlike scenery is a feeling of desolation and isolation. Human life seems to have deserted the street and the buildings. As a boy in 1946 and as a man years later, Perec meets practically nobody he knows in what is still a crowded neighborhood. Except for a neighbor of his parents, he sees no passersby, no shopkeepers, and no children going to school. Noticeably, rue Vilin is associated twice with the memory of outdoor children's games before and after the war. Perec remembers that in his early childhood rue Vilin might have been covered with wooden pavement. And he adds, "Perhaps there was even a great heap, somewhere, of nice cubic wooden paving blocks with which, like the characters in Charles Vildrac's L'Ile rose, we built castles and cars" (47). Whether real or imaginary, this scene implies the presence of playmates ("we"). But after the war, these playmates disappear. In 1969 and 1971, for his project called *Lieux*, Perec had already told the memory of his postwar visit to rue Vilin twice. In both versions he alludes to a boy he played with while his aunt was talking with one of his parents' neighbors.[1] In *W*, this boy is no longer present. The playmate has been erased if not from the narrator's memory, at least from his narrative. Young Perec plays alone. Rue Vilin equals loneliness.

Finally, in chapter 10, the uncertainty of his memories—"I have no childhood memories" (10)—reaches its climax. Phrases expressing the narrator's doubts, such as "I think" and "perhaps" are methodically repeated; these formulas corroborate his declaration of amnesia: "The street brought back no sharp memories, only a vague awareness that it might possibly be familiar" (48). Physical traces of the past have disappeared or faded out. If they remain, Perec is prone to elude them. For instance, in "La rue Vilin," a piece of memory collected in the posthumous publication titled *L'Infra-ordinaire* (The Infra-ordinary),[2] on February 27, 1969, after he has noted that the sign "Hairdressing salon" (Salon de coiffure) is still visible at number 22, he adds, "the salon was my mother's" ("le salon de coiffure était celui de ma mère") (19).[3] In *W*, the sign remains, but we hear no more mention of the fact that the salon was his mother's. Other testimonies are ignored or willingly displaced. On January 13, 1971, Perec meets a woman who tells him that she remembers perfectly well "la coiffeuse du 24" (the hairdresser at number 24). On other occasions, he sees two old men, a little girl, a boy, two Algerians, and two black people. All these traces of life—past and present—we do not find any more in the final version of *W*. The foreign workers are alluded to as proofs of objective knowledge, not as a parts of the narrator's empirical experiment. He knows for sure that foreign workers (Portuguese and African) now occupy the buildings, though he does not testify that he has seen them there.

Does that mean then, as it has been suggested,[4] that Perec is lying, distorting the truth? Obviously not, and scholars such as Lejeune or Burgelin have already made this point clear. More than collecting memories and traces, Perec is attempting to build and convey, through his vision of Paris, a feeling of radical loss. Thus, his return to rue Vilin awakens no memory, or at least no reliable memory. Infantile amnesia is to blame, but not only that. As Maurice Halbwachs has emphasized in *Les cadres sociaux de la mémoire* (*On Collective Memory*), one does not remember alone. One remembers inside a social framework, within the limits of one's family, one's community, one's professional group. There is no such thing as solitary memory. To Perec, almost nobody is left to help him in this memory-building process. In the drafts for the fictional parts of *W* we find these words that Perec intended to put into Gaspard Winkler's mouth: "je reviens plus personne" (I come back nobody's there).[5] Maybe all Perec's relations to urban spaces and urban places, and specifically his relation to the city of Paris, derive from this initial traumatic experience of returning to an empty nest.

The image of Paris that Perec constructs in chapter 10 is bound to the global structure of the text. As we know, *W, or the Memory of Childhood* unfolds along two—arguably, three—narrative tracks. Perec alternates his narrative autobiography with fiction. The autobiographical part describes the author's wartime boyhood, while the fictional tale itself is divided into two parts. One consists of following Gaspard Winkler's inquiry into the search for a child—also named Gaspard Winkler—lost in a shipwreck; the other part describes life on the Island of W, an island of sportsmen dedicated to the Olympic ideal. Although these two story lines seem disconnected, they are tightly related fictions, through metaphor and allegory, of what the "I" of the autobiography is unable to utter, namely the horror and pain of the Holocaust. "A boy lost in a shipwreck" can indeed be interpreted as a relevant metaphor of Perec's own childhood and the island of sportsmen, where famished inhabitants are governed by pitiless laws, stands for an efficient representation of a concentration camp. Some elements in chapter 10 are intertwined with this large echoing system. For instance, at the age of six, Georges Perec was sent to Villard de Lans in the Alps, where he hid until the end of the war. Phonetically, in French, Villard is close to Vilin and to W (pronounced V). In fact, graphically, the first two letters of each word V[ilin]-[V]illard form a W. Moreover, Villard is a *village*, in which many *villas* (cottages) are located, some of them occupied by Jewish refugees, among them Perec's relatives (75).[6] The Island of W is composed of "four settlements simply called *villages*" (71). All these words, *Villard*, *village*, *villa* are consonant with *Vilin* and with the letter W. This enables us to stress the existence of a phonetic chain in which Paris's rue Vilin is tied to the war/Holocaust experience, both on an autobiographical level and on a fictional level.

Another set of episodes draws our attention. In chapter 10, Perec recalls three school memories. In one of them, he remembers himself rushing down Couronnes Street (dévalant la rue des couronnes) holding in his hands a picture of a bear he has just drawn at school. He is "drunk with excitement" (53) and yelling, "Here come the cubs! Here come the cubs!" (53). It is one of the rare moments in which the narrator is depicted as physically active in the city; Paris usually stands as mere material for observation and description, or for static scenes; here, it is connected to the narrator's motion and emotion. But, the narrator insists, the boy has a very special way of running: "at each stride I do a hop on the foot that is forward; it's a running style, halfway between proper running and hopping" ("à mi-chemin de la course proprement dite et du saut à cloche-pied").

In chapter 16, the racing system on the Island of W is detailed. Because of the poor physical condition of the contestants, as we are told, some mock contests have been organized: "the 200 meters is run three-legged" ("le 200 mètres se court à cloche-pied") (85). In both cases, the original French version uses the same expression: "à cloche-pied"—a repetition that is unfortunately lost in translation. Yet it helps us to establish a link between the child and the athlete, and between rue Vilin and the Island of W. Paris is not a concentration camp, but it is invaded by the imaginary of the concentration camp.

Outside Belleville, Paris is reduced to street names linked to the names of Perec's relatives. Rue des Eaux, near Porte de Versailles, was Fanny's address. Boulevard Delessert near Passy was Esther's. Rue Cadet and rue Lamartine were Esther, David, and Icek's first home and work addresses. Perec tries to imagine the subway lines and connections he probably used to go from one address to the other. After the war there were no established routes anymore. In his uncle's car, young Georges Perec goes from Gare de Lyon to avenue Junot and then to rue de l'Assomption. "Rue de l'Assomption has become 'home'" (157). The city seems to be dislocated, like the family. Landmarks are lost. Only one landmark remains, Gare de Lyon, mentioned three times in *W*'s autobiography. Gare de Lyon is the train station through which he left and came back to Paris. It is also the last place where he saw his mother, the last space he shared with her. Maybe that's why he mistakes it for a monument (157).[7]

Perec imagines that Paris was particularly meaningful for his mother. In chapter 8 of his autobiography and, more precisely in one of the two texts in bold type written "more than fifteen years ago" (26), Perec writes that the announcement of her departure for Paris was the only event in his mother's life (31). She would then dream of Paris, fancy it as a feast, as a postcard. Rebuilt through the author's own narrative topoi, Cyrla Szulewicz's Paris is reduced to a collection of stereotypes, both touristic and ethical. It is a common place, in the rhetorical sense of the word, since it is designated by its monuments, such as the Eiffel Tower or the Arc de de Triomphe, and given symbolic power, namely, the promise of peace and happiness, of no more slaughters, ghettos, or poverty. Reality brought a cruel denial of this dream. Life in rue Vilin was as much of a struggle as it was in Poland and his mother will be rounded up and murdered in Auschwitz. The city of light has become a lethal trap.

W, or the Childhood of Memory summarizes the main characteristics attributed to France's capital city in Perec's works in general, while providing interesting insights into the author's urban practice. His sense of urban dislocation, his fear of being disoriented feeds his need to rationalize the city and enclose it within a tight grid pattern. Thus, he experiments through his characters in *A Man Asleep* as well as in *Things* with all kinds of possible routes leading from one point to the other inside the limits of Paris. In these two novels, he describes ways of relating to the urban space, such as wandering along the streets, strolling on the waterfront of the Seine, shopping on rue de la Madeleine, and so on. Behind his so-called *Lieux* project lies Perec's own experience of spacial instability and disappearance. The project consists of Perec's intention of selecting twelve spots in Paris, all meaningful to him. Twelve times during twelve years he will describe these twelve places, once by remembering them, once through living observation. In both *Things* and *A Man Asleep* Paris transforms itself. From a feast it turns into a nightmare, from a city of light into a ghost city.

We can observe a similar metamorphosis in *Things: A Story of the Sixties*. Published in 1965, it is generally considered to be a documentary and sociological novel. The author himself has not failed to accredit such an interpretation. It is supposed to be a story the 1960s, a novel about consumer society, a radiography of a generation fascinated by objects and in search of material satisfaction.

Inspired by Flaubert's *Sentimental Education*, Perec's urban topography obeys an implicit sociology. The city of *Things* is thus divided into separate areas between which the characters, Jerôme and Sylvie, revolve in order to pursue their different activities. According to the concept of urban functions developed in the twentieth century by geographers and city planners, Paris is divided into a residential, an economic, a recreational, and a political zone. The couple resides in the residential area, consumes in the economic city, goes to the movies in the recreational district, and joins a demonstration against the war in Algeria inside the political city. Yet in this—Perec's first novel— Paris turns insidiously into a frightful place haunted by memories of war.

This impression is striking when one closely examines the commercial city. Perec and his commentators have repeated so many times that *Things* is a romance of the consumer society that readers are convinced that we are witness to a portrait of the urban consumer at the time of the "thirty glorious years." But this is partly a collective hallucination. Consumer society not only means a fit of shopping fever, but also a production circuit for the mass market in need of both cheap and technical products. This is not the case in Perec's novel. Caught in a distinctive strategy, Jerome and Sylvie despise consumer products and technical items, and instead focus on scarce, traditional, and expensive goods, such as Chesterfield sofas. The weekly magazine *L'Express* and its supplement *Madame Express*, which is supposed to be, as Perec himself stresses in his interviews, the main arbiter for the couple's purchases, display a far more eclectic taste. It is true that the magazine may praise, at times, a "pure wool carpet" as "a luxury temptation" with its "braids, fringes and tassels."[8] However, modern items are far from overlooked. Advertisements for Swissair and Fiat stand alongside those of stereo systems. Year after year, articles and photographs reporting on the "Salon des Arts ménagers" (Ideal Home Show) inform the public of the latest available models of refrigerators, stoves, washing machines, electric mixers, and vacuum cleaners. Instead of this, remodeled by Jerome and Sylvie's desires, the merchant city becomes a city of antiques, of caterers selling salmon and *pâtés*, of stores proffering secondhand clothes and chic suits. It is more reminiscent of a prewar Paris, or even of the society described in Emile Zola's *Au Bonheur des Dames*, than of a city of the second half of the twentieth century.

The same attachment to the past seems to extend to the cultural city and the residential city. The characters turn their backs on artistic modernity and on urban modernity. As moviegoers, they will only see old movies, attending retrospectives. During their wanderings, they do not visit the new districts, are not attracted to urban sites, even though the Radio Building (la Maison de la radio) was erected in 1963 and the Center for the New Industries and Technologies (CNIT) was opened in 1958. At the same time, large swaths of slum demolition and renovation had begun, particularly affecting the Belleville area. *L'Express* is passionate about architectural transformations, to which it regularly devotes articles. On January 7, 1960, the magazine is interested in the "Spark Operation," a building project "built in less than a month at Asnieres"; on January 28, 1960, it gives advices to Parisians who settle in the suburbs. For comparison again, the characters in *Les Belles images* by Simone de Beauvoir are much more representative than Jerome and Sylvie of this new urban class that Perec, or at least his narrator, claims to depict. De Beauvoir's characters drive cars, buy stereo systems, adore the young authors and their "books that talk about nothing."

How then to explain the paradox of Sylvie and Jerome who are supposedly well adjusted to their time but who carefully avoid the present? In truth, the city of *Things* is frozen in the memory of World War II. Twice at least, there is a regressive slide into what can legitimately be called the scene of a trauma. The war in Algeria first awakens the memory of these dark years. The militant engagement it generates is apprehended by the actors through the categories of the previous era: fascism, antifascism, resistance, martyrdom. Moreover it brings back urban scenes in which the atmosphere of food shortages and violence refers, beyond their narrative stereotypes, to the Nazi occupation: "Housewives stocked up with sugar in kilos, bottles of cooking oil, tins of tuna, coffee and condensed milk. Squads of helmeted security policemen . . . patrolled at ease up and down Boulevard Sébastopol" (73); "they were being followed, their number-plates were being taken down, they were being watched, being framed: five wine-sodden foreign legionnaires were going to set upon them and leave them for dead in a dark alley, on the rain-washed pavement, in a neighbourhood of ill repute" (73). These images of "blood, explosions, violence, terror" are meant to conjure up the visions of the horror of World War II more than to represent the Parisian unrest during the war with Algeria. Thus, the squads of riot police who are seen patrolling "at ease" along the Boulevard Sebastopol might obliquely designate a column of German soldiers.

The second twist occurs in chapter 10 when, during an investigation, Jerome and Sylvie discover agricultural France. With Lorraine farmers and the grain growers of Beauce, the two young people discover abundance. "The silos were full of wheat" (89); "In unending cellars they would be welcomed by tons of hogsheads, vats full of oil and honey, barrels of preserves in brine, juniper roast-ham, kegs of rough brandy" (89). This visit triggers a series of mirages with visions of "[s]talls of mangoes, figs, honeydews and water melons" (90); of "columned temples with ceilings groaning with hams and sausages" (90); of "double ranks of suckling pigs and wild boars hanging by their feet" (90); of "wondrous patisseries" (90). This enumerative technique, borrowed perhaps from Zola (*Le Ventre de Paris*) and Flaubert (*Madame Bovary, Salammbô*) is used here to configure an imaginary war. The starving city, in contrast to the eating countryside, is a topos of the Occupation. Behind the fields full of food stands a hungry Paris abandoned to the black market. Such delusions of food satiety recall other hungry people: those imprisoned in the concentration camps of Nazi Europe. This explains the reference to Robert Antelme, whom Perec quotes as being an inspiration for *Things*, alongside Flaubert, Barthes, and Nizan. In *The Human Race*, Antelme writes of the food obsession that tormented the deportees: one person would recapitulate what he had eaten before his deportation; another would dream aloud of the pudding and the café au lait that his mother used to prepare (50–51). Many stories of deportation tell of how the concentration camp slaves invoked the feasts of freedom. The Paris of *Things* is a famished society hallucinating dreams of abundance.

At the end of the novel, Jerome and Sylvie make a trip to North Africa, as many romantic heroes had done before them. Leaving their apartment in front of the Mosque of Paris, they settle in Sfax, in Tunisia. Foreigners are strangers in the Arab town as much as they are in the European district—they experience there an empty, disused place that awakens no desire. There they discern "[n]ot a soul stirring" but "metal roller blinds, high wooden fences, a world of squares that were not squares, of non-streets, of phantom avenues" (110). This is already the city of *A Man Asleep*, in which work sites are transformed into mass graves. This ghost city that is supposed to be the opposite of the Parisian feast, reveals itself, in fact, as an extension and an unveiling of the Parisian experience. Paris itself, where no passerby ever seems to be met, where no inhabitant is ever embodied, which instead of the promised treats offers only tasteless meals (126), resembles a depopulated city, as it probably appeared to little Georges when in 1944 he returned from Villars de Lans to Belleville and found out that his whole family was missing.

Notes

1. "Je sais, parce que ma tante me l'a dit, que je suis retournée [*sic*] une ou deux fois rue Vilin après la guerre, que j'y ai revu un garçon de mon âge qui avait été mon voisin et mon copain de jeux, que je suis allé jouer avec lui dans la rue cependant que ma tante, je suppose, parlait avec ses parents de l'arrestation de ma mère, des grands-parents etc.[*sic*]." (I know, because my aunt told me so, that I went back to rue Vilin once or twice after the war, that I met again with a boy of my age who had been my neighbor and my playmate, that I went to play with him in the street while my aunt, I suppose, would talk with her parents of my mother's arrest, about the grandparents, and so on), in Lejeune, "Vilin souvenirs, Georges Perec," 127–51, 135. My translation. See also pp. 143–44, in which the memory of the scene is depicted as "very vague," but the playmate himself is remembered rather precisely as "plump" ("*grassouillet*").

2. "La rue Vilin" is part of a project that Perec called *Lieux*, which he refers to in *W*, in *Espèces d'espaces* (1974), and in a letter to Maurice Nadeau. *Lieux* was supposed to consist of two kinds of texts: "Souvenirs" (memories) and "Réels" (pieces of reality). "La rue Vilin" belongs to the second. It was first published in the Communist Party daily newspaper *L'Humanité*, November 11, 1977, and later, after Perec's death, in *L'Infra-ordinaire*.

3. My translation.

4. See David Bellos's biography of Perec, *Georges Perec: A Life in Words*.

5. See Lejeune, *La Memoire et l'oblique*, 107.

6. It is also relevant to note that Michel de M'Uzan, one of Perec's psychoanalysts, lived in villa de l'igloo in Paris.

7. The other possible reason for this mistake is that Gare de Lyon is monumental. It looks like a monument indeed, but only from outside, not when you are inside. And Perec was coming from inside the station when he asked his relatives which monument it was.

8. *L'Express*, February 18, 1960, 21.

Bibliography

Robert, Antelme. *The Human Race*. Translated by Jeffrey Haight and Annie Mahler. Evanston, IL: Marlboro Press/Northwestern University Press, 1998.

Bellos, David. *Georges Perec: A Life in Word*. Boston, MA: David R. Godine, 1993.

Burgelin, Claude. *Georges Perec*. Paris: Seuil, 2002.

Jablonka, Ivan. *A History of the Grandparents I Never Had*. Translated by Jane Kuntz. Stanford, CA: Stanford University Press, 2016.

Lejeune, Philippe. *La memoire et l'oblique*. Paris: P.O.L, 1991.

————. "Vilin souvenirs, Georges Perec." *Genesis* 1 (1992).

Perec, Georges. *Espèces d'espaces*. Paris: Galilée, 1974.

————. *L'Infra-ordinaire*. Paris: Seuil, 1989.

————. *Things: A Story of the Sixties* [With *A Man Asleep*]. Translated by David Bellos. London: Harvill, 1991.

————. *W, or the Memory of Childhood*. Translated by David Bellos. Boston, MA: David R. Godine, 1988.

14

Street Walking Paris

SARA R. HOROWITZ

In his 1971 poem, "In a Chinese Antique Shop" ("In a khinezishn gesheft fun antik") the Yiddish poet Abraham Sutzkever imagines an overheard conversation between the proprietor and a ninety-nine-year-old customer in a shop located on rue Monsieur Le Prince in Paris (7–9). Although the two men converse in Chinese, the narrator finds that he can miraculously "understand their language, understand their expression as though I had been born in China." The elderly customer—whom the poem repeatedly refers to as a "mummy"—complains that his children impatiently await his death: "[T]hey're already waiting, waiting to bury me, / just as you see me, in my rags / among horse carcasses outside the city." Presumably assimilated into Paris habits and conforming with what Gérard Noiriel terms the "French cultural norms" that permit immigrants to call France home, his children value neither the traditional Chinese esteem for ancestors nor the funereal practices of Chinese religion. The proprietor attempts to comfort his customer. Were he the old man's son, he would honor him with a proper Paris funeral; he would "ornament your grave with coral, / and bury you in Père-Lachaise" (7), the largest cemetery in the city. But a proper Paris funeral at a venerable cemetery in the city's Belleville area is not what the elderly man desires: "I don't want to lie with those corpses in the Père-Lachaise, / but among my ancestors the Chinese" (8). Instead, he proposes that after his death, the proprietor cut off the man's finger, place it in a small ivory box, "and send it across to my ancestors / in the village of Chu-Hi / on the River Yangtze, / and I'll bless you with my dusty lips" (8). In death he imagines a recuperation of what he lacks in exile: home.

Sutzkever's poem, set in Paris but written neither in France nor in French, serves as an unlikely but apt portal to interrogate Paris as dynamic space in the postwar Jewish imaginary. Like many of Sutzkever's poems of the 1970s, it contemplates vanished communities and unraveled societies, mediating memory through depictions of landscape and cityscape, and negotiating the interdependence of time and space in the human and the Jewish experience. Arguably the most important Yiddish poet of the past century, Sutzkever was born in Belarus, escaped with his wife from the Vilna Ghetto, fought partisan fighters, and testified against Nazi war criminals in the Nuremberg trials. After the war, Sutzkever spent half a year in Paris before immigrating to Tel Aviv in 1947, where he remained until his death in 2010. In the period just after the war, Jan Schwarz writes in *Survivors and Exiles: Yiddish Culture after the Holocaust*, Paris was "an important hub" for Yiddish belles lettres. Like many other war refugees, Yiddish writers were drawn to the city not only because, in their statelessness, the city was a move in the right direction (westward), but also because of the important place of Paris in the Jewish imaginary. Paris was the emblem of French revolutionary values, of emancipation, of the birth of a modernity that promised citizenship, human rights, and diversity in civic space. For many Yiddish writers arriving in Paris soon after the war, the Parisian cityscape permitted them to transgress the restrictive yeshiva traditions of their youth, to reembrace the jouissance of sexuality and artistic freedom, to imagine a future that was different from the immediate past.

It is perhaps the context of this city's promise of belonging and pleasure that drew Sutzkever to rue Monsieur Le Prince, in an area of narrow, winding streets on the Left Bank of Paris, in the center of the Quartier Latin, in the 6th arrondissement. Monsieur Le Prince is the title accorded to the Princes of Condé—a line of French princes associated with the royal House of Bourbon. In the sixteenth century, Louis de Condé led the Huguenot Wars, or Wars of Religion, a series of battles on behalf of Protestant rights in Catholic France. The war concluded with the adoption of the Edict of Nantes, recognizing Protestant freedom of worship, although in limited circumstances. While providing for continued Catholic dominance, the Edict of Nantes is viewed as an early move toward religious tolerance. A hundred years later, Louis XIV revoked the edict, and fierce persecution of Protestants ensued. The fragility of the hard-won toleration gained on behalf of the Protestants by the Prince of Condé may have struck Sutzkever as a prelude to the successive gains and setbacks of the Jews of France. In the general area around rue Monsieur Le Prince, a thousand years before the French Revolution and the emancipation of the Jews of France, was what is thought to be the earliest Jewish settlement in the city.

It may be that the checkered history of the Jews of Paris—the successive exiles and returns—allowed Sutzkever to easily blur the boundaries between Chinese and Yiddish in yearning for a remembered past and a recollected cultural ease that, for refugees of the Nazi genocide, is attainable only in the imagination and, perhaps, in death. The Yiddish phrase that he uses for the elderly Chinese man's ancestors—*mayne oves*—can equally well connote the Biblical forefathers (Abraham, Isaac, and Jacob) in the Holy Land, and the poet's more recent predecessors in Poland. By the time Sutzkever composed the poem, he was already ensconced in Tel Aviv, where he edited a Yiddish literary journal. One could say that Sutzkever achieved what the Chinese exile could only yearn for: he returned to the land of his biblical *oves* and the language of his diaspora *oves*. But the poem gestures back to an earlier poem written in 1947 during a more unsettled time in Sutzkever's life. Sutzkever's composed "The Woman of Marble in Père Lachaise" (*"Di Froy fun mirml afn Per-lashez"*) during his postwar sojourn in Paris. Like all of Sutzkever's poems composed during the war years and immediately after, the poem includes a time and place notation: "Paris, 1947." These notations are effectively part of the poem, grounding them in personal and collective history. In this earlier poem, the speaker makes a pilgrimage to the grave of the Polish-born composer Frédéric Chopin. Although Chopin lived half of his life in Paris, his music—especially his polonaises, based on the music of Polish folkdance—is said to reflect a deep and abiding attachment to his homeland. For many Poles in moments of crisis, his music was understood as an expression of his and their patriotism and love of Poland, and as a resistance to political conquest and cultural erasure.[1] Chopin's tomb in Père Lachaise features a sculpture of a grieving Euterpe, the muse of music; this is the "woman of marble" of the poem's title.

Reading the inscription on Chopin's gravestone, the poet is overwhelmed by a sense of kinship with this other Polish expatriate in Paris. Born in neighboring cities, although separated by decades, the poet sees Chopin as "almost a brother." The stone statue of Euterpe above Chopin's tomb comes to life and explains to the poet that while the dust of Chopin's body lies interred here in Père Lachaise, the composer's heart rests in his "homeland"—buried, that is, in Warsaw. Indeed, at the composer's request,

Figure 14.1. Tomb of Frédéric Chopin, Père Lachaise Cemetery, Paris. (*Photograph by Michael Dan*)

his sister placed his heart in an urn and smuggled it out of France. The statue asks the poet where his own "heart should be taken?" The question leaves the poet mute, *on-loshn*, literally without language—a charged description in 1947, given the destruction of the centers of Yiddish culture.

> I turned numb in Père Lachaise,
> speechless:
> Was it worth it to count up
> some thirty years,
> losing those dear to me,

> hanging by a hair, emerging from the ovens
> with unburnt tears,
> only to hear just now at Père Lachaise,
> that my strong heart isn't even worth a sou?

If triangulation is a stable navigational means of determining location, in Sutzkever's poem the triangulation of space, time, and language locate a cemetery in Paris as the grounds for both home and exile, in enduring oscillation. Together, Sutzkever's two Père Lachaise poems unravel, reconstruct, and unravel again relationships among space, time, memory, identity, and nation. For the celebrated Chopin, as for the unnamed Chinese "mummy," home is where the heart (or the finger) is; the unending yearning of the exile for a return surfaces and comforts as death approaches. But the pilgrim to Chopin's grave has no such comfort. He no longer has a home toward which to direct his heart. The 1947 poem concludes:

> . . . if I were to make a will
> so someone should bring my heart home—
> the entire Diaspora,
> the sad Diaspora—
> will laugh.

For the Jewish refugee in Paris, the very idea of home has been destroyed.

Despite these sober reflections, there is a trace of flânerie—that quintessential Parisian form of seduction and movement—in the stations of Sutzkever's postwar Paris poems. Wandering freely through urban spaces like the nineteenth-century poet Charles Baudelaire's flâneur, he observes ordinary people in their everyday environment. In Sutzkever's poems, the movement through Parisian space reveals the poet's own dislocation and disillusion. But if the exile cannot settle down, blend in, and find home after the war, the city itself is not to blame.

Paris opens itself up to him and he wanders freely.

In the postwar reconstruction of Jewish movement in Paris *during* the Occupation, however, we see a different aspect of Paris. Call it an anti-flânerie. As Patricia Ferguson observes in her discussion of Paris and revolution in nineteenth-century writing, "The flâneur's movement within the city, like his solitude, points to a privileged status" (84). In other words, the privilege of roaming freely in the city is reserved for those already privileged. For those without status, mobility itself is suspect. Women might be assaulted, the poor might be harassed, and the Jew? The contrast is sharp between the flâneur, who wanders the city at his pleasure, and the Jew in occupied Paris, who walks the streets fearfully or not at all. In Sarah Kofman's memoir of her wartime childhood in Paris, *Rue Ordener Rue Labat*, for example, Kofman's mother remains confined to the apartment of the Catholic woman who hides her and her daughter. Their host and rescuer walks the streets with little Sarah, who is blond enough to "pass." Similarly, for example, in Patrick Modiano's retrospective imagining of a Jewish adolescent arrested in Paris, Dora Bruder does not so much move through as transgress forbidden space. Or, to put it differently, every space is forbidden to the Jewish teenager except the death camp in Poland to which she is eventually deported.

Both Kofman's and Modiano's works negotiate memory through spacial practices, through an alternation between movement and stasis. Looking back at the war years from the perspective of almost half a century, Kofman's belated memoir is built on a series of forced movements—her father's deportation to Auschwitz, where he will be murdered; her siblings' clandestine move to safer places in the north; her mother's sudden abandonment of the family home to elude roundup. Kofman's recounts a series of undesired separations from her mother until the two are taken in by a French Catholic woman whom she calls Mémé. During the period of time

Figure 14.2. Rue Labat. (*Photograph by Sara R. Horowitz*)

that the pair is sheltered by Mémé, most of the narrative unfolds in interior spaces. Although Sarah is sometimes permitted to accompany Mémé outdoors, and is familiar with the neighborhood, she seldom specifies the places they pass. Given the geographic precision of some of her memories, it is curious that she does not supply the building number on rue Labat. We know that she remembers it—she supplies it in the 1987 testimony that she writes to Yad Vashem attesting to Mémé's act of rescue.

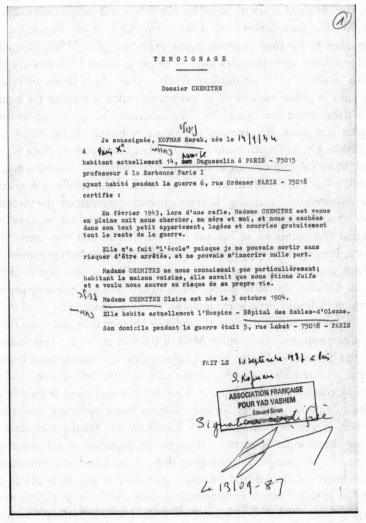

Figure 14.3. Letter from Sarah Kofman requesting that Mémé be recognized as Righteous Among the Nations. (*Source*: Yad Vashem)

By contrast, Kofman's earlier memories are punctuated with street names, Métro stations, squares, and landmarks, as she retraces the long walk home from synagogue on the Sabbath, or the route to school, or to a friend's home, or a favorite teacher's house. Her father's synagogue was on the rue Duc (5). She played with the Adler boys who lived on rue Simart; her deported classmate lived on rue Emile-Duployé (18). Her school was located on rue Doudeauville (17); her teacher lived at 75 or 77 rue de la Chapelle (20). She almost lost her mother in the garden of the Sacré-Cœur (27); she collected cigarette butts for her father and bought him cigarette paper on rue Jean-Robert (11). One is reminded of the distinction that geographer Yi-Fu Tuan draws between space and place. "What begins as undifferentiated space becomes place as we get to know it better and endow it with value. . . . [I]f we think of space as that which allows movement, then place is pause; each pause in movement makes it possible for location to be transformed into place" (6). The experience of space, the rendering of space into place, he observes, is product of human desire, attachment, and action. Or, as French anthropologist Marc Augé puts it, place is "relational, historical, and concerned with identity" (63). In specifying where she walked, played, and studied, and with whom, Kofman recollects *her* Paris, a place saturated with meaning. Kofman's narrative remembers the displaced, those whose place has been taken from them either because they were deported and murdered, or because they fled homes that they could never reclaim. Pausing in the spaces they once inhabited, associating remembered activities and personalities with points on the Paris streets, one might say that in Kofman's narrative people are re-placed and places are re-peopled. A little girl's Jewish Paris is repopulated, restored, re-storied.

In contemplating the literary symbiosis between time and space that he terms "chronotopes," philosopher Mikhail Bakhtin explains, "Time takes on flesh and becomes visible for human contemplation; likewise, space becomes charged and responsive to the movements of time and history and the enduring character of a people. . . . Chronotopes thus stand as monuments to the community itself, as symbols of it, as forces operating to shape its members' images of themselves" (7). Like Kofman, Modiano explores the shifting chronotopes of memory through the depiction of a haunted and haunting Paris cityscape. Intermingling shifts of space and temporality, *Dora Bruder* layers recollected and imagined narratives of the same places over time: the Jewish teenager in Montmartre, near the Porte de Clignancourt, emerging from the Métro at Marcadet Poissoniers, or at Nation. The narrator's remembrances of the wanderings of his own childhood, his adolescence, his adulthood give way to an imaginative reconstruction of Dora's more fraught wandering, always already back shadowed by her deportation and murder at Auschwitz. Like a multiple exposure on a camera in which the film mechanism is stuck, Modiano's narrative insists that we see multiple time frames simultaneously: Dora Bruder's defiant wandering in a city no longer hers to possess, her parent's apartment, the Catholic school where she boarded, the nineteenth-century boundaries of the city, the narrator's later unintended or purposeful retracing of Dora's possible routes. He reflects, "From day to day, with the passage of time, I find, perspectives become blurred, one winter merging into another. That of 1965 and that of 1942" (6). He had been, it turns out, to the Bruder's neighborhood long before was aware that the family had ever existed, taken by his mother to a local market in the 1950s. And of course, by then, they no longer existed. Times change, places change. Still, he muses, "Already, below the surface, they were there" (6). As French philosopher Gaston Bachelard reminds us, one important psychic function of space is to serve as a repository for the emotions of memory. In recollecting a familiar space, we describe not so much the precise physical place, but an imagined, desired, dreamed space. But the disappearance of Dora Bruder unsettles the narrator's spatial memory, destabilizing

Figure 14.4. Rue Ordener. (*Photograph by Sara R. Horowitz*)

both time and space. Jewish place is no place at all. The spacialization of loss that runs through Modiano's narrative imagines urban geography as bereft. The narrator internalizes Jewish placelessness. Repeatedly, he notes a feeling of "absence," "a sense of emptiness," in the city and in himself.

The Paris cityscapes haunted by the Jewish no-place pose questions about what it means to be a refugee, to be displaced, to be replaced. Once lost, can home ever be recovered or reconstituted? For Bachelard, the memory of home provides a protective and enduring psychic structure. "We comfort ourselves by reliving memories of protection. . . . the house shelters day-dreaming, the house protects the dreamer, the house allows one to dream in peace" (28). Jean Améry, the Austrian-born essayist whose mixed parentage defined him as a Jew under Nazi law, would agree. In an essay first published in 1966, "How Much Home Does a Person Need?" Améry several times states, "Home is security." Bachelard's poetics of space emanates from his childhood home in the French countryside. For him, the idea of "home" is pastoral, rural, and French. Its architecture offers a stability that is unsettled in urban spaces like Paris. Although Améry's roots were in urban Vienna, for him, too, home is tied to landscape and language, to regional habits, to native tongue, but also to time. "Just as one learns one's mother tongue without knowing its grammar, one experiences one's native surroundings. Mother tongue and native world grow with us, grow into us, and thus become the familiarity that guarantees us security" (48). Although the memory house sustains Bachelard while he lives in a claustrophobic Paris apartment away from his beloved countryside, Améry insists "that there is no return, because the re-entrance into a place is never also a recovery [of] the lost time" (42). Indeed, in reaction to being rejected by his fatherland and mother tongue, Améry renounced them: "since the day when an official decree forbade me to wear the folk costume that I had worn almost exclusively from early childhood on, I no longer permitted myself the dialect" (43). For Améry, it is not simply that "home"—like any place—changes over time, or that one cannot reenter one's childhood once an adult. It is that Améry's home—his home town, his homeland—disowned him, cast him out, redefining him as a Jew and not an Austrian, and so proved to be no home, after all.

In the flow of time, the psychic space of Améry's childhood home morphs into a Jewish no-place, the no-place that reached across borders into the Paris no-place of Dora Bruder and Sarah Kofman. Those who survive recognize profoundly, according to Améry, "that they had been made homeless, and . . . they could perceive more clearly how much a person needs home" (46). For Améry, the condition of homelessness is linked to the state of exile. Resonating with Sutzkever's inner dialogue with Chopin's muse in Père Lachaise, he observes, "I have twenty-seven years of exile behind me, and my spiritual compatriots are Proust, Sartre, Beckett. Only I am still convinced that one must have compatriots in village and city streets if the spiritual ones are to be fully enjoyed, and that a cultural internationalism thrives well only in the soil of national security" (46). Much like the Yiddish poet at Père Lachaise, Améry has no home to which he can send his heart or even a severed finger.

Little Sarah, too, emerges as an exile of sorts in Kofman's memoir, even though she remains in Paris. Before the Occupation, the girl seamlessly negotiated the overlay of Jewish space and French space in the city. Like other Jews, she circulated freely throughout a multi-ethnic Paris. She took long Sabbath walks with her father and excursions to the zoo with her teacher. She spoke Yiddish to her parents, French to her friends and teachers. When the Paris space of Jewish émigrés becomes a no-place, Mémé integrates her into French Paris, assimilating the girl to French cultural practices and re-creating her in her own image. She renames her Suzanne, "the saint's name closest to hers (Claire) on the calendar" (39), restyling her hair, her clothing, and her diet, insisting that the girl eat—and like—pork, horsemeat, lard, and other foods forbidden by Jewish law. She detaches the girl from Jewish religious and cultural habits. For Sarah, the loss of hybridity transforms what was once a simultaneity—Jewish and French—into a tension between Jewishness and Frenchness. The denaturalization of home is emblemized by the transformation of Yiddish in Kofman's narrative. The Kofman family conversations are narrated in flawless French, although we are told that her parents spoke mostly Yiddish to the children. This allows Kofman to represent her parents' speech as articulate. Afterward, what had been the intimacy of a mother-tongue becomes an alien and oppressive language, the pull of unwanted origins, the shouts of a brutal mother.

Several years before composing her memoir, Kofman published a more philosophical book that contended with the legacy of the war years without directly discussing her own experiences. In *Paroles suffoquées*, or *Smothered Words*, Kofman discusses the moral imperative to talk about Auschwitz, where her father was murdered, and the impossibility of doing so adequately. In it, she retells a 1936 *récit*, or first-person story, by the writer Maurice Blanchot. Her discussion of "The Idyll" (*L'Idylle*) reframes it, so that—although she does not say so directly—it offers an implicit commentary on her childhood in occupied Paris. Blanchot's story focuses on

Figure 14.5. View of the rue de Hôpital St. Gervais in the Jewish quarter of Paris, 1930s; United States Holocaust Memorial Museum, courtesy of National Archives and Records Administration, College Park. Walking through the Jewish neighborhoods of Paris before the Occupation, Sarah Kofman encountered sights similar to this. (*Source*: USHMM)

a foreigner given refuge in a new city. Wanting to fit in, to belong—one might even say, to survive—he submits to the tutelage of a lady who has offered him shelter in her manor. Under her mentorship, he adopts local habits, suppresses his emotions, agrees to remake himself. He understands the need to obey, to accept, to please, to appear happy—a situation uncannily resembling Kofman's wartime experience. Améry's meditation on home and the precariousness of the refugee makes clear the stakes of being seen as different. Améry recollects, "Faces, gestures, clothes, houses, words (even if I halfway understood them) were sensory reality, but not interpretable signs. . . . I staggered through a world whose signs remained as inscrutable to me as Etruscan script. Unlike the tourist however, for whom such things may be a piquant form of alienation, I was dependent on this world full of riddles" (47). When read alongside her memoir, Kofman's description of Blanchot's refugee offers an intimation of little Sarah's inner life, with

Blanchot's unnamed city standing in for a de-judified Paris. Kofman quotes from Blanchot's story: "If you miss your country, every day you'll find more reasons to miss it. But if you forget it and begin to love your new place, you'll be sent home, and then, uprooted once more, you'll begin a new exile" (21). You might say that her citation of Blanchot plots the coordinates of her own trajectory: the Kofman home, then Mémé's, then—after the war—her mother's, losing the possibility to call any place home.

It is no coincidence that the cityscape of Paris occupies a central role in the French intellect and the French imagination, or that the notion of the flâneur emerged there and remains connected with the city. Novelists, poets, philosophers, politicians, revolutionaries—for them, Paris is both itself and a potent symbol of France and all that it stands for. Paris is the center of the country, geographically and emotionally. Its streets hold the cafés where intellectuals gather to argue, the garrets where artists create, the barricades where successive revolutions unfold. Its museums display the country's heritage and treasures; its parks provide natural respite. Paris is the heart of France. To think about its meaning is to penetrate the French soul. In "Walking in the City," Michel de Certeau, a twentieth-century French Jesuit priest and cultural theorist, described the way that individual walkers move through city streets. Although the essay speaks of cities as a general category, and opens with a view of Manhattan, Paris is the crux of his consideration. While governments and other institutions create a sense of the city as a unified space—through maps, street names, planned use, and other means—each walker moves in his or her own way. Walkers thus redefine official space and give it personal meaning. The walker may, for example, literally go off the grid of mapped streets. De Certeau refers to this wandering and detouring way of moving through city streets as "surreptitious creativities" (96), pedestrian movements that "weave places together" (98) in unforeseen and unanticipated ways. The walker's choices, the meanings she assigns to street names, how he uses public places, the stories she associates with different locales "transform" (98) the city, making it tell a story that is different from the official one shaped by governments and other institutions. In walking the streets, using the city, remembering, experiencing, de Certeau suggests, the walker articulates "a second, poetic geography on top of the geography of the literal, forbidden or permitted meaning" (105).

Drawing on de Certeau's analysis, you might say that French Jewish writing after the war re-creates a Paris that disappeared as Jewish walkers were under interdiction, a Paris later suppressed by French ways of remembering the war years. De Certeau, in fact, compares city walking to language, to "unorganized poems" (93) that together "compose a manifold story that has neither author nor spectator, shaped out of fragments of trajectories and alterations of space" (93). As Kofman, Modiano, and others seek to reconstruct the Jewish experience in Paris, to walk is to transgress. Being denied the right to wander freely and unharmed becomes an apt emblem for the larger denial: to write one's own story, to live it out, to live at all. It falls then, to those like Kofman and Georges Perec, who eluded the genocidal net, or to those like Modiano and Henri Raczymow, who came later, to walk the city, to give it narrative and poetic shape, to supply the

Figure 14.6. The Town Hall in the 18th arrondissement, Paris, where the families of Sarah Kofman and Dora Bruder resided. The words above the doors promise "Liberty, Equality, Fraternity." (*Photograph by Sara R. Horowitz*)

fragments of memory and imagination that restore the disappeared to the streets, homes, and parks they were denied.

Let me come back briefly to Sutzkever. The space of Yiddish, one might say, is located not in Paris but in what Jeffrey Shandler has called Yiddishland, a borderless homeland defined by language rather than by territory. But looking at the place of Paris in works by Sutzkever and other Yiddish writers sharpens the way in which the image of the city comes to connote different things to refugees like Sutzkever who arrive in Paris after liberation, and those like Kofman whose wartime catastrophe begins there. As Henri Raczymow writes in *Contes d'exile et d'oublie*, "What happened in Poland happened in France."

In *Paris Insolite*, Jean-Paul Clébert's arresting account of wandering in postwar Paris as a vagabond among the down and out, the Yiddish-speaking ultra-Orthodox Jews of the Marais pose an impenetrable world. Despite his ability to blend into a range of milieux, "to ape the demeanor, tics, language and habits of others, to the point where I can pass just as easily in the relevant environment, for a truck driver, an antique dealer, a pimp, or an intellectual—despite this, I have never managed to penetrate the Jewish milieu, and every time I visit I feel like an outsider, almost like a tourist. . . ." Indeed, he concludes, "the Jewish quarter is strictly speaking not in Paris at all." Although it is clear that he thinks kindly of the oddly dressed Yiddish speakers of the Marais, the opacity of their world for him resonates with the trope of indelible otherness that characterizes a strain of European discourse about the Jew. Yiddish, then, comes to represent textually the unassimilable. In that sense—and I am stretching here, but with a purpose—one could say that Yiddishland encompassed even Dora Bruder, even though there is no suggestion in Modiano's text or the documents he uncovers that she knew the language at all.

Like an ethnographer venturing into an unknown milieu with foreign cultural habits, Clébert yearns for an informant to bring him inside. If the flâneur observes the daily habits of the city's residents, remaining simultaneously part of it and apart from it, then Yiddish Paris is the place that denies entrance, disrupts the flânerie, exposes the pretensions of identification and observation that define flânerie. But the textual representation of Yiddishland in Paris functions as a potent symbol for the endurance of the traumatic past, the instability of home, the unspeakability of the deportation and genocide of the Jews which could not (yet) be brought fully into public discourse about the war.

Note

1. In Ida Fink's autobiographical novel, *The Journey*, for example, the Jewish protagonist—a former university student posing as a Polish peasant—cannot resist playing a Chopin polonaise on the piano in the presence of German soldiers, although it endangers her life.

Bibliography

Améry, Jean. "How Much Home Does a Person Need?" In *At the Mind's Limits: Contemplations by a Survivor On Auschwitz and Its Realities*, translated by Sidney Rosenfeld and Stella P. Rosenfeld. Bloomington: Indiana University Press, 1980, 41–61.

Augé, Marc. *Non-Places: An Introduction to Supermodernity*. Translated by John Howe. London: Verso, 1995; *Non-lieux: Introduction à une anthropologie de la Surmodernité*. Paris: Editions du Seuil, 1992.

Bachelard, Gaston. *The Poetics of Space*. Boston, MA: Beacon Press, 1964.

Bakhtin, Mikhail. *The Dialogic Imagination: Four Essays*. Translated by Caryl Emerson and Michael Holquist. Austin: University of Texas Press, 1981.

Blanchot, Maurice. "L'Idylle," In *Le Ressassement iternel*. Paris: Minuit, 1951.

Clébert, Jean-Paul. *Paris Insolite*. [Unusual Paris]. Paris, Atilla, 2009. (Text reprinted from *Paris Insolite*, Paris: Éditions Denoël, 1952.) Translated into English as *Paris Vagabond*. New York: New York Review of Books, 2016.

De Certeau, Michel. "Walking in the City." In *The Practice of Everyday Life*, translated by Steven Rendall. Berkeley: University of California Press, 1984 [*L'invention du quotidien, tome 1: Arts de faire* (1980)].

Ferguson, Priscilla Parkhurst. *Paris as Revolution: Writing the Nineteenth-Century City*. Berkeley: University of California Press, 1997.

Fink, Ida. *The Journey*. Translated by Joanna Weschler and Francine Prose. New York: Farrar, Straus, Giroux, 1992.

Kofman, Sarah. *Paroles suffoquées*. Paris: Galilée, 1987. Translated into English as *Smothered Words* by Madeleine Dobie. Evanston, IL: Northwestern University Press, 1998.

———. *Rue Ordener Rue Labat*. Paris: Galilée, 1994. Translated into English as *Rue Ordener Rue Labat* by Ann Smock. Lincoln, NE: University of Nebraska Press, 1996. All quotations are from these editions.

Modiano, Patrick. *Dora Bruder*. Paris: Editions Gallimard,1997. Translated into English as *Dora Bruder* by Joanna Kilmartin. Berkeley: University of California Press, 1999.

Noiriel, Gérard. "French and Foreigners." In *Realms of Memory: Rethinking the French Past*, edited by P. Nora. New York: Columbia University Press, 1966, 145–80.

Raczymow, Henri. *Contes d'exile et d'oublie.* Paris: Gallimard, 1979. Translated into English as excerpts from *Tales of Exile and Forgetfulness.* Translated by Alan Astro. "Discourse of Jewish Identity in Twentieth-Century France." *Yale French Studies* 85: 91.

Schwarz, Jan. *Survivors and Exiles: Yiddish Culture after the Holocaust.* Detroit: Wayne State University Press, 2015.

Sutzkever, Abraham. "In a Chinese Antique Shop." Translated by Ruth Whitman. *Massachusetts Review* 30, no. 1 (Spring 1989): 7–9.

———. "The Woman of Marble in Père Lachaise." In *With Everything We've Got: A Personal Anthology of Yiddish Poetry*, edited and translated by Richard Fein. Austin, TX: Host Publications, 2009, 164–67.

Tuan, Yi-Fu. *Space and Place: The Perspective of Experience.* Minneapolis: University of Minnesota Press, 2001.

15

The Afterlife of
Irène Némirovsky's *Suite française*

SUSAN RUBIN SULEIMAN

By now, many people have heard of Irène Némirovsky and may have read her novel, *Suite française*. A Russian-Jewish émigré to France born in Kiev in 1903, into what was then the Russian Empire, Némirovsky and her parents left Russia after the 1917 revolution and arrived in France when she was sixteen years old. In 1929, at age twenty-six, Némirovsky earned instant fame as the author of a novel about a Russian-Jewish businessman, *David Golder*, that received glowing reviews and was adapted into a successful film and a stage play.

Over the decade that followed, she published ten more novels and dozens of short stories, and became one of the rare women writers in France whose works were both commercially successful *and* commanded the respect of the literary establishment. In 1926, she married another Russian Jewish émigré from a middle-class family, Michel Epstein, with whom she had two daughters. Personally as well as professionally, Némirovsky's life was an extraordinary success—but was cut short by the horrors of World War II. In July 1942, she was deported to Auschwitz as a "foreign Jew" (she and her husband had never obtained French citizenship) and she died there a month later, at age thirty-nine. Her husband followed her a few months later and suffered a similar fate. Their two daughters, who were young

221

Figure 15.1. Poster for the film version of *David Golder*, directed by Julien Duvivier, 1930.

children at the time (Denise was twelve and Elisabeth, five), survived the war in hiding, in the care of a woman who had worked for the family and whom Irène and Michel trusted enough to appoint as the children's legal guardian in the event that they disappeared.

In the decades after the war, Némirovsky's name sank into obscurity. But it emerged spectacularly in 2004 when *Suite française*, a novel she had only partially completed at the time of her death, was published and became an international bestseller. *Suite française* is a brilliant novel, even in its unfinished state. Written in the last two years of Némirovsky's life along with numerous short stories and four other books, this novel has the strange quality, for a reader today, of a letter found in a bottle on the sand. The novel is set in France during World War II, from June 1940 to June 1941—a time that for Némirovsky was the present. Tolstoy, one of her literary heroes, wrote *War and Peace* half a century after the historical events he recounted. Némirovsky wrote *her* war novel when the war had just begun and she never lived to finish it. This fact makes *Suite française* anomalous among the books treated in this volume—for, unlike the works by Kofman, Modiano, Perec, and Raczymow, this novel cannot be called a work of memory, written by an author looking back. But it has a place in our exploration of postwar memory precisely because of its "message in a bottle" quality: although it was not a memory work for the writer, it is definitely one for its readers. Knowing what we know—or, if we are old enough, what we may remember—about the first year of the German occupation in France, we can only wonder at the sharpness of Némirovsky's vision of her own time.

There is yet another way in which *Suite française* is an anomaly when compared to the other works considered in the pages of this book: very little of it deals with Paris. Part 1, "Storm in June," is all about the *exode* of June 1940, when people were fleeing Paris; and part 2, "Dolce," takes place in an occupied village in the center of France, based on Issy-l'Evêque, the village where Némirovsky and her family were living when she was arrested. Instead, the postwar Jewish memory of Paris in this novel is found on the side of readers rather than the writer.

After the success of *Suite française*, which literally brought Némirovsky back to life, all of her earlier works were reissued, including *David Golder* and several others that focus on Jewish protagonists. This led to some lively debates and bitter controversies. A number of readers—in France, in the United States, and elsewhere—consider her portrayals of Jewish characters to be antisemitic. These readers have condemned her as a "Jewish antisemite" or a "self-hating Jew." Placing *Suite française* in the context of postwar Jewish memory highlights the question of Jewish identity in Némirovsky's life and work, but also in the lives of her two daughters, who eventually became the primary agents of Némirovsky's return to public memory. Elisabeth Gille, who had built a highly successful career as a literary editor in Paris during the 1970s and 1980s, published a book about her mother in 1992, *Le Mirador*, that created a flurry of interest in the press and on radio; she went on to write two more books before her premature death from cancer in 1996. Denise Epstein Dauplé, who spent most of her adult years as a housewife and occasional political activist for left-wing causes, transcribed the manuscript of *Suite française* quite early on and published it after her sister's death, whereupon her own life was spectacularly transformed.

This brief sketch points to two of the most interesting aspects of the "afterlife of *Suite française*": first, the role that Némirovsky's daughters played in bringing their mother back to life as a writer, with the consequences that followed for their own lives and those of their children and grandchildren, and second, the role this novel played in calling attention to Némirovsky's earlier works, with the resulting controversy about her portrayals of Jews. That there are no Jewish characters in *Suite française* itself has fed into the accusations against her.

Both of these are large and complicated subjects. I will therefore focus only on the story of the daughters' role in Némirovsky's literary rebirth, and even that in a condensed form. But as we'll see, the question of Jewish memory, and of Némirovsky's attitude toward Jews, is very much a part of the story.

Let us begin with the most obvious question: why did it take so long for *Suite française* to be published? According to a widespread legend, the manuscript, written in a notebook in tiny lettering to save paper, lay for decades in a suitcase, unread. The suitcase had been handed to twelve-year-old Denise by her father on the day he was arrested, with the admonition never to let go of it. After the war, she and her sister continued to treasure it, but thought that the notebook contained their mother's personal journal and could not bring themselves to read it. Then one day, after decades had passed, Denise opened the notebook, saw that it was a novel, transcribed it—and the rest is history.

The story is "beautiful and tragic," wrote journalist Macha Séry, who repeated it in *Le Monde* as recently as October 2014. But like all legends, it has only an approximate link to reality—which in this case is just as compelling and has the advantage of being true. In fact, Denise and Elisabeth knew about their mother's novel from early on and did not try to hide it. Denise mentioned "a fat manuscript in my possession" on a radio program in 1992, when Némirovsky's name started to crop up again after the publication of Elisabeth's *Le Mirador*. And Elisabeth mentions *Suite française* in her book more than once, citing it by its title.

But the existence of *Suite française* was already known to Denise, and undoubtedly to Elisabeth as well, in 1956 or at the latest 1957. Elisabeth was then nineteen years old, studying English language and literature at the Sorbonne. Denise was married, living in the banlieue with her husband and two young boys—her daughter, Irène, would be born a few years later. The family had very little money and Denise sometimes wrote to Albin Michel to ask whether any royalties on her mother's works were outstanding. By then, Némirovsky's name was all but forgotten and Albin Michel had no royalties to pay. They had published two posthumous works by her in 1946 and 1947, books that she had written during the war but could not be published at the time. The Nazis had put a veto on all books by Jewish authors. These posthumous works, the novel *Les Biens de ce monde* and a biography of Chekhov, *La Vie de Tchekhov*, had been sparsely reviewed, by critics who remembered Némirovsky in her glory days. But the war had swept away those days and brought to prominence a whole new set of writers from a very different milieu than the one Némirovsky had cultivated. Her role models had been the members of the Académie Française or those aspiring to be—many of whom were not only much older than the post-war stars but had discredited themselves by their less than stellar record of resistance to the Occupation during the war. The new stars—Sartre, Camus, Beauvoir, Romain Gary, Elsa Triolet—were all identified with the resistance, rightly or wrongly (in Beauvoir's case). They represented a different literary world. By 1956, yet another new world was in the making, with the rise of experimental writers of the *nouveau roman*, who had no use for the social and psychological realism in fiction that Némirovsky had excelled at.

In 1956, the woman who had taken care of Denise and Elisabeth during the war, Julie Dumot, died in her native Bordeaux. Curiously, she had had little contact with them in the intervening years—she had found new employment after the war and spent several years in the United States before returning to France. It appears, however, that she had hung on to the famous suitcase, for it was only after her death that the suitcase came into Denise's possession. Denise Epstein was always quite negative when she spoke about Julie Dumot, even while recognizing that Julie had saved her and her sister. She never wanted to explain exactly what she held against her, saying only that Julie had "done some bad things" after the war. It's possible that Julie's hanging on to the suitcase for so long, even after Denise was a grown woman, was one such bad thing. In any case, Denise did finally receive the suitcase, which contained not only the notebook with the manuscript of *Suite française* but other documents as well, including the manuscript of a novel that Némirovsky had finished before she died, *Les Feux de l'automne*. One reason for Némirovsky's astonishing output in the last two years of her life is that she had become the family's sole breadwinner when her husband was fired from his job at a bank in June 1940. Her letters and diaries from that time show that anxiety over money was uppermost in her mind. *Les Feux de l'automne* reprised themes from her other works and appears to have been written for quick publication. In the end, it, too, waited a long time—but Denise must have taken it to Albin Michel as soon as it turned up, for they paid an advance on royalties to her and her sister in November 1956 and published the book a few months later. Unfortunately, it went almost totally unnoticed. But in April 1957, soon after the novel appeared, the French-language Swiss newspaper *Tribune de Lausanne* ran a long article on Némirovsky in its Sunday edition. Signed by one J. Claude Daven, it was actually written by the journalist Catherine Descargues, who had interviewed Denise and corresponded with her in preparing it. Illustrated with two photos of Némirovsky furnished by Denise, the article was headlined: "AU MOMENT OÙ PARAÎT SON DERNIER LIVRE: SOUVENEZ-VOUS D'IRÈNE NÉMIROVSKY" (At the moment when her last book appears: Remember Irène Némirovsky). And it began thus: "There was no news of her since 1939, but with this publication we see the reappearance of one of the most famous women novelists before the war." The journalist goes on to evoke Némirovsky's death in Auschwitz, then gives a detailed, very positive review of the new book. More important from our point of view, she refers to the writer's "older daughter," who had told her about the family's refuge in a village during the war. "*The Fires of Autumn* were written then, under those conditions, along with another book, unfortunately unfinished, which would no doubt have counted among the writer's major works: *Suite française*." The journalist explains that these works were discovered only recently, in a suitcase found after the death of the woman who had been the girls' guardian after their parents were deported.

When I discovered this obscure article in the online archives of a paper that no longer exists under that name, I experienced one of those moments that researchers long for: an important piece in a puzzle had fallen into place. Now we can pinpoint exactly when Denise and Elisabeth learned of the existence of their mother's great work. And we also know that the story about the wartime suitcase revealing its contents after many years is not completely wrong; it merely exaggerates the number of years for greater dramatic effect. But that fact is actually important, for it raises the question of what would have happened if *Suite française* had been published when it first came to light, around 1957. Denise had apparently sent the manuscript to Catherine Descargues with the idea of publishing it and the journalist wrote to her a few days before the *Tribune de Lausanne* article appeared, saying that she had read the manuscript and found it "altogether remarkable"—then added, "c'est navrant qu'étant inachevé, on ne puisse l'éditer" (it's really a pity that, being unfinished, it can't be published).[1]

In fact, *Suite française* as it currently exists has a perfectly acceptable ending: the departure of German troops from the occupied village after Hitler's invasion of the Soviet Union, almost exactly one year after the story begins. Némirovsky made copious notes for a sequel, but the novel as it is, spanning the first year of German occupation, stands on its own. However, it is not at all certain, given the literary and cultural climate at the time, that *Suite française* would have been received with the admiration in 1957 that it received in 2004. The *nouveau roman* was just gaining momentum and *Suite française* was definitely not that. Nor was there much interest in fiction about World War II or the Holocaust. The first French novel to evoke the Holocaust, André Schwarz-Bart's *Last of the Just*, did not appear until 1959; even nonfiction works that we now consider classics, like Wiesel's *La Nuit* (*Night*) or Charlotte Delbo's *Aucun de nous ne reviendra* (*None of Us Will Return*), or Primo Levi's *Se questo è un uomo* (*Survival in Auschwitz*), were either unknown—Levi's book, published in Italy in 1946, had sold only a few hundred copies and was not translated into French until 1961—or not yet published—*La Nuit* appeared in 1958, translated into English two years later, and Delbo's book, written quite early, was not published until 1970.

Besides, *Suite française* was not a book about the Holocaust. It was a historical novel about French civilian life during the first year of German occupation. Realist historical fiction about World War II that did not deal with heroic feats, preferably by men, was not much of a sell in France of the 1950s. Simone de Beauvoir's *Les Mandarins*, which won the Prix Goncourt in 1954, could be considered an exception—but its subject was the postwar years, with only glancing references to the Occupation. Historian Henry Rousso has called the 1950s the period of "repression" about the Vichy years in France. The silence that greeted the publication of *Les Feux de l'automne* in 1957 bears out this view; Albin Michel had advertised the book as the posthumous work of a "great woman novelist who died in deportation." *Les Feux de l'automne* is not as good a novel as *Suite française*, but the tragic fate of its author could have been a selling point. It wasn't. By the time *Suite française* appeared fifty years later, the French public had acquired a huge appetite for works related to Vichy and the Jews—so huge that Rousso has qualified it as an "obsession." Even though *Suite française* was not a Holocaust work, the excerpts from Némirovsky's wartime diary and correspondence that were included as an appendix drew readers' attention to the author's tragic end and no doubt influenced their response to the novel. Within three months of its publication, it had already sold 200,000 copies.

The French "obsession" with the Holocaust had started quite a bit earlier, in the 1980s, and one may wonder why *Suite française* was not published then. It could probably have found a publisher, especially with Elisabeth Gille's connections to the Paris publishing world. The people I spoke with offered various explanations for the delay, none of them documented. According to some, Elisabeth was against publication because she, too, considered the novel to be unfinished and not as good as it would have been if her mother had lived to complete and revise it; others claim that Elisabeth wanted to write her own book about Némirovsky before publishing the novel. No doubt a whole host of factors, some based on conscious choice, some on the demands of everyday life that took precedence, and some on pure chance, created the delay.

There could have been another factor as well. The second part of *Suite française*, about life in the occupied village, is very close to being a personal chronicle—the chronicler does not appear in the action but she is everywhere present by her observations, her sharp-eyed way of depicting the various villagers' responses to the Occupation and to the Germans. The narrator's disenchanted gaze is that of an ironist, an outsider. And no one was more of an outsider in occupied France than a "foreign" Jew, the category inflicted on Némirovsky and her husband by the Vichy regime. So although there are no Jewish *characters in Suite française*, there is definitely something that can be called a Jewish presence. Reading the manuscript must have evoked very painful memories—if not for Elisabeth, who was too young at the time to be aware of much, then for Denise, who wore the yellow star to school in Issy-l'Evêque in the late spring of 1942. The legend that the Denise and Elisabeth couldn't bring themselves to read the notebook seems to have a grain of truth in it.

Indeed, the "repression" of memory that occurred on a collective level in France in the 1950s and later also occurred on the level of individuals. For many years, Jews in France who had suffered persecution did not talk about their experiences—or if they did, they laid all the blame on the Nazis, not on the French policemen who stamped the letter *J* on their identity cards and later came to arrest them or their loved ones. Repression was even more apparent among Jewish children, especially those who had lost a parent during the war, as many psychological studies as well as testimonies by child survivors have documented. Neuropsychiatrist Boris Cyrulnik, in his slender book of reflections on how he survived the war after the deportation of his parents when he was six years old, explains that the compulsion to "always keep going forward" (*"aller toujours de l'avant"*) became his strategy of survival, a defense against depression and helplessness (49).[2] This ability to bracket off the most painful aspects of the past is an important component of what Cyrulnik and other theorists of childhood trauma call resilience, but it generally comes at a cost.

With a few notable exceptions, most of the memoirs and testimonies by French child survivors of the Holocaust date from the 1990s or later. During the years following the war, many children were not only too young to give coherent accounts of their experience, but were unable to talk about it, even with those who had lived through similar events. The writer Berthe Burko-Falcman, whose family were Jewish immigrants from Poland and whose father was deported to Auschwitz in 1942, recounts in her memoir, *Un prénom républicain*, that in the Yiddish-speaking summer camps where she and other Jewish orphans were sent after the war, none of the children talked about what they had gone through: "Maybe we didn't know that what had happened to us was unusual. With a few variations, we all had the same story. There was therefore nothing to say, and we didn't speak about it" (92).[3] (The memoir appeared in 2007, when Burko-Falcman was seventy-three years old.) Psychoanalyst Denise Weill, who as a teenager was active in a group of Jewish scouts who took care of orphaned children in 1942, told me that after the war, she and her surviving friends would get together to dance all night and have a good time: "We had worn the yellow star, we had lost parents, but we never talked about the past. We wanted to study, get married, have children," she said. Later, as an analyst, she realized that many child survivors (including herself) did not talk about their past even in analysis. "Repression is a useful defense mechanism," she observed. "It allows you to go on living."[4]

Like so many others, Denise and Elisabeth remained silent about their childhood suffering for many years, even with each other—or maybe especially with each other. Elisabeth's son Fabrice Gille told me, when I interviewed him in 2010: "My aunt and her sister, my mother, found it very hard to speak about all that, for decades." According to him, Elisabeth especially resisted speaking about the war, perhaps because she had so few personal memories of that time. "They had some fairly stormy conversations, when my mother said, 'Listen, I can't talk about it. I don't have your memories, I can't talk about it. It's not possible.'" The spell was broken, Fabrice Gille said, one night when Denise was visiting them, sometime in the late 1970s: "I had had enough of those conversations that didn't go anywhere. So I sat down with my aunt and said to her, 'Tell me my story.' My aunt started to talk and my mother was listening from the kitchen, and she started to hear things they had never been able to discuss between them. . . . but it was a story told to me, not face to face between the two sisters."[5] The importance of this moment was confirmed by Denise Epstein in 2011, when I interviewed her for the last time. Toward the end of our conversation, she remarked that a life never moves in a straight line, but rather in zigzags, especially for people who "lived through that." Her sister, for example, was focused on her career as an editor for many years, which was understandable. And then she told me about that evening long ago, when Fabrice sat her down and asked her to "tell the story."

This anecdote illustrates beautifully what theorists of testimony have devoted many pages to explaining. In order for a story of trauma to be told, a sympathetic listener must ask to hear it, and it may take many years for that to happen. Denise Epstein's daughter Irène told me that her mother almost never spoke about her childhood with her children, but spoke about it freely with some of their friends. The friends asked, whereas her children, who were aware of how painful the subject was to her, made a point of not asking. "With someone who has suffered a lot," Irène said, "it's hard to say to them, 'Tell me. What exactly made you suffer?' So I have the impression that my own history is something I learned in fragments. And then, little by little, I glued the pieces together."[6] The feeling of a past cut off, one that can be reassembled only in pieces, is experienced not only by child survivors but also by their children and grandchildren.

If remembering and telling the story came late to Denise and Elisabeth, so did a proclaimed identification with Jewishness. Their parents had married in a synagogue, according to the wishes of Michel Epstein's parents. But neither he nor Irène had any attachment to Jewish identity or practice. Although some of Némirovsky's most insightful novels feature Jewish protagonists, her view of Jewish existence was bleak. Anxiety and insecurity, bred by centuries of persecution; poverty, struggle, and continual displacement; decisions about whether to flee pogroms or to try to make a better life; and, with all that, the bitter awareness that one would never be fully accepted into non-Jewish society, no matter how hard one tried—those were the main features in her depictions of the lives of the European Jews, who, in her novels, were all born into the ghettoes of eastern Europe. In February 1939, Irène and Michel converted to Catholicism and converted their daughters—a fact that Denise usually explained as their attempt to protect themselves. The actual reasons were somewhat more complicated than that and, of course, their conversion did not protect them at all in the end. But it did have important repercussions on Denise and Elisabeth's lives, starting with the fact that after the war they both attended a Catholic boarding school, Notre Dame de Sion—Denise for just a couple of years before obtaining her *baccalauréat* and Elisabeth for several years more. Although Denise often said, when she was interviewed after the success of *Suite française*, that her baptism meant nothing to her, and that soon after she arrived at Notre-Dame-de Sion she insisted on no longer going to mass because she was Jewish, her public behavior for many years suggests a fear of being identified as a Jew. She herself emphasized that for a long time she felt anxious and afraid, eager to get the Catholic "stamp" on her papers. She had a church wedding, made sure that all of her children were baptized, sent them to catechism to prepare them for their first communions (which they all had), and used the name Epstein only on occasion. Even in her last years, when she was very outspoken about her Jewishness, her mailbox in Toulouse bore the name Dauplé, not Epstein. Her son Emmanuel recalls that until age fourteen he was quite religious, going to church with his mother; he thought of the family as "left-wing Catholics" and, even after he had started "asking questions" and become an atheist, it never occurred to him that they might be Jewish. Denise was afraid that the "whole thing could start over," he said, and she wanted to protect her kids, make sure they were "just like everyone else." Her reaction was not at all unusual for that generation of Jews, he remarked. In fact, more Jews changed their names to sound "less Jewish" during the decade after World War II than in the preceding century and a half combined.

As for Elisabeth, she rebelled against the conventional Catholicism of her upbringing as soon as she arrived at the Sorbonne. She did not marry in church, did not have her children baptized, and declared herself an atheist, as did her husband. She knew the story of her mother and father, of course, and had already read all of her mother's books as a teenager—but the question of Jewishness or Jewish identity did not concern her much, according to her own account as well as those of her friends whom I interviewed. For a long time, she held the view that Sartre had made famous in his *Réflexions sur la question juive* (Antisemite and Jew): a Jew is someone whom others call "Jew," that there is no positive content to the term. She later said that she began to change after the birth of her children; at that point, she "felt a genuine continuity" and "accepted the heritage of [her] parents."[7] Elisabeth's son was born in 1963 and her daughter in 1972, but her interest in Jewish history and culture, as well as in her own past, started in the late 1970s, precisely at the time when Jewish memory of the Holocaust became a widespread collective phenomenon in France. It was not by pure chance that young Fabrice Gille asked his aunt to "tell the story" just around then: a desire to know, and to tell, was in the air.

Meanwhile, Némirovsky's name continued to languish in oblivion. Grasset, the publisher of *David Golder*, continued to keep that book in print, but nothing else by her was available. In July 1983, however, Albin Michel received a letter from someone who was doing research on Némirovsky and wanted to know which of her books were still available. A few years later, they started, somewhat cautiously, to reissue her works. No one noticed these books, but at least they were available. And in the meantime, Elisabeth and Denise were talking seriously about writing a biography of their mother. Both women were divorced by then and their children were grown up. Elisabeth's career as a Parisian editor was at its height and she had access to many people working in journalism and publishing. Someone had contacted Albin Michel with a proposal to write a biography—but she and her sister didn't like that idea and decided to write one together. It was to be a "classic biography, coauthored, based on documents," Elizabeth later recalled.[8] The two sisters, who had led very different lives, were drawn closer by this project. But in the end, they settled on a different version: Elisabeth would write the book, while Denise researched documents and contributed personal memories, many from before Elisabeth was born. And it would not be a "classic biography" but something between a biography and a first-person novel. *Le Mirador* is subtitled "mémoires rêvées" (Dreamed Memories). Irène is the presumed memoirist, but Elisabeth was the dreamer/author—and historian as well, for she incorporated many documents from Némirovsky's archives into the book (this is where Denise's help was precious). Adding yet another layer, Elisabeth inserted occasional brief fragments about "the child"—herself—bearing dates from March 1937 (just after her birth) to October 1991 (the time of writing). The book opens and closes with these fragments, which are written in the third person, as if to emphasize the difficulty of drawing clear boundaries between history and dream, or invention. It is the autobiographical fragments that appear as history, told by an "objective" voice, while the "subjective" account of Irène Némirovsky's life and thoughts is a literary invention, even if based on historical research.

Elisabeth Gille was a great admirer of Georges Perec's *W, ou le souvenir d'enfance*, which consists of two parallel narratives, one totally fictional and one autobiographical. Perec is famous for this formal innovation, which allowed him to compensate for his lack of childhood memories—he lost both of his parents during the war—by inventing a fictional story that could be read as a metaphor for the missing facts. Elisabeth created her own version of a split narrative by interspersing Irène's reconstructed story with her own and Denise's scattered but real memories.

There was another problem she had to confront, however: how to tell her mother's story, most of which took place "before Auschwitz," without imposing on it her own post-Holocaust perspective, without judging it? Seen from today, some of Irène Némirovsky's choices during the 1930s and even in the first year of the war appear unfortunate, if not downright reprehensible. But Elisabeth, in writing about her mother, did not want to adopt the position of a judge, which is the inevitable consequence of what Michel André Bernstein called "backshadowing"—expecting a person in the past to have known what we know later. This is a problem that confronts anyone writing about Némirovsky, or about many other assimilated Jews in Europe during the interwar period, but it is especially vexing if the writer is the subject's own daughter. Elisabeth Gille solved the problem by dividing the book into two parts. In part 1, she imagines Irène writing about her life in November 1929, shortly after the birth of her daughter Denise. She recounts her childhood in Kiev, the upheavals of the Revolution and exile, and ends on a highly optimistic note: her family had made the right choice by settling in France, "the country of moderation and freedom" that had "definitively adopted" her as she had adopted it.

After this bit of tragic irony, we skip to July 1942: Irène is sitting in her favorite spot for writing, the woods outside Issy-l'Évêque, wearing the yellow star—and she is no longer optimistic. By constructing the book this way, Elisabeth told an interviewer, "I could have my mother say things in 1929 that she no longer recognized in 1942."[9] More to the point, she could have her mother say things in1942 that showed remorse over her earlier choices. Némirovsky herself never did that, in fact—her diary and letters during the war manifest anger and despair, but not remorse. In *Le Mirador*, however, Elisabeth imagines Némirovsky just days before she was deported, "crying with rage" when she rereads the pages written by her younger self. How could she have been so blind to what was happening around her? Even if certain obliviousness was excusable in a "frivolous young girl" who had already seen too much death and destruction, was it not downright "criminal on the part of the happy and fulfilled woman I was in 1929, and that I remained until I arrived here?" (287). The "crime" she reproaches herself for was her indifference to the rise of right-wing, antisemitic movements in France as early as the 1920s, and her later hostility to "foreigners" fleeing Hitler's Germany. Actually, Némirovsky was not a political writer, so Elisabeth is projecting onto her the public attitudes of some established Jews in France toward foreigners—such as Emmanuel Berl, whom Némirovsky knew quite well. Elisabeth even imagines her mother foreseeing her daughters' dilemma, for on the same page that Némirovsky calls her earlier self practically a "criminal," she asks, "If things go badly, very badly, what will my daughters think of me? What will they reproach me for, with good reason, in ten or twenty years, when they will be grown women?" One has the impression, at moments like this, that Elisabeth Gille wanted to "tell all" about her mother, holding nothing back, but also wanted to protect her and, in a sense, to excuse her—or at least, to explain her choices to a later generation.

Le Mirador was published in February 1992 and received admiring reviews in major newspapers and magazines, from *Le Monde* and *Libération* to *L'Express*, *Elle*, and the Jewish weekly *Actualité Juive Hebdo*. Their focus was on Elisabeth Gille as author and daughter, but above all on Irène Némirovsky, whose name suddenly reappeared in the press after a decades-long absence. The reviewers all emphasized her tragic death at age thirty-nine, but many also praised her work. Among other media appearances, Elisabeth and her sister Denise were featured in a lengthy radio program devoted to Némirovsky.

Despite this flurry of interest, Némirovsky's work remained largely unknown for another decade. But her daughter's book had breathed new life into her and she returned the favor: with Le *Mirador*, Elisabeth Gille became a writer. In the too-few years that remained to her before dying of cancer in 1996, she published two more books, including a novel, *Un paysage de cendres*, that has entered the canon of autobiographical fiction by child survivors of the Holocaust.

Next was Denise's turn. After moving to Toulouse in the late 1970s, she had started to frequent "liberal" (Reform) Jewish groups and to visit schools to talk about the persecution of Jews in France during the war, including her parents and herself. Before Elisabeth died, the two sisters donated what they possessed of their mother's papers to the Institut Mémoires de l'Édition Contemporaine, an archive of writers and publishers, thus making them available to researchers. While the general public was still unaware of Némirovsky's name, her work had started to be discussed by scholars of modern French literature, at home and abroad. In 2000, the Stock publishing firm brought out twin volumes bound in their signature dark blue covers: Elisabeth Gille's *Le Mirador* in a new edition; and *Dimanche*, a selection of short stories by Némirovsky published in newspapers during her lifetime that Denise had unearthed during her research. The two books were often reviewed together.

Not long after that, Denise found a small publisher near Toulouse to bring out another selection of her mother's stories in a limited edition for which she wrote the preface. Denise Epstein had a very strong sense of her role as a witness to her parents' tragic history. Twice in this brief text, she expresses her desire to bring her mother back to life, with "her talent and her personality at once tender but often cruel (*à la fois tendre, mais souvent cruelle*), with her clear-eyed gaze on the world around her." The importance of memory and testimony, which has dominated public discourse about the Holocaust worldwide in the past half-century, had acquired a particular resonance in France during the 1980s and 1990s, when a number of highly publicized trials brought the Vichy period—most notably, Vichy's responsibility in the deportation of Jews—back into the limelight. The "duty to remember" (*devoir de mémoire*) became a slogan that Denise, like many others, adopted with fervor. In her case, the duty to remember was reinforced by the particular status of her mother, a writer once celebrated but now forgotten. She ended her preface with a hopeful declaration: "I am the only one left now who still speaks of them [her parents], but every work of my mother's that is published brings her back into the world of the living."[10]

This book of stories, aptly titled *Destinées* (the title of one of the stories), appeared in April 2004. A few months later, Irène Némirovsky returned to the "world of the living" with a bang. Denise had made a new transcription of the manuscript of *Suite française* and had spoken about it with the writer Myriam Anissimov, who was visiting Toulouse on a book tour. Anissimov read the typescript and showed it to her publisher at Denoël, Olivier Rubinstein, who took it immediately. Denise had also typed up excerpts from Némirovsky's journal and correspondence, which were added as an appendix. A preface by Anissimov, outlining Némirovsky's brilliant career and tragic end, completed the volume, which appeared in bookstores at the end of September 2004. Right from the start, the novel garnered excellent reviews in France and a great deal of interest from foreign publishers at the Frankfurt Book Fair. But major success came when it was awarded the Prix Renaudot in November of that year. A few writers and journalists criticized the posthumous award, for which there was no precedent—the literary prizes were awarded, they pointed out, in order to "encourage living writers." But the general opinion about the prize and the book was enthusiastic. By the beginning of December, *Suite française* had earned a place among the top twenty bestsellers of 2004.[11] And it had made Denise Epstein, at age seventy-five, into a minor literary celebrity.

In fact, a whole new life had begun for her. For the first time, she found herself free of financial constraints. She bought a large, airy apartment on the top floor of a modern building in Toulouse, after years of living in more cramped quarters, and she "worried over the high taxes she had to pay, after years of not paying any!" her son Nicolas Dauplé told me with a laugh. Over the next eight years, she traveled the world as her mother's representative and published a book of conversations about her own life, *Survivre et vivre*, with the writer Clémence Boulouque. She participated as the guest of honor in the ceremony that took place in Issy-l'Évêque in September 2005, when a memorial tablet was placed on the wall of the

Figure 15.2. The street sign on Place Irène Némirovsky in Issy-l'Evêque. (*Photograph by Susan Rubin Suleiman*)

house where the Epstein family had lived in 1941–1942, and the square in front was renamed Place Irène Némirovsky.[12] If some people who had known Denise years earlier remembered her as a sad woman, that certainly could not be said of her in the last decade of her life. Elisabeth's old friend, writer René de Ceccatty, used the word "radiant" to describe the impression Denise made on him when they met again after many years. Denise's son Nicolas described her as "transfigured" after the success of *Suite française.* "It was as if she had been on radio and television all her life," he said.[13]

The last time I interviewed Denise, in June 2011, we spent a while talking about the funeral of her sister, Elisabeth—but despite the solemn subject, our conversation was full of laughter. Denise took delight in recounting her efforts to organize a Jewish ceremony despite her ignorance of traditional rituals. The requirement of a minyan, a quorum of ten Jews to say the prayers, was news to her, she said. Luckily, the "liberal" rabbi who had been recommended to her was very understanding, even when she told him that Elisabeth had been a convinced atheist! As for herself, Denise said, she had reserved a place next to her sister.

Figure 15.3. Place Irène Némirovsky, Issy-l'Evêque, France, June 2014. Némirovsky and her family were living in the house in the background when she was arrested in 1942. (*Photograph by Susan Rubin Suleiman*)

Figure 15.4. Denise Epstein (center) with her daughter Irène (left), and her grand-daughter Juliette (right), Toulouse, June 2011. (*Photograph by Susan Rubin Suleiman*)

The following year, Denise was diagnosed with lung cancer, the same illness that had killed Elisabeth. Despite the debilitating chemotherapies, she continued her email correspondence as long as she could, always interested in work about her mother. Up to the very end, according to her son Nicolas, she maintained her courage and good humor, and her love of life. A favorite photo that her daughter Irène sent to friends after her death shows Denise sitting on a fall day on a beach in Hendaye, her childhood vacation spot, where her children had taken her as a surprise gift for her eightieth birthday. She is bundled up in a sweater and scarf, with a bottle of champagne at her feet. Her arms are raised in a gesture of victory and she is smiling.

Denise Epstein died on April 1, 2013, at her home in Toulouse, surrounded by her children and grandchildren. Her ashes are buried in the Jewish section of the Belleville cemetery next to her sister, Elisabeth, and next to an inscription that records the deaths of their parents at Auschwitz.

Figure 15.5. Family tombstone, Cimètiere de Belleville, June 2013. The inscriptions on the stone include the names of Irène Némirovsky and Michel Epstein with the notation "Died in Auschwitz." (*Photograph by Susan Rubin Suleiman*)

Notes

1. Catherine Descargues to Denise Epstein Dauplé, April 12, 1957. Personal archives of Denise Epstein.

2. In 2012, Cyrulnik published a full-length memoir about his childhood and youth, in which he juxtaposes his personal story with general observations about the psychology of trauma and survival: Cyrulnik, *Sauve-toi, la vie t'appelle* (Paris: Odile Jacob, 2012).

3. An earlier quote, about feeling Catholic in her own way, is on page 203. Burko-Falcman's earlier works are novels, loosely based on her wartime experiences: *La Dernière vie de Madame K.* (1982), *Chronique de la source rouge* (1984), and *L'Enfant caché* (1997).

4. Interview with Denise Weill, Paris, 10 July 2010. Denise Weill, mother of the journalist and essayist Nicolas Weill, was born in 1926 and died in March 2015.

5. Interview with Fabrice Gille, San Diego, April 29, 2010.

6. Interview with Irène Dauplé, Toulouse, June 23, 2011.

7. "Pentimento," radio program, France Inter, April 4, 1994.

8. Myriam Anissimov, "Les filles d'Irène Némirovski," 70. This interview provides the most details about the original project and its evolution. Denise spoke about it with me in personal interviews in June 2008 and June 2009.

9. Ibid., 72–73.

10. Denise Epstein, "Une photographie," in Elisabeth Gille, Le Mirador, 10; the other quotes in this paragraph are on pp. 7–8.

11. Christine Rousseau, "La Fiction au 'top,'" Le Monde, February 10, 2005, http://abonnes.lemonde.fr/archives/article/2005/02/10/la-fiction-au-top_397, accessed online on April 29, 2015. Criticisms of the posthumous award were reported in an unsigned article in Le Monde: "Le Renaudot attribué, à titre posthume, à Irène Némirovsky," November 9, 2004; http://abonnes.lemonde.fr/archives/article/2004/11/09/le-renaudot-attribue-a, accessed online on April 29, 2015. See also Josyane Savigneau, "Renaudot, Goncourt et marketing littéraire," Le Monde, November 11, 2004; Savigneau mentions the book's success at the Frankfurt Book Fair. http://abonnes.lemonde.fr/archives/article/2004/11/11/renaudot-goncourt-et . . . Accessed online on April 29, 2015.

12. Letter from Denise Epstein to Gilbert Vachet, then mayor of Issy-l'Évêque, September 6, 2005, in which she thanks him for the "unforgettable day" of the ceremony. Given to me in June 2014 by the current mayor's office, along with other materials relating to the ceremony.

13. Interview with René de Ceccatty, Paris, July 7, 2010. Interview with Nicolas Dauplé, Volnaver le Bas, near Grenoble, June 6, 2014; interview with Léa Dauplé, Paris, June 9, 2014.

Bibliography

"Au moment où paraît son dernier livre: Souvenez-vous d'Irène Némirovsky," Tribune de Lausanne, April 14, 1957, 7. http://scriptorium.bcu-lausanne.ch/#. Accessed online on April 8, 2015.

Burko-Falcman, Berthe. Un Prénom républicain. Paris: Seuil, 2007.

Cyrulnik, Boris. Je me souviens. Paris: Odile Jacob: 2010.

Conan, Eric, and Henri Rousso. Vichy: un passé qui ne passe pas. Paris: Pluriel, 2013.

De Beauvoir, Simone. Les Mandarins. Paris: Gallimard, 1954.

Delbo, Charlotte. Aucun de nous ne reviendra. Paris: Minuit, 1970.

Epstein, Denise, with Clémence Boulouque. Survivre et vivre. Paris: Denoël, 2008.

Gille, Elisabeth. Le Mirador. Paris: Stock, 1998.

———. Un Paysage de cendres. Paris: Point, 2011.

Levi, Primo. Se questo è un uomo. Torino: De Silva, 1947.

Némirovsky, Irène. Les Biens de ce monde. Paris: Albin Michel, 1947.

———. David Golder. Paris: Grasset, 1929.

————. *Destinées et autres nouvelles.* Toulouse: Sables, 2004.

————. *Dimanche.* Paris: Stock, 2000.

————. *Les Feux de l'automne.* Paris: Albin Michel, 1957.

————. *Suite française.* Paris: Denoël, 2004.

————. *Suite Française.* Translated by Sandra Smith. New York: Knopf, 2006.

————. *La Vie de Tchekhov.* Paris: Albin Michel, 2005.

Sartre, Jean-Paul. *Réflexions sur la question juive.* Paris: Paul Morihien, 1946.

Schwartz-Bart, André. *Le Dernier des Justes.* Paris: Seuil, 1959.

Séry, Macha. "Le Pays où l'archive est reine." *Le Monde*, October 10, 2014, 6 [of book section].

Wiesel, Eli. *La Nuit.* Paris: Minuit, 1958.

Contributors

Julia Creet is professor of English at York University. She is the author of *The Genealogical Sublime* (2020), coeditor of *Memory and Migration: Multidisciplinary Approaches to Memory Studies* (2011) and of *H. G. Adler: Life, Literature, Legacy* (2016). She is also the director and producer of *MUM: A Story of Silence* (2008), a documentary about a Holocaust survivor who tried to forget. Creet has published broadly on Holocaust literature, testimony, and memory.

Amira Bojadzija-Dan is research associate at the Koschitzky Centre for Jewish Studies at York University. Her dissertation deals with issues of memory, trauma, and identity in post-Holocaust memory narratives, and she has an expertise in French literature and culture. She is the coeditor of *H. G. Adler: Life, Literature, Legacy* (2016), a collection of essays examining the place of absence, trauma, and memory in Adler's oeuvre.

Maxime Decout is cofounder of the ongoing scholarly seminar on Écrivains juifs de langue française at Université Lille III, where he teaches French literature. He is the author of *Albert Cohen: les fictions de la judéité* (2011); *Écrire la judéité: Enquête sur un malaise dans la littérature française* (2015); and *En toute mauvaise foi: Sur un paradoxe littéraire* (2015); and edited special editions of the journal *Europe* on Perec (2012) and Modiano (2015).

Sarah Hammerschlag is assistant professor of religion and literature at the University of Chicago Divinity School and the author of *The Figural Jew: Politics and Identity in Postwar French Thought* (2010) and *Broken Tablets: Levinas, Derrida and the Literary Afterlife of Religion* (2016), and is editing an anthology of French Jewish thought for Brandeis University Press.

Sara R. Horowitz is professor of comparative literature and humanities at York University. Her work on Holocaust literature focuses on fictional, autobiographical, and testimonial narrative and on issues of gender. She is the author of *Voicing the Void: Muteness and Memory in Holocaust Fiction* (1997); editor of *Lessons and Legacies of the Holocaust X: Back to the Sources* (2012); coeditor of *Encounter with Aharon Appelfeld* (2003) and *H. G. Adler: Life, Literature, Legacy* (2016), which was awarded the Canadian Jewish Literary Award; founding coeditor of the journal *Kerem: A Journal of Creative Explorations in Judaism* (1994–2015); and founding senior editor of the Azrieli Holocaust Memoir Series (2007–2009).

L. Scott Lerner holds an endowed chair in Humanities, chairs the Judaic Studies Program, and teaches French and comparative literature at Franklin and Marshall College. His research interests include representing loss in French literature, and trauma in the modern Jewish imaginary. He edited *Modern Jewish Literatures: Intersections and Boundaries* (2011) and *The Dreyfus Affair in the Making of Modern France* (1997), and is currently working on "After Exile: Narrative and Jewish Experience From the French Revolution to Proust" and "Proust and the Profanation of the Jewish Mother: Memory, Mourning, Subjectivity."

Nadia Malinovich is the author of *French and Jewish: Culture and the Politics of Identity in Early Twentieth-Century France* (2008) and coeditor of *The Jews of Modern France: Images and Identities* (2016). Her research focuses on the integration and evolving identities of graduates of the schools of the Alliance Israelite Universelle in France, Canada, and the United States.

Ruth Malka has completed a PhD at McGill University in French literature and Jewish studies. Her thesis dealt with three antisemitic texts published in the late 1930s and the early 1940s by Louis-Ferdinand Céline. She is also interested in the French Jewish answer to antisemitism and in postwar Jewish literature.

Gary D. Mole is associate professor of French at Bar Ilan University. He is author of *Beyond the Limit-Experience: French Poetry of the Deportation, 1940–1945* (2014) and *Levinas, Blanchot, Jabes: Figures of Estrangement* (1997); editor of a special issue of *Essays in French Literature and Culture* (2014) titled *Représenter la Grande Guerre: les écrivains et les artistes face à l'épreuve*; and member of the editorial board of *Dalhousie French Studies*.

Thomas Nolden is professor of comparative literature at Wellesley College and author of *In Lieu of Memory: Contemporary Jewish Writing in France*, and coauthor of *Contemporary Jewish Writing in Europe: A Guide* and *Voices from the Diaspora: Jewish Women Writing in Contemporary Europe*.

Henri Raczymow is an award-winning French literary author. He has published more than twenty novels, including *Un Cri sans voix/Writing the Book of Esther*, as well as short story collections, and literary memoirs. He also writes as a literary and cultural critic, and has published on twentieth-century French Jewish writing, culture, and experience.

Annelies Schulte Nordholt has published extensively on twentieth-century French literature, with a special interest in postwar memory, Jewish writing, and Holocaust representation. She is the author of *Perec, Modiano, Raczymow. La génération d'après et la mémoire de la Shoah* (2008), *Témoignages de l'après-Auschwitz dans la littérature juive française d'aujourd'hui* (2008), and *Maurice Blanchot. L'écriture comme expérience du dehors* (1995).

Susan Suleiman is the C. Douglas Dillon Professor of the Civilization of France and professor of comparative literature at Harvard University. She is a renowned literary critic and theorist whose work encompasses twentieth- and twenty-first-century French literature, Holocaust literary memory, and women's studies. Her books include the memoir *Budapest Diary: In Search of the Motherbook* (1996), *Crises of Memory and the Second World War* (2006), and *The Némirovsky Question: The Life, Death, and Legacy of a Jewish Writer in Twentieth-Century France* (2016). Her edited volumes include *Exile and Creativity* (1998) and *French Global: A New Approach to Literary History*. She has won many honors, including the Radcliffe Medal for Distinguished Achievement (1990), and a decoration by the French government as Officer of the Order of Academic Palms (Palmes Académiques) in 1992. During the 2009–2010 academic year, she was the invited Shapiro Senior Scholar-in-Residence at the Center for Advanced Holocaust Studies of the U.S. Holocaust Memorial Museum.

Nelly Wolf is professor of French literature at the Université Charles de Gaulle-Lille III, France. Her research interests are focused on the interrelationship between politics and the novel, and on French Jewish literature. She has published *Le peuple dans le roman français de Zola à Céline* (1990); *Une* *littérature sans histoire: Essai sur le Nouveau Roman* (1995); *Le roman de la démocratie* (2003); and *Proses du monde: les enjeux sociaux des styles littéraires* (2014). She is also the author of articles on Perec, Némirovsky, Modiano, and on the presence of Yiddish in French literature. She has supervised, with Maxime Decout, the publication of an issue of the French journal *Tsafon* dedicated to French Jewish writers, she is the organizer, also with Maxime Decout, of a monthly research seminar, "French Contemporary Artists and Writers," at the university Charles de Gaulle-Lille III.

Index